The Final Revolution

Other Books by George Weigel

Peace and Freedom: Christian Faith, Democracy, and the Problem of War

Tranquillitas Ordinis: The Present Failure and Future Promise of American Catholic Thought on War and Peace

Catholicism and the Renewal of American Democracy

American Interests, American Purpose: Moral Reasoning and U.S. Foreign Policy

Fieles y Libres: Catolicismo, Derechos Humanos y Democracia

Freedom and Its Discontents: Catholicism Confronts Modernity

Just War and the Gulf War (with James Turner Johnson)

Books Edited

Retos Contemporáneos: Reflexiones desde el realismo bíblico de la tradición católica

A Century of Catholic Social Thought: Essays on Rerum Novarum *and Nine Other Key Documents* (with Robert Royal)

The American Search for Peace: Moral Reasoning, Religious Hope, and National Security (with John P. Langan, S.J.)

A New Worldly Order: John Paul II on Human Freedom—A Centesimus Annus *Reader*

Being Christian Today: An American Conversation (with Richard John Neuhaus)

The
Final Revolution

THE RESISTANCE CHURCH
AND THE COLLAPSE OF COMMUNISM

George Weigel

New York Oxford
OXFORD UNIVERSITY PRESS
1992

Oxford University Press

Oxford   New York   Toronto
Delhi   Bombay   Calcutta   Madras   Karachi
Kuala Lumpur   Singapore   Hong Kong   Tokyo
Nairobi   Dar es Salaam   Cape Town
Melbourne   Auckland

and associated companies in
Berlin   Ibadan

Published by Oxford University Press, Inc.
200 Madison Avenue, New York, New York 10016

Oxford is a registered trademark of Oxford University Press

Library of Congress Cataloging–in–Publication Data
Weigel, George
The final revolution : the resistance church and the collapse of
communism / George Weigel
p. cm.   Includes index.
ISBN   0-19-507160-3
1. Communism and Christianity—Catholic Church—Europe, Eastern.
2. Revolution—Religious aspects—Christianity. 3. Europe,
Eastern—Politics and Government—1945–
I. Title.   BX1396.4.W45   1992
261.7´0943´09048—dc20   92-9607

9 8 7 6 5 4 3 2 1

Printed in the United States of America
on acid-free paper

For
Richard John Neuhaus
"Ecce quam bonum et quam iucundum
habitare fratres in unum."
(Psalm 133.1)

Sursum corda (Lift up your hearts!)

—*The Roman Liturgy*

"Man surpasses man, infinitely."

—*Blaise Pascal*

What does the political scientist know?
The political scientist knows the latest trends
The current states of affairs
The history of doctrines

What does the political scientist not know?
The political scientist doesn't know about desperation
He doesn't know the game that consists
Of renouncing the game

It doesn't occur to him
That no one knows when
Irrevocable changes may appear
Like an ice-flow's sudden cracks

And that the natural resources
Include knowledge of the venerated laws
Ability to wonder
And a sense of humor.

—*Artur Miedzyrzecki*

"It may be that God and His Holy Mother intend to blind the enemy on purpose . . . so that he'd go so far in his lawlessness and rapacity. Otherwise he'd never dare to raise the sword against this holy place. He didn't conquer this country by himself alone; our own people helped him. But no matter how low our nation has fallen, or how deeply steeped in sin it might be, there is a limit . . . which none of our people would ever go beyond. They turned their backs on their King and the Commonwealth but they never ceased to honor and worship their Patroness and Mother who has always been the true Queen of Poland. . . .

"The enemy jeers at us and despises us, asking what's left of our former virtues. And I'll tell him this much: we've lost them all but one, and that is our Faith and the honor we show to the Holy Mother, and that is the foundation on which we can reconstruct the rest. . . . [Our enemies] understand what is at stake here. . . . [And] if God hasn't blinded them by design, they'd never dare strike at Jasna Góra. Because that day would be the beginning of the end of their supremacy and the beginning of our awakening."

> — Father Kordetzki's speech to
> the defenders of the monastery
> of the Black Madonna,
> 1655: recounted by
> Henryk Sienkiewicz in
> *The Deluge*

"The pope? How many divisions has the pope?"

> —*Josef Stalin*

Preface

This is a book about revolutions. But it treats more of priests than of politicians, takes the worlds of the spirit more seriously than the worlds of economics, and argues that a religious institution typically regarded as cautious and conservative was instrumental in demolishing one of the twentieth century's greatest (and most despicable) concentrations of aggressively secular political power.

Things are not always what they seem: in history, as well as in everyday life. Francis Parkman, perhaps the most distinguished of American historians, suggested that "it is the nature of great events to obscure the great events that came before them." And if that was true in a less frenetic era, it is even more the case in our own times, when the rapidity of historical change has been little short of breathtaking.

All the more reason, then, to look carefully into the human geology beneath the upheavals that have riveted the world's attention in recent years: the disintegration of the Union of Soviet Socialist Republics, the collapse of the Warsaw Pact and the post–World War II European order, and the end of Marxism-Leninism as an ideological force. These things did not just happen. The communist crack-up was gestated over many years. A lot of that revolutionary incubation took place in an institution despised and persecuted by Lenin and Stalin and their heirs: the Roman Catholic Church. How the Church helped foment and shape the Revolution of 1989 in central and eastern Europe by preaching a revolution of conscience, a revolution of the human spirit, is the story unfolded here.

There is much credit to be distributed in the aftermath of the collapse of communism. The Catholic Church had many partners in resistance. Nor was Pope John Paul II the lone impresario of this new kind of revolution, in which a corrupt and cruel tyranny was overthrown, in the main, without violence. But the Church and the pope were indispensable to what became the Revolution of 1989—according to many, many people, across the full range of religious and political opinion in central and eastern Europe. Their testimony weighs heavily in this book: as indeed it should. Those who were there—those who put their lives on the line—have a special claim on our attention.

My own life has been immensely enriched by hundreds of conversations with the people of the Revolution of 1989. They are not superheroes. They are simply men and women of conviction and conscience who, under relentless pressure, stuck fast to their beliefs, and by doing so challenged the tyrants at their maximum point of vulnerability. One need not agree with everything these people have done since 1989 to understand what a debt they are owed by everyone who cares about freedom.

There are few moments in history, particularly in this bloodiest of centuries, when the good guys win, cleanly, and against great odds. That is what happened in central and eastern Europe in the Revolution of 1989. This is the story of one great part of the revolution of conscience that made the political revolution possible.

Washington, D.C.   G.W.
February 14, 1992
Feast of Sts. Cyril and Methodius

Acknowledgments

I have incurred more than the usual number of author's debts in the course of preparing *The Final Revolution*. I am particularly grateful to the following for discussing the Church's role in the Revolution of 1989 with me, for their help on my research trips, for providing materials, and/or for reading earlier drafts of the book:

Rome: Father Edward Buelt, Cardinal Edward Idris Cassidy, Archbishop Giovanni Cheli, Bishop Pierre Duprey, M. Afr., Msgr. Antonio Franco, Father Robert Graham, S.J., Father John Hilton, Dr. Karl Krčméry, Cardinal Pio Laghi, Msgr. Diarmuid Martin, Margaret Melady, Ambassador Thomas P. Melady, Dr. Joaquin Navarro-Valls, Father John Navone, S.J., Bishop George Pell, Msgr. John Radano, Cardinal Joseph Ratzinger, Father Ronald G. Roberson, C.S.P., Archbishop Jan P. Schotte, C.I.C.M., Msgr. Salvatore Scribano, Victor and Daniella Simpson, Archbishop J. Francis Stafford, Father Terry Tekippe, Cardinal Jozef Tomko, Wilton Wynn.

Poland: Ferdinand and Danuta Chrobok, Stanisław and Barbara Galata, Dr. Bronisław Geremek, Bishop Tadeusz Gocłowski, C.M., Michael Hornblow, Zbigniew Janas, Father Kazimierz Jancarz, Wiesław Klisiewicz, Piotr Konczewski, Cardinal Franciszek Macharski, Father Mieczysław Maliński, Father Stanisław Małkowski, Dr. Krzysztof Michalski, Andrzej Miciewski, Andrew Nagorski, Janusz Onyszkiewicz, Piotr Pacewicz, Barbara Paluch, Father Jacek Salij, O.P., Father Józef Tischner, Jerzy Turowicz, Jacek Wojnarowski, Kazimierz Wóycicki, Antoni Zięba, Father Maciej Zięba, O.P., Bishop Józef Życiński, and the gentleman selling T-shirts at the papal Mass in Warsaw's Agrikola Park.

The Czech and Slovak Federal Republic: Ivana Albrechtová, Kamila Benda, Dr. Václav Benda, Pavel Bratinka, Jiří Burdyck, Archbishop Giovanni Coppa, John Evans, Ondřej Fischer, Msgr. Thomas Gullickson, Father Tomáš Halík, Tomáš Holub, Cardinal

Franz König, Jan Kotas, Miroslav Kratochvíl, Dr. Silvester Krčméry, Dr. Vladimir Krčméry, Maria Langschova, Bishop František Lobkowicz, O. Praem., Father Oto Mádr, Father Václav Malý, Dr. František Mikloško, Ladislav Nádvorník, Jiří Pechar, Father Karel Pilík, Michal Semín, Dalibor Slavíček, Tomáš Svoboda, Zuzana Szatmary, Bishop Jaroslav Škarvada, Pavel Tobek, Cardinal František Tomášek, Ján Truban, Dr. Václav Vaško, Archbishop Miloslav Vlk, Father Vladimír Vyhlídka.

Elsewhere: Dr. Frans A.M. Alting von Geusau, Dr. Shlomo Avineri, Dr. James H. Billington, Dr. Bohdan Bociurkiw, William C. Bodie, the Rev. Michael Bourdeaux, Paloma Cabetas, Archbishop Agostino Cacciavillan, Sarah Davis, Midge Decter, Dr. Larry Diamond, Dr. E.J. Dionne, Jr., Dr. Nadia Diuk, Paula Dobriansky, Dr. Jude Dougherty, Carl Gershman, Professor Mary Ann Glendon, Dr. Patrick Glynn, Father J. Bryan Hehir, Dr. Kent Hill, Ambassador Max M. Kampelman, Father Joseph A. Komonchak, Dr. Maciej Kozłowski, Dr. Charles Krauthammer, Raina Lewis, Jonathan Luxmoore, Francis X. Maier, Msgr. William Murphy, Victor Nakas, Rabbi Dr. David Novak, Michael Novak, Gerard Powers, Brad Roberts, Robert Royal, Ambassador Richard Schifter, Andrew J. Strenio, Jr., Dr. Judith F. Strenio, Bishop Sigitas Tamkevicius, S.J., Joan B. Weigel.

Richard John Neuhaus suggested the image of the "final revolution" and pointed me toward Norman Cohn's study, *The Pursuit of the Millennium*. For those kindnesses, and for so many others over fifteen years of friendship and collaboration, I am deeply grateful. The dedication of this book is a small payment on a very large debt.

Rodger Potocki came with me to Poland and was a splendid traveling companion and a fine translator. Thanks, too, to his wife Magda for lending him to me, and to Magda's parents, Fred and Danuta Chrobok, for their hospitality in Nowa Huta.

Christopher Ditzenberger, my executive assistant (and first baseman) at the Ethics and Public Policy Center, prepared the manuscript for publication (with some indexing help from Gwyneth Weigel) and kept my office in order while I was exploring the Revolution of 1989 on site.

Cynthia Read of the Oxford University Press and I have now done two books together: despite the mutual antipathy endemic between New York Mets and Baltimore Orioles fans after what we in the latter category remember as the late unpleasantness of October 1969. I remain grateful for her enthusiasm about this project, her support, and her wise editorial counsel.

And last, but by no means least, I should like to thank my family—Joan, Gwyneth, Monica, and Stephen Paul—for their steady support and love.

Contents

Introduction: The Final Revolution, 3
The Quest for the Millennium, 4
Back to the Present, 6
The Tyranny of the Political, 10
The Priority of Conscience, 12

ONE   *Not by Politics Alone:*
Unwrapping the Revolution of 1989, 15
The Standard Account: Mikhail Gorbachev Did It, 18
The Realist Account: Ronald Reagan Did It, 21
The Diplomatic Account: The Helsinki Final Act Did It, 26
The Great Ideas: Economics and/or History Did It, 30
The Heart of the Matter, 33

TWO   *Calling Good and Evil by Name:*
The Communist Lie Confronted, 37
Signs Among the Onions, 39
The Web of Mendacity, 41
From Complicity to Resistance, 47
Revolutionary Morality, Reconsidered, 50
Breaking the Fever of Fear, 55

THREE   *Catholics and Commissars: 1917–1978,* 59
Opening Gambits, 60
The Confrontation Intensified, 64
John XXIII and the Spirit of Dialogue, 67
Vatican II and the Catholic Human Rights Revolution, 70

A New *Ostpolitik:* The Quest for a Reasonable
   Accommodation, 74

   FOUR   The Wojtyła Difference, 77
Whose Humanism? 78
A Man for This Season, 79
"Breathing Space", 85
A Changed Game, 88
Training for Moral Combat, 90
Going on Offense: The *Ostpolitik* of John Paul II, 93
Questions of Conviction, 96

   FIVE   Poland: Igniting the Revolution, 103
Saddling the Cow: Stalinist Poland, 1944–1956, 104
The Years of the "Great Novena": 1956–1970, 111
Prelude to Revolution: 1970–1978, 122
The Rise of Solidarity: 1978–1981, 128
The Hard Road to Freedom: 1982–1989, 145
The Challenge of the Free Society, 155

   SIX   Czechoslovakia: A Church Reborn
             in Resistance, 159
From Gigantism to "Normalization", 161
A Taste of Ashes, 166
Rebirth in Resistance, 174
St. Agnes's Gentle Revolution, 183
The Lazarus Church, 185

   SEVEN   No Monopolies on Virtue: Christian Conviction
                and the Democratic Prospect, 191
The Communist Hangover, 193
The Church Being Itself, 195
Truth and Freedom, 199
The Peace and Freedom Connection, 203
Surprises from the Lord of History, 205

Notes, 211
Index, 247

Photographs follow page 110

The Final Revolution

Introduction:
The Final Revolution

The Revolution of 1989—the collapse of the communist regimes in central and eastern Europe—was one of the most extraordinary events in a century filled with the unexpected. What was this historic cataclysm that changed the very meaning of the word *revolution*? How did the Lenin Shipyards in Gdańsk become the twentieth century's version of the Bastille? How could a nonviolent resistance movement topple an empire that had been built on violence, cruelty, and repression? How did people divided by an iron curtain for forty years come to dance together atop the Berlin Wall?

The people who made the Revolution of 1989 are among the genuine heroes of freedom in this, or indeed any other, century. Their voices have a special claim on our attention. What did they think they were doing? Why did they do it? Who were their heroes and role models? Why were they willing to take the risk of resistance?

In the West, the Revolution of 1989 seemed to be many things at once. It was "people power," it was high political drama, it was the victory of democracy over totalitarianism.

But according to the brave men and women who overthrew communist tyranny in the captive nations of Stalin's empire, the Revolution of 1989 was also something else, and something more. Listen to them and you will be told, time and again, that theirs was first and foremost a revolution of conscience, a revolution of the spirit.

In fact, the Revolution of 1989 was an embodiment of the final revolution.

And the final revolution is the human turn to the good, to the truly human—and, ultimately, to God, who alone can make all things new.

Understanding the Revolution of 1989 requires a careful listening to the stories told by those who made the revolution: in 1989 and in the years of resistance that led up to that year of miracles.

That is what we shall do, in the later parts of this study. But it also requires an appreciation of the moral passions that often drive politics. And that means a brief visit back into history.

The Quest for the Millennium

Deep within the subsoil of human consciousness and culture, in the recesses of our common memory where the most profound and ancient yearnings of the human spirit are lodged, lies the image of the Millennium: the incarnation of the perennial human hope for a redeemed world and a redeemed, or cleansed, or recreated humanity—for a new earth (or a new age) in which righteousness and truth will meet, justice and peace will kiss, swords will be beaten into plowshares, and every tear will be wiped away. Hundreds of millions of human beings, across time, nations, and cultures, have been touched in the depths of their souls by this imagery. No one who has pondered the deaths of innocents; no one who has watched, helplessly, as human lives were ruined by prejudice, cruelty, or madness; no one who has tasted the joys of human love and community can fail to have been stirred by the power of the quest for the Millennium.

The image of the Millennium has also had public consequences. Indeed, the quest for the Millennium has been one of the most formative, and powerful, images driving the history of the West from the days of the Hebrew prophets down to our own time. Yet within the western stream of millenarian consciousness, there have been two, largely antithetical, tendencies: a transcendent or spiritual school, and a mundane or political school. According to the former, the Millennium will occur because of God's action, not man's. And while human beings can participate, in an anticipatory way, in the life of the Millennium (through prayer, by observance of the Torah, in festivals and liturgies, by incorporation into the Church), the Final Age is, in the final analysis, the consummation of history, and its coming cannot be "forced" into the here and now (or the immediate future) by human action. According to the latter construal, humanity—or that small, elite part of humanity that has discerned the truth of things—can accelerate the millennial reconstitution of the human condition. Indeed, on this understanding, those who have been

illuminated—those who have grasped the possibility of an imminent Millennium brought about by human action—have no
choice but to act on that insight: to redeem the times, and thereby
to hasten the arrival of the time that completes time.

Since the late eighteenth century, the quest for the Millennium
has intersected in the modern imagination of the West with that
magical, talismanic word, *revolution*. According to historian
James H. Billington, faith in the revolution—faith in the mundane, terrestrial, historical-political form of the quest for the
Millennium—has in fact been *the* characteristic faith of modernity, or at least of modern intellectuals and publicists.[1] Thus Karl
Marx, one believer in the revolutionary faith, sought "a politics
to end all politics."[2] Lenin, another believer, adopted as his motto
(and the epigraph for his revolutionary newspaper), "From the
spark comes the fire."[3] An earlier, and much greater, Russian,
Dostoevsky, reflecting on the millenarian passions of his age (on
which Lenin would, of course, feed) described those furies as a
"fire . . . in the minds of men."[4] Remembering the depth of the
millenarian aspiration in western culture, it is not going too far to
suggest that, in describing the quest for the Millennium in terms
of fire, both Lenin (doubtless unconsciously) and Dostoevsky
(perhaps intentionally) evoked deeply entrenched cultural memories of the sacrificial holocausts in the Temple and of the Easter
candle, that "flame divided yet undimmed" which is the symbolic
centerpiece of the axis of Christian worship, the liturgy of the
Easter Vigil.

The modern quest for the worldly Millennium—the revolutionary quest for secular salvation through political action[5]—has
brought unspeakable suffering in its wake; the death toll in the
twentieth century alone reaches well over 100 million lives.
Thankfully, and at the end of this most sanguinary of centuries,
we may discern a waning of the millenarian passion in its modern
revolutionary form in the collapse of communism in central and
eastern Europe and the late Soviet Union. But we shall miss the
full force of these historic cataclysms if we do not see that the
(largely) nonviolent revolutions that brought down the kingdoms
of Lenin's mundane revolutionary millenarians drew their inspiration, not from politics, or from the quest for a politics to end all
politics, but from a transcendent source.

The Revolution of 1989 and the New Russian Revolution of

1991 were revolutions of the human spirit before they were revolutions with worldly consequences. They were revolutions that, by reversing Marx and Lenin, overthrew them. They were revolutions in which the transcendent hope which communism understood as an expression of human alienation became the motive force behind great acts of human liberation.

Back to the Present

The revolutionary convulsions of the twentieth century can be read through the prisms of economics, sociology, political science, and psychology. And doubtless there is much to learn from each of these disciplines as one tries to untangle the thick knot of human striving, human wickedness, and human courage that is the history of the contemporary quest for the just society. Yet one also had the eerie sense, during the Revolution of 1989 and the New Russian Revolution, that there was something strangely familiar about the struggles we were witnessing. And in fact a good case can be made that the Marxist-Leninist revolutionary fantasy and its concrete political expression, the totalitarian communist state, were prefigured in the history of western millenarianism, and specifically in the revolutionary chiliasm of the Middle Ages.[6] In this sense, one gets at least as profound an insight into the energies and passions engaged by modern totalitarianism by reflecting on Joachim of Fiore, Jan Bockelson, John Ball, the Drummer of Niklashausen, and the Bohemian Taborites as by studying the economic etymology of Marx's theory of surplus value, or the historiographic rationale for Lenin's claim that imperialism was the last stage of capitalism. For the past is often prologue, and the politicization of the ancient hope for the coming of the Millennium was all the more tenacious in its grip on the twentieth century because of this largely forgotten aspect of the cultural history of the West.

In their quest for the final purification of the world,[7] medieval millenarians could reach back into a religious and cultural history embodied in the eschatological and apocalyptic literature of the Hebrew Scriptures and the New Testament, especially the Book of Daniel and the Book of Revelation. Nor, for all its exotic imagery, was this literature beyond the doctrinal pale: the concept of the coming messianic Kingdom, the kingdom of the Millennium, is a stable feature of post-exilic Jewish, and later Christian, orthodoxy.[8] But ideas, as ever, have consequences. And the very consequential question this concept sharpened was the question of *now*: What is the relationship between the promised messianic Kingdom and our activities in this world? That there were controversies over this in biblical times is evident from the debates over the claims of the Essenes, the Sicarii, and Bar Kokhba in the First and Second Jewish Revolts, and from the arguments over the "signs of the times" and their meaning for religious practice within the early Christian Church. Indeed, one defining moment in the break between synagogue and Church occurred when Jewish Christians fled (or, on the Jewish understanding, deserted) Jerusalem for Pella during the siege of Titus in A.D. 70 in anticipation of the Second Coming of Jesus Christ and the inauguration of his Kingdom.[9]

Following Constantine's reconciliation with the Christian Church, the orthodox Christian "solution" to the "problem" of the Millennium came from Augustine of Hippo. In *The City of God*, Augustine taught that the Book of Revelation was to be read allegorically and spiritually, rather than as a road map for navigating contemporary history. Moreover, according to Augustine, the Millennium "had begun with the birth of Christianity and was . . . realized in the Church."[10] Christians, in other words, experienced the grace and peace of the coming Kingdom in an anticipatory, or proleptic, way in the life and communion of the Church. But the fullness of the messianic age in the City of God would be realized in the consummation of history, in God's good time and through God's redemptive action—not in this world, and not through human agency, especially human political agency.

This is precisely what the medieval chiliasts rejected. These millenarians appeared in a fascinating, indeed fantastic, array of styles and guises. Yet the common denominator among them was that each was a distinctive variation on a more general revolt against the Augustinian "solution." And the themes and images of that revolt would reverberate through the centuries down to our own time.

What was the great hope of the medieval millenarians? It was for salvation: salvation in the here and now. And the salvation they sought had five special characteristics.

It was collective and egalitarian: it was to "be enjoyed by the faithful as a collectivity," and the ranks of the "faithful" were open to men and women regardless of their lack of worldly estate. Medieval millenarians influenced by this egalitarian ethic showed an early and persistent antipathy toward the primitive commercial economy, and many of them believed that the elimination of private property would lead to a new form of justice.[11]

It was worldly or "terrestrial" or mundane: salvation was to be enjoyed, and the messianic kingdom inaugurated, on this earth rather than in "some other-worldly heaven."[12]

It was "imminent": salvation and the Millennium were not for the distant future, but would come swiftly and suddenly.[13]

It was "total": life on earth would be utterly transformed, such that millennial life would be no mere improvement but "perfection itself."[14]

And it was "miraculous": men could accelerate the coming of the Millennium, but those who would succeed in this epochal task would do so "with the help of supernatural agencies."[15]

The achievement of this salvific Millennium required the completion of certain premillennial tasks. Chief among these was the elimination of disbelief, misbelief, and misbehavior. Those who did not share the millennial faith as interpreted by medieval chiliasts, or those who persisted in their sinful ways (again as construed by the millenarians), were not simply misguided souls: they were obstacles to the coming of the Kingdom, and they had to be eliminated.[16] In practice, of course, eliminating sin meant eliminating sinners.[17] The Bohemian Taborites in the fifteenth century gave this a proleptically modern twist by identifying the obstacles to the Millennium as "all lords, nobles, and knights"—in other words, "the great," against whom a class war had to be waged.[18] Later, in the New Jerusalem of Jan Bockelson's sixteenth-century Münster, terror and propaganda as means of social control (although always rationalized as being in service to the millennial kingdom) made a crucial premodern appearance.[19]

The egalitarianism and anticommercialism of the medieval millenarians; their commitment to a renewal of the earth that first involved shattering the old order; their foreshadowing of the modern totalitarian "party" that recognizes no claims but its own;[20] and some of their tactics (terrorism, and systematic control of the means of communication for the purposes of propagandizing the population)—all of these would linger on in European consciousness in what historian Norman Cohn has described as a "dim, subterranean existence,"[21] only to achieve a new lease on life in the modern period. But perhaps even more influential over time—because it created the imaginative space in which these other teaching and tactics could flourish, given the right circumstances—would be the historical and eschatological speculations of the great medieval mystic, Joachim of Fiore (1145–1202).

Joachim, a good trinitarian, taught that history was an "ascent through three successive stages" which paralleled the three Persons of the Holy Trinity. The Age of the Father was the time of the Law and obedience. The Age of the Son was the time of the Gospel and discipleship. His time, Joachim believed, was the third stage, the Age of the Spirit: an age of "love, joy, and freedom" in which "the knowledge of God would be revealed directly in the hearts of all men" in a "Kingdom of the Saints [that] would endure until the Last Judgment."[22] It was, and remained, a powerful vision of the present and the future.

Joachim was a deeply pious man who wanted to remain orthodox and who had no desire, unlike other medieval millenarians, to overthrow the Church. Yet his theory was baldly antithetical to the Augustinian "solution," and would be understood as such by some of his less scrupulous (or more fanatical) followers. More to the point for our purposes, Joachim's image of the "three stages" would have a profound, long-term influence on crucial schools of thought in the western philosophy of history, including schools deeply hostile to Christianity. As Norman Cohn has put it,

> Horrified though the unworldly mystic would have been to see it happen, it is unmistakably the Joachite fantasy of the three ages that reappeared in, for instance, the theories of historical evolution expounded by the German Idealist philosophers Lessing, Schelling, Fichte, and to some extent Hegel; in Auguste Comte's idea of history as an ascent from the theological through the metaphysical up to the scientific phase; and again in the Marxian dialectic of the three stages of primitive communism, class society, and a final communism which is to be the realm of freedom and in which the state will have withered away.[23]

The Tyranny of the Political

The bridge between Joachim of Fiore and Lenin (and the Gulag)—
the bridge between the revolutionary chiliasm of the medieval millenarians and many of the convulsions of twentieth-century history—was built in the late eighteenth and early nineteenth
centuries by European intellectuals and publicists who radically
secularized and politicized the millennial hope and thus transformed it into what James Billington has called the "revolutionary
faith." Jean-Jacques Rousseau, who revived the medievals' image
of a pristine state of nature to which millennial man would return,
and whose concept of the "general will" would be crucial to modern totalitarian pretensions, played a large role in this development, as did less well-remembered men such as Nicholas
Bonneville and Filippo Buonarotti.[24] But however one weighs the
relative influences of these (and a host of other) revolutionary figures, what remains is the fact that their intention was Promethean:
as Prometheus had stolen fire from the gods, so it might be said
that the adepts of the modern revolutionary faith tried to steal the
Millennium from God. The final revolution, in their imaginings,
would be an "ultramundane" revolution: a revolution $99\,{}^{44}\!/_{100}$ percent transcendence free.

There were, to be sure, certain secularizing tendencies among
the medieval millenarians, as might have been seen in the revolutionary New Jerusalem of Jan Bockelson's Münster, a favorite
reference point for generations of Marxist historians.[25] But secu-
larity, and millennial hope, the West could handle—as it had
since Augustine distinguished the City of God and the earthly
City. The really new element (some would say, poison) that
entered the western bloodstream with Rousseau and his disciples
was the apotheosis of the *political* as the vehicle for creating the
New Jerusalem in this world.

Furthermore, this was not "politics" in a merely instrumental
sense: this was politics as ontology, politics as metaphysics, politics as the object of faith. For Rousseau and those who pursued
the trail he blazed sought not simply utopia *through* politics, but
utopia *against* all forms of traditional authority, and especially
religious authority.[26] There was, of course, a curious symbiosis
here. For "at a deep and often unconscious level, the revolutionary faith was shaped by the Christian faith it attempted to replace.

Most revolutionaries viewed history prophetically as a kind of unfolding morality play. The present was hell, and revolution a collective purgatory leading to a future earthly paradise."[27] But there would be no need, and thus no room, in that paradise for God.

After the initial revolutionary hopes of Rousseau and the early nineteenth-century intellectuals and publicists were dashed by the Thermidore that restored traditional monarchical (and religious) authority, the flame of revolutionary faith was tended by what Billington has termed "a new species of man, the professional revolutionary."[28] And while professional revolutionaries subscribed to a number of mundane millennial theologies, the most influential of these belief systems was the creed first defined by Marx and Engels, and then refined (if such be the term) into a powerful instrument of revolutionary agitation and, later, social control by Vladimir Ilyich Ulyanov, more familiarly known by his Bolshevik nom de guerre, Lenin.

Marxism-Leninism was (and I think we can now, safely, say "was") many things. In power, and on the proceeding analysis, it was medieval Münster, albeit without God. It embodied, in an especially cruel and odious form, the tyranny of the political that was inevitable in any social system born from Rousseauian presuppositions. As a doctrinal system, Marxism-Leninism included a theory of economics (generally quite silly), a theory of history (reaching, as we have seen, back into the cultural subsoil first tilled by Joachim of Fiore), and a theory of radical politics (perhaps the most successful example of the genre in modern history, at least in terms of its capacity to inform a minority in its seizure and maintenance of power).

But we miss the essence of Marxism-Leninism—the essence that accounts for its mythic power and its ability to hold on to what it had seized over time—unless we understand it as a religion. It was a secularized religion, to be sure; a false religion, certainly; but a religion—a *religio*, a binding together of its adherents in a common faith from which grew a powerfully attractive community—without a doubt.

The revolutionary faith of Marxism-Leninism had all the elements of a traditional religion. For all that it was often explicated in stultifying prose, communism had a doctrine and particularly a soteriology (a theory of salvation—in this case, through revolution) and an ecclesiology (a theory of the Church—in this case, the party). Within the party, it had a discipline and a theory of apostolic succession.[29] It had sacred texts (the *Manifesto*, *Das Kapital*, *What Is to Be Done?*). It had a ritual, including a ritual of expurgation (in which misbelievers and disbelievers were "exterminated"—a favorite word of Lenin's—for the sake of the revolutionary faith). It had, in its own cruel way, an ethics, of which Feliks Dzerzhinsky, founder of the Cheka/NKVD/KGB, was a leading theoretician. It had, as we have seen, an eschatology: a theory of the "last things." It had the power of the anathema (although it used this, not only against individuals, but against whole classes of people who embodied a putative sin—the "kulaks," peasants who employed others on their farms, for instance). It had heretics (democratic socialists, "left-wing deviationists," and Trotskyites, prominent among them).

And all of *that*, far more than its ability to force the pace of economic modernization in backward lands, gave Marxism-Leninism its power in history. Marxism-Leninism—communism—was the ultimate modern expression of the tyranny of the political. But because it was a tyranny in the service of an ancient eschatological ideal, and because it ironically provided what it denied men needed—a faith and a community of faithful that was universal in scope—it had staying power far beyond that managed by the other political fantasies of the nineteenth and twentieth centuries, including its demonic twin, Nazism.

The Priority of Conscience

On some readings of history, the twentieth century was to have seen the triumph of the revolutionary faith. Yet to the surprise of those who expected the dawn of the earthly Millennium, humankind seems to have learned some rather different things about itself and its prospects since Lenin, in his famous question, asked what was to be done.

We have learned that politics is important, but penultimate, and that those who assert its ultimacy do terrible damage to human beings, to human society, and to the earth's ecology.

We have learned that millennial hope is a fixture of the human psyche and the human spirit, but that Augustine's explication of that great hope is wiser than Joachim of Fiore's.

We have learned, or relearned, that faith is an indispensable component of a truly human life. But we have been reminded that faith untethered from a transcendent point of reference means tyranny, and that tyranny under modern means of social control means suffering without end.

The quest for a "politics to end all politics" is one with which many people (and particularly those obliged to involve themselves in politics) can sympathize. But reflecting on the wretched results of Real Existing Marxism, surely one can draw two lessons from the experience of the twentieth century. The first is that the absolutizing of the political necessarily yields the tyranny of the political. The second is that only a reality that transcends politics can truly transform politics: or, better, transform the human condition.

At the end of the 1970s, James Billington closed his history of the revolutionary faith with a provocative set of questions. Could this "secular creed, which arose in Judeo-Christian culture . . . ultimately prove to be only a stage in the continuing metamorphosis of older forms of faith"? Might it be that "the belief in secular revolution, which has legitimized so much authoritarianism in the twentieth century" could in fact "dialectically prefigure some rediscovery of religious evolution to revalidate democracy in the twenty-first"?[30]

As things turned out, Billington was simply off by a decade or two. For the Revolution of 1989 in central and eastern Europe was precisely that—a revolution of the human spirit, frequently informed by a reinvigorated Christian (often Catholic) faith, which proved to be the irresistible force that the communist enterprise could not finally withstand. That the Catholic Church, long identified by modern millenarian revolutionaries as the great bastion of the hated ancien régime, and mocked by Stalin with his dismissive question about the power of the "pope's divisions," should have helped give birth to the final revolution added piquancy to the world-historical mix. And that the Bishop of Rome, a Slav no less, should have been the principal evangelist of the final revolution—well, to some it seemed to suggest that the One whom Christians worship as the Lord of history had a finely edged, and deliciously ironic, sense of the proprieties indeed.

If human freedom has in fact been given a new lease on life as we approach the twenty-first century, it is because the tyranny of politics was successfully resisted in the twentieth, and on the basis of a transcendent affirmation of the human person in the plenitude of his or her humanity. Religion, far from withering away, is an ascendant reality in human affairs. Democracy, that impressive and yet most fragile of experiments in self-governance, is now warranted by religiously grounded moral conviction across wide expanses of the globe: no news, perhaps, to the heirs of the Puritans (long accustomed to thinking of their faith as a buttress for democracy), but good news indeed to the children of Rome, who have played a great, if underappreciated, role in that development. The paradigm for what the twenty-first century should *not* be can be found in the mad totalitarianisms that have beset humankind in the twentieth. Can we discern a paradigm for what public life ought to be in the final revolution, the revolution of the spirit, which put an end to the tyranny of the political and reminded the world that politics is a function of culture—and that the heart of culture is cult, or religion?

How the final revolution informed the Revolution of 1989, and what that might mean for the future of democracy, is the business of this book.

ONE

Not by Politics Alone: Unwrapping the Revolution of 1989

The collapse of the communist regimes in central and eastern Europe and their replacement by democratic governments in Poland, Hungary, the German Democratic Republic (GDR), and Czechoslovakia dramatically changed the face of the twentieth century. Moreover, the Revolution of 1989 was the work of courageous men and women who self-consciously identified their cause with the larger cause of human freedom: by which they meant the political values whose protection had been understood, since 1945, to have been the special charge of the countries called "the West." And yet in the United States, and more generally throughout western political, media, and academic circles, there has been a curious lack of agreement on the sources of the Revolution of 1989: the combination and correlation of forces that led (nonviolently no less) to what had long seemed so difficult as to be virtually impossible—the disintegration of Stalin's post–World War II empire, and the return of what used to be called "captive nations" to the house of Europe. Indeed, and judging from the timorous reactions of many in its political elite, the West has barely begun to grasp the very good news that the Revolution of 1989 happened. But it has not even begun to grapple seriously with the questions of *why* the revolution happened, when it did, and how it did.

When did the Revolution of 1989 begin? Did it have a chief instigator? Who lit the match that ignited the flame?

Here is one possible answer, in the dry prose of the chronology of world events published annually by *Foreign Affairs*:

June 2–10 [1979]. Pope John Paul II visits Poland, celebrates first pontifical Mass in a communist country, and meets with Polish political leaders.[1]

But given the high drama of the Revolution of 1989, perhaps the case should be put more provocatively:

What Lenin started at Petrograd's Finland Station on April 16, 1917, and what Stalin thought he had guaranteed at the Yalta conference in February 1945, and what Brezhnev brutally reconfirmed by invading and subjugating Czechoslovakia in 1968, Pope John Paul II began to dismantle at the Jasna Góra monastery in Częstochowa, the shrine of the Black Madonna, Queen of Poland, on June 4, 1979.

That, at any rate, and to take symbolic reference points that embody key elements in the larger drama, is the thesis of this book.

What follows is certainly not a comprehensive history of the Revolution of 1989 in all its multiple facets. Nor is it being claimed here that the pope, or the Roman Catholic Church, were the only factors in igniting the revolution in the late 1970s and early 1980s and carrying it through to a successful conclusion in the *annus mirabilis*, 1989. The claim is more modest, although perhaps none the less controversial for that: the claim is that it is impossible to understand both the *why* of the revolution (the fact that, in 1989, at this discrete point in history, and after more than forty years of totalitarian oppression, the people of central and eastern Europe cast off the political chains that had bound them since the end of the Second World War) and its *how* (its nonviolent and democratic character) without taking considerable account of the Catholic Church and, pre-eminently, of its supreme pastor, Karol Wojtyła of Kraków, latterly the Bishop of Rome, John Paul II.

A moral and cultural revolution preceded, and in fact made possible, the political Revolution of 1989. Clerical and lay leaders and members of the Catholic Church in central and eastern Europe, inspired and led by Pope John Paul II, were crucial, and in some cases determinative, figures in the moral and cultural revolution. The impact of the moral and cultural revolution on the political revolution (in which, of course, Catholics also figured prominently) was decisive. Missing that, we miss the distinctiveness of this most singular of revolutionary upheavals.

This is not, to put it gently, a claim that has dominated American and other western discussions of the Revolution of 1989. Neither Zbigniew Brzezinski nor Jeane J. Kirkpatrick, two of the most astute American commentators on central and eastern European affairs throughout the 1980s, takes very much account of the role of the Church and the pope in the revolution, in their books on the subject.[2] Nor, on the other side of the Atlantic, does Sir Ralf Dahrendorf, warden of St. Antony's College, Oxford, former director of the London School of Economics, and author of *Reflections on the Revolution in Europe*.[3] *Foreign Affairs* published some twenty-one articles analyzing aspects of the Revolution of 1989 and its aftershocks in the first two years after the iron curtain fell; only three of them even mentioned the Church's role in the revolution, and the lengthiest discussion of the phenomenon occupied one paragraph.

There have been occasional (and distinguished) exceptions to this general trend. Throughout the 1980s, the journalism of the young Briton, Timothy Garton Ash, available to Americans in the *New York Review of Books*, showed a marked sensitivity to the roles of the Church and the pope in challenging, and finally overthrowing, Real Existing Socialism.[4] The Librarian of Congress, James Billington, broke ranks by decrying the "pitifully tubular" and narrow-gauged "economic and political behaviorism" that had dominated western analysis of the Revolution of 1989.[5] Another dissident was Aaron Wildavsky, former president of the American Political Science Association, who insisted that the collapse of communism was fundamentally a moral collapse.[6]

But these were, in fact, exceptions. Far more frequently, and at the higher altitudes of the U.S. government as well as among policy analysts and commentators, one encounters explanations of the *why* and the *how* of the Revolution of 1989 that ignore or radically minimize the religious (or, perhaps more neutrally, moral-cultural) dimension of the revolution, and focus instead on more familiar political personalities, economic issues, and/or political-military-diplomatic processes.

Several of these more familiar explanations are worth a brief exploration here. Each of them has elements of insight and truth in it. But each is finally unsatisfactory: because none of them takes sufficient account of the *why* and the *how* of the revolution of the spirit, the moral and cultural revolution, that was the heart and soul of the Revolution of 1989.

The Standard Account: Mikhail Gorbachev Did It

A striking array of commentators seem agreed that primary credit for the Revolution of 1989 must go to Mikhail Gorbachev: the "Man of the Decade," as *Time* magazine's editors put it in 1990 with unrestrained enthusiasm. But *Time* was hardly alone in its celebration of the Soviet leader. The same Norwegian Nobel Committee that had honored Lech Wałęsa and Andrei Sakharov for their resistance to Soviet totalitarianism honored Gorbachev in 1990 with its Peace Prize—precisely for what the Committee regarded as his crucial role in the democratic transitions in central and eastern Europe (transitions that Gorbachev seemed markedly reluctant to introduce into his own country until the dramatic events of August 1991 ended, in effect, the "Soviet Union"). Then there was pundit Sidney Blumenthal, a bellwether of left-liberal opinion in the United States, whose admiration for Gorbachev was, evidently, boundless: Gorbachev, *pace* Blumenthal, not only liberated eastern Europe; he destroyed communism in the USSR, saved Ronald Reagan's presidency, spared George Bush from being dragged down by the Iran-contra affair, and created "the preconditions for the revival of liberalism" in America.[7]

A far more serious case for Gorbachev as the sine qua non of the Revolution of 1989 was made by Ralf Dahrendorf in his aforementioned *Reflections*. Without Gorbachev and his "remarkable approach," Dahrendorf argued, "the events of 1989 . . . would not have happened and in the particular way in which they occurred." And what was the Gorbachev difference? It featured, according to Dahrendorf, two revolutionary tenets: that "the Soviet army will no longer intervene when its allies go their own way," and that "the Soviet party will not insist on the monopoly of the Communist Party" in the countries of central and eastern Europe. "It would not be too farfetched," Dahrendorf concluded, "to say that Gorbachev is above all an opener of hitherto closed doors" who hopes that his erstwhile "allies" will end up with "some kind of 'democratic socialism,'" but who above all "wants to unlock the door into an open future."[8]

Dahrendorf's view was shared by many other prominent commentators; three may be taken as representative of the wider Gorbachev caucus. According to Sir Michael Howard, not even Gorbachev's mentor and patron, Yuri Andropov, could have foreseen the skill with which Gorbachev would consolidate and maintain his internal authority and the boldness with which he would unleash the forces of revolutionary change. . . . Even to chronicle the events of 1989 leaves one breathless, and it is still too soon to appreciate their full significance for the future of East-West relations. One thing, however, is clear. The liberation of eastern Europe occurred not in face of objections from Moscow, but with positive Soviet support.[9]

William H. McNeill agreed: Gorbachev had "initiated changes that may well turn out to be [as] important" as the Tennis Court Oath in 1789 and Lenin's revolution in 1917.[10] Robert G. Kaiser, who believes that Gorbachev was in some respects a failure because he created a revolution he could not subsequently control, was yet in no doubt that Gorbachev had in fact created the revolution:

In just over five years, Mikhail Gorbachev transformed the world. . . . He tossed away the Soviet empire in eastern Europe with no more than a fare-thee-well. He ended the Cold War that had dominated world politics and consumed the wealth of nations for nearly half a century. . . . These are the most astounding historical developments that any of us are likely to experience.[11]

With the advantage of more temporal distance from the extraordinary events of late 1989, perhaps a less breathless, more measured judgment is possible.

Mikhail Gorbachev ought to be given a measure of the credit for the fact that the Revolution of 1989 took place without bloodshed and without overt interference from the Soviet Union (the question of covert interference, indeed of Soviet attempts to manipulate the revolution, remains open). The minimal, ungrudging statement about Gorbachev's contribution to the revolution, from the time he took power in March 1985 through the dramatic events of late 1989, would run something like this: Gorbachev was unwilling to risk World War III in order to preserve Stalin's imperial system in central and eastern Europe. Thus Gorbachev injected into Soviet foreign policy the critical measure of realism that permitted the USSR to disentangle itself from the spider's web of the Brezhnev Doctrine, which taught the permanence of communist regimes and the special role of the USSR in enforcing that irreversibility. Put yet another way, and taking due account of the worlds from which he emerged, Gorbachev deserves credit for not doing in 1989 what Brezhnev unhesitatingly did in 1968: send in the tanks.

But it would be a grave mistake to think that Gorbachev's relative restraint vis-à-vis the restive nations of central and eastern Europe involved some sort of noblesse oblige toward those whom Dahrendorf describes (inaccurately, it must be said) as his "allies." Various mythologies and other forms of wishful thinking notwithstanding, there is virtually no evidence to suggest that Mikhail Gorbachev ever broke in a fundamental way with Marxism-Leninism prior to the New Russian Revolution of August 1991— at which point Gorbachev's convictions became rather an irrelevance. No doubt Gorbachev wanted communism with a human face—which would surely have been an improvement over communism with a Stalinist or Brezhnevite face. But it would still have been communism. Indeed, the way in which Gorbachev stubbornly clung to certain Marxist-Leninist orthodoxies even after August 21, 1991, is cast into even sharper relief when set against what seem to have indeed been the genuine breaks with the past made by several of Gorbachev's former allies in the post-Brezhnev-generation Soviet leadership.

In brief, the weight of the evidence suggests that, during the events which led to and culminated in the Revolution of 1989, Mikhail Gorbachev was never anything but a reform communist. His goal, in the satellites of central and eastern Europe as in the Soviet Union, was what Berkeley Sovietologist Martin Malia has described as "controlled liberalization . . . an expanded but still limited right to tell the truth about the past and to criticize the shortcomings of the present; a measure of participation in public affairs by groups outside the party; and a modest degree of managerial and financial autonomy for state enterprises, together with the emergence of a small sector of semi-private businesses providing services." But reform communism "never was intended to mean full cultural freedom, constitutional government, or a market economy with private property. And it never envisaged abandoning the hegemony of the party, even though other political groups might be tolerated as part of a reform 'popular front.' "[12]

To return to the minimalist proposition: when General Wojciech Jaruzelski's reform communism (which, Malia argues, was instigated by Gorbachev's perestroika) failed in Poland, and when the unreformed communism of East Germany's Erich Honecker and Czechoslovakia's Gustáv Husák imploded, Gorbachev did not send in the Red Army; he may even have done more in terms of the GDR, perhaps going so far as to restrain the East German internal security troops from using deadly force against demonstrators. But it is not ungracious, simply realistic, to suggest that by the time the Revolution of 1989 gained critical mass in the fall and winter of that year, Gorbachev really had no choice but to acquiesce in the demise of the Soviet outer empire and to put the best possible face on it. His own image as a great international statesman was, ironically, one restraint on Gorbachev's menu of policy options in the late 1980s. But by 1989 the Soviet economic crisis had become so desperate, and the Soviet need for western financial and other economic assistance so great, that Gorbachev simply had no rational alternative but to cut his losses and, out of the loss cutting, to gain whatever degree of leverage was possible for the next phase of his attempt to salvage reform communism in the USSR.

Still, and notwithstanding the kernel of truth within it, the standard account that "Gorbachev did it" is ultimately unsatisfactory as an explanation of the Revolution of 1989 for reasons more profound than the fact that Gorbachev was no democrat during the mid-to-late 1980s. For the Gorbachev-as-catalyst model fails to explain how it was that Mikhail Gorbachev was presented with an unprecedented situation—a revolt of both workers and intellectuals, often operating in tandem, determined to bring about a transition to democracy through nonviolent means—in 1989. No reasonable analyst would suggest Gorbachev created that fact. And yet that fact, the "pre-revolution" before the revolution, was the human and organizational basis of the Revolution of 1989.

"Gorbachev did it" explains one facet of the nonviolence of the revolution: the fact that the tanks didn't roll. But it does not explain the revolution in its origins, in its staying power, or in its most powerful human dynamics. The answers to those foundational questions must lie elsewhere.

The Realist Account: Ronald Reagan Did It

The obverse of the notion that "Gorbachev did it" is the claim—encountered far more frequently in central and eastern Europe than in North America—that Ronald Reagan "did it": that

Ronald Reagan was, if not the catalyst, then the indispensable condition for the possibility of the Revolution of 1989.

There is more than a little truth here. Indeed, when the passions of present controversies fade, the notion that "Reagan did it" will probably be regarded as having far more plausibility than the now dominant claim that "Gorbachev did it."

How did Reagan "do it?" One way he did it was through the power of rhetoric: a political weapon much esteemed when wielded by John F. Kennedy, but curiously ignored (or deprecated) when deployed by Ronald Wilson Reagan (who was, as we know, "only" an actor). And yet listening to the reminiscences of central and eastern Europeans, as well as to those Soviet democrats who completed the Revolution of 1989 in August 1991, one cannot but be struck by the impact that Reagan's rhetoric had on the morale of what were then called "dissidents" in the countries behind the iron curtain. Indeed, the most bitterly controverted phrase of the Reagan presidency, the president's description of the Soviet Union as an "evil empire," is still regarded in many central and eastern European democratic circles as nothing more than a statement of the obvious: albeit a welcome statement that cleansed the rhetorical and moral atmosphere of fustian, cut through the Orwellian babble of the Brezhnevite "era of stagnation," and heartened those struggling to break out from under the rubble (as Solzhenitsyn graphically put it) of the totalitarian system. The dissidents were convinced that theirs was, above all, a moral struggle: a contest not merely between alternative power systems but between drastically different conceptions of the human person, human community, human history, and human destiny—in short, between two very different concepts of good and evil. And they were (and remain) grateful for a president of the United States who seemed to agree with them and who gave voice to his agreement—and to their aspirations.

But the politics of nations is not motored by rhetoric alone, and there are other, more tangible accomplishments of the Reagan presidency which give credibility to the claim that "Reagan did it."

One of these was the deployment of intermediate-range Pershing II and cruise missiles in western Europe, fulfilling the commitment made to NATO in the late 1970s by the Carter administration. The INF (intermediate-range nuclear forces) debate was heated and bitter, in the United States, Great Britain, and the Federal Republic of Germany. Protesters frequently filled the streets and liberal political leaders throughout the West rushed to embrace the talismanic proposal of the renascent peace movement, the "nuclear freeze." Those who argued that the freeze would lock in a situation of Soviet nuclear superiority, or who suggested that the real source of conflict along the Yalta fault line was not the weapons but rather communism and its abuse of human rights, were informed that they were too little concerned about the threat of nuclear war. These were the days when ABC-TV broadcast "The Day After," a melodrama about a nuclear war that began with an American INF launch; when anti-nuclear Physicians for Social Responsibility chapters sprang up from one end of the United States to the other; and when International Physicians for the Prevention of Nuclear War (led by a privileged Soviet apparatchik and an American who had been singularly silent in the face of the persecution of Soviet democrats like Andrei Sakharov) won the Nobel Peace Prize. The Brezhnev Doctrine, it seems, had been internalized far more by leading elements in the American and west European political classes than by those who would later make the Revolution of 1989.

Ronald Reagan, of course, said a resounding "No" to this agitation. In doing so he laid down an empirical marker that Soviet military and political leaders could not ignore, while challenging at a political-psychological level the myth of the irreversibility of Soviet power. And all of this, it has to be said again, gave heart to the dissident community in central and eastern Europe, even to those who shared western concerns about the proliferation of nuclear weapons in Europe: indeed, especially to those committed to the pursuit of peace through freedom.

Here, of course, is one of the paradoxes of the endgame of the Cold War. The anti-INF forces in the West were vocally supported, indeed celebrated, by the official, regime-sponsored "peace movements" throughout the Warsaw Pact. But they were not applauded, and one would be hard pressed to say that they were supported, even by those dissidents who were very much men and women of the left. Why?

Václav Havel gave a sharp answer to that question in one of the more remarkable essays to issue from the underground literature of this period, "The Anatomy of a Reticence."[13] Why were the dissidents reticent about western "peace movements"? Because the very word *peace* had been so debased by communist propaganda that it had lost its moral power: it had "been drained of all content."[14] Because the "struggle for peace" in the Warsaw Pact had been another instrument of Stalinist and Brezhnevite social control, and western agitators and activists had done little to challenge that. Because the dissidents in central and eastern Europe understood that one could not speak truth to power in the same way, and with the same effect, in democracies and in totalitarian states: asymmetrical pressures would inevitably result, to the advantage of the totalitarians and the disadvantage of the democrats. Because the western agitators and activists often had the "wholly erroneous impression that the only dangerous weapons are those surrounded by encampments of demonstrators."[15] Because the western activists seemed blind to the germ of totalitarianism that lurked within their utopianism. Because too frequently western "peace" activists linked the problem of disarmament to other ideological enthusiasms (including feminism) in ways that were simply incomprehensible to dissidents (including women) in the Warsaw Pact countries.[16] Because, wrote Havel, the dissidents had "learned only too well, from their own fate, where a policy of appeasement can lead": namely, to more violence as well as to personal and social moral degradation.[17]

But at the most fundamental level of politics, dissidents in the Warsaw Pact countries were profoundly skeptical of western "peace" activists because there was a deep cleavage in analysis between these two groups of dissenters, a cleavage that was geopolitical, tactical, and moral. Dissidents like Havel believed, on the basis of hard personal experience, that "the danger of war is not caused by weapons as such but by political realities . . . in a divided Europe and a divided world." Moreover, the dissidents were convinced that "no lasting, genuine peace can be achieved simply by opposing a particular weapons system, because this deals with consequences, not with causes." The only way to peace lay through a fundamental "restructuring [of] the political realities that are at the roots of the current crisis": which meant the evolution of "free and independent nations" comprised of "free, self-respecting, and autonomous citizens." As Havel put it, a "state that ignores the will and rights of its citizens" could not make peace: because it could not guarantee that it would "respect the will and rights of other peoples, nations, and states." In short, "a state that denies its citizens their basic rights" is "a danger to its neighbors as well. . . . A lasting peace and disarmament can only be the work of free people."[18]

That was the view the Reagan administration brought to American foreign policy: the human rights issue and the disarmament issue could not be sundered in devising U.S. policy toward the Soviet Union and its satellites. Václav Havel and Ronald Reagan may still seem, to some, an odd couple. But on this crucial point—that the chief threat to European security lay, not in military hardware per se but in the nature of the regimes imposed on central and eastern Europe by the Yalta imperial system—they were of one (very determined) mind.

Three other distinctive elements of Reagan administration policy had an impact on the Revolution of 1989. One was the creation of the National Endowment for Democracy, a congressionally chartered, governmentally funded nonprofit corporation that provided financial support and technical assistance to democratic dissidents in central and eastern Europe throughout the mid-and-late 1980s. Then there was the Reagan Doctrine of supporting anticommunist resistance forces around the world—a policy that cost the USSR dearly, particularly in Afghanistan, but also in Africa and Central America. The relationship between the weakening of the Soviet economy and the Soviet military caused by this U.S. policy, and Soviet behavior in the last six months of 1989, can only be speculated upon: but a weaker Soviet Union was surely in a less advantageous position relative to its central and east European satellites than it had been during the revolts of 1953, 1956, and 1968.

Finally, there was the Strategic Defense Initiative (SDI). Here, too, causal chains of a mathematical sort are difficult to construct. But one cannot help but be impressed by the number of political and religious leaders in central and eastern Europe who, when asked what accounts for the shift in Soviet behavior in the late 1980s, say, simply, "SDI." (One hears the same thing, far more discreetly, from some senior officials in the Vatican.) By "SDI" here is meant, of course, a cluster of hypotheses about the decisions that shaped events from 1983 through 1989: that the Soviet Union knew it could not compete with the United States on a new technological frontier without bankrupting itself; that the

Soviet leadership, having failed to kill SDI through a massive propaganda campaign, decided to try to cut the project down by an abrupt turn toward amiability on the matter of offensive nuclear arms control; and that the threat of full-bore SDI development, which the Soviets judged would follow hard on the heels of any overt military intervention to enforce the Brezhnev Doctrine in central and eastern Europe, helped keep the tanks from rolling in 1989. There is no way to know, with any degree of certainty, about the truth of these hypotheses. But they are not implausible. And they are widely held among the people who were there during the revolution.[19]

So there were numerous ways in which Reagan administration policy contributed to the Revolution of 1989. But even the most enthusiastic Reaganite would make a mistake by loading too much weight onto the claim that "Reagan did it." The Yalta imperial system had withstood great military and political pressures before: at the time of the formation of NATO, during the Marshall Plan, at the time of the revolts in Hungary (1956) and Czechoslovakia (1968), during the various western nuclear and conventional force modernizations that defined one dimension of the rhythm of the Cold War. This time, though, in 1989 and in the decade that preceded the *annus mirabilis*, things were different: the "dissent" was more widespread, more flexible, more effective. It was nonviolent. It drew on explicitly religious symbols, and appealed openly to moral warrants and norms in international law, in an unprecedented way. The Reagan administration did a lot to help make the Revolution of 1989 possible; but it cannot be given credit for the distinctive character of the revolution. The sources of that singularity must lie elsewhere.

The Diplomatic Account: The Helsinki Final Act Did It

On this question of the distinctiveness of the Revolution of 1989, one way to give credit where credit is long overdue is to acknowledge the crucial impact of the 1975 Helsinki Final Act and the "Helsinki review process" that it mandated under the umbrella of the ongoing Conference on Security and Cooperation in Europe (CSCE).

When he signed the Helsinki Accords on August 1, 1975, Leonid

Brezhnev quite probably thought that he had secured Stalin's bastard patrimony, the Yalta imperial system, for the foreseeable future. Interestingly enough, the secretary of state of the Holy See (Cardinal Jean Villot, a Frenchman who declined to represent the Vatican at the signing of the document), conservative commentators in the West, and "captive nations" activists agreed: the principal effect of the Helsinki Final Act was to codify the post-1945 status quo (and the Brezhnev Doctrine) in central and eastern Europe. On this view, and if chuckling is permitted where he is now resident, Stalin was chuckling on the evening of August 1, 1975.

Foreign policy liberals were not enthusiastic about the Helsinki Final Act either. On the left, "arms control" had emerged as the Grail in pursuit of which all other issues had to be subordinated. And the Final Act said little about "arms control," although it did say agreeable things about consultation and negotiation as the means for settling intra-European grievances. And so, while the conservatives deprecated Helsinki as appeasement, the liberals yawned, so to speak, and then got back to the real business of trying to negotiate controls on nuclear and conventional weapons in Europe.

As things turned out, though, August 1, 1975, was the beginning of the terminal phase of the Yalta imperial system. Leonid Brezhnev had signed, not the guarantee, but the death warrant of Stalin's empire. For the Helsinki Final Act contained, in its famous "Basket Three," a set of human rights provisions and compliance review procedures that gave a new, and ultimately irresistible, impetus to the political dynamics that eventually created the Revolution of 1989 in central and eastern Europe. How, is a story of courage and fortitude that should inspire those who care about freedom a century from now.

The tale may be told here far more briefly than justice requires. Shortly after the Final Act was signed, "Helsinki monitoring groups" sprung up throughout the communist world. The list of leaders of Soviet monitoring groups reads like a *Who's Who* of the heroes of Soviet human rights activism: Yelena Bonner; Yuri Orlov; Alexander Ginzburg; Anatoly (Natan) Sharansky; Anatoly Marchenko; Petyor Grigorenko; Ludmilla Alexeeva. In central Europe, the Helsinki Final Act was crucial to the formation of Charter 77 (spokesman: Václav Havel) in Czechoslovakia, while in Poland the Final Act's provisions were cited by Solidarity leaders in defense of their organizing activities. Throughout central and eastern Europe and in the USSR itself, church activists and authorities cited Basket Three's clear statement on religious freedom (for which the Holy See had pressed hard during the negotiations that led to the Final Act) as the legal justification for their resistance to further state persecution of believers.

The original Helsinki monitoring groups were met with ferocious repression. Nothing like these organized and linked groups of human rights activists had ever been seen before behind the iron curtain. And while the communist authorities could (and did) accuse the monitors of being agents of western propaganda, the inescapable fact was that the activists were holding their governments accountable to human rights norms that those same governments had publicly embraced (in what they had assumed to have been their hour of triumph) in signing the Helsinki Final Act. Moreover, repression produced an important "catacomb effect": many human rights leaders, when jailed, made their incarceration the occasion to think through in detail the strategic and tactical issues involved in replacing totalitarian with democratic regimes; the prison writings of Havel and Poland's Adam Michnik are two of the most eloquent examples of how much of the Revolution of 1989 was intellectually gestated under lock and key.[20]

That the human rights movement energized by the Helsinki Final Act was not simply crushed was due primarily to its members' unflagging courage. But that courage got an unprecedented degree of visibility and support in the West through two other byproducts of the Final Act: western human rights organizations explicitly linked to the work of the Helsinki monitors in communist countries, and the periodic "Helsinki review conferences" mandated by the Final Act itself. Western organizations such as Helsinki Watch, Scientists for Sakharov, Orlov, and Sharansky, and Lithuanian Catholic Religious Aid provided material and moral support to embattled human rights activists behind the iron curtain and, through their own pressure (and that of the bipartisan congressional Commission on Security and Cooperation in Europe, a kind of Capitol Hill Helsinki watch group), helped the Carter and Reagan administrations keep the glare of publicity on Soviet and Warsaw Pact human rights violations at the Helsinki review conferences in Belgrade (1977–1978), Madrid (1980–1983), and Vienna (1986–1989). The review conferences provided unprecedented opportunities to remind western audiences of the linkage between human rights and "security and cooperation in Europe," while reassuring activists in communist countries that their lifeline to the West (the activists knew full well that their physical survival often revolved around their visibility west of the Elbe River) had not been cut.

The CSCE review process regularly clarified the moral stakes in the Cold War at crucial points when many in the West (both conservatives and liberals) were inclined to regard that struggle as but one more variant on the Great Game of great powers. The Helsinki monitoring groups were themselves intellectual and organizational incubators for much of the leadership of the Revolution of 1989. The review process was not only crucial to the safety of the monitors in communist countries; it provided the occasion to vigorously press human rights issues on the countries of the Warsaw Pact in an arena that was slightly off the center stage of the superpower drama. The fact of the monitors and their persecution, and the reality of the review conferences, forced western liberals to confront the realities of totalitarian societies, while it compelled western conservatives to think beyond the sterilities of Realpolitik and to consider the possibility that there were also nonmilitary ways to confront the Yalta imperial system.[21] For all of these reasons, CSCE played a major role in preparing the moral, intellectual, and political ground for the Revolution of 1989. Ignorance of that role among western political leaders, pundits, and political scientists is but another sign of the tone deafness toward the music of freedom that seems so sadly characteristic of these worlds. But ask the people of central and eastern Europe, and particularly the leaders of the Revolution of 1989: they will tell you that "Helsinki" made an enormous difference.

Yet "Helsinki" or "CSCE" does not, in and of itself, provide a wholly satisfactory explanation of the *why* and the *how* of the Revolution of 1989. Granting its impressive contribution to the cause of freedom, there is yet no way to explain, within the documents and structures of the Helsinki process itself, why *this* effort to press human rights took hold.

What created the conditions for the possibility of the "reception" of CSCE? Why did Basket Three not go the way of the

1948 Universal Declaration of Human Rights and the U.N. Covenant on Civil and Political Rights, both of which were promptly signed, and just as promptly ignored, by the regimes within Stalin's empire? What, in other words, explains the "staying power" of the human rights provisions of the Helsinki Final Act, and the fact that, this time around, so many people were willing to put their careers, and even their lives, in harm's way for the sake of basic moral principles?

There are surely many answers to that question, or perhaps better, many dimensions to the answer. But it may well be that a more compelling authority than international legal documents was at work this time, giving those documents a breath of life that could not be extinguished by the usual processes of repression. The very success of the Helsinki process, in other words, is suggestive of the possibility that a moral revolution did indeed precede, and make possible, the political Revolution of 1989.

The Great Ideas: Economics and/or History Did It

One indicator of just how disorienting the Revolution of 1989 was for opinion makers in the West was the eagerness with which denizens of those circles reached for Great Idea answers to their perplexities. The most frequently heard of these was "Economics": the Revolution of 1989 was a matter of "delayed modernization," inevitable because of the technological and managerial sluggishness of the command economies of the Warsaw Pact.

No doubt there is an element of truth here. The idiocies of Real Existing Socialist economics made the odds on the successful, long-term application of the Brezhnev Doctrine longer than they might have been in a pre-microchip age. But there is something unpersuasive, even faintly obscene, about what is finally a soft Marxist answer to the crisis of Marxism-Leninism. Moreover, the notion that men and women would suddenly, after forty years of sullen acquiescence to oppression, rise up nonviolently and overthrow communist dictatorships for the sake of VCRs, refrigerators, and BMWs is inherently implausible (particularly in Czechoslovakia and the German Democratic Republic, where the regimes in question had perfected a modern bread-and-truncheons strategy of political control). Food shortages and grim working conditions had led to rioting in the countries of the Yalta imperial system before: but these uprisings had been violent; they had not brought workers and intellectuals together; and they had been quickly suppressed. The Revolution of 1989, in Poland, the GDR, Hungary, and Czechoslovakia was nonviolent, sustained, ecumenical (in that workers, intellectuals, and churches acted together), and effective. None of these distinctive characteristics of the Revolution of 1989 can be satisfactorily explained by the lure of western consumer goods. Something else—something more—had to be going on.

Then there was Francis Fukuyama's solution to the puzzle of the late 1980s: "History" did it; the revolution was in the cards all along. Such a brisk formulation does little justice to Fukuyama's elegant and notorious essay, "The End of History?", first published in the summer of 1989 and later developed into a book. But it probably captures the popular and media "reception" of his hypothesis: we (the West) had "won" because we were right from the start; or, because we were "on the right side of history."[22]

Even those who disagreed with his high-octane Hegelianism and his peremptory conclusion had reason to be grateful for Fukuyama's attempt to explain "1989." In an environment still dominated by policy intellectuals who pride themselves on a sharply empirical (others would say, empiricist) cast of mind, Fukuyama argued that ideas count: ideas generate the energy of history. This was not only a helpful antidote to the economic determinism of the "delayed modernization" school; it was also a hopeful sign that the long, dark night of the numbers crunchers might be drawing to a close in international relations theory. Moreover, Fukuyama alerted the policy community to the fact that the democratic capitalist revolution had a firm empirical basis in many parts of the world. A remarkable consensus on the requirements for an effective and humane modern society was being built, across nations and (to a lesser extent) cultures, throughout the 1980s: a consensus in favor of decentralized decision making in economics (the market, basically) and in politics (democracy, in one form or another). Fukuyama quite reasonably suggested that the West ignored this good news at peril of missing the chief story line of late twentieth-century political history.

But both of these Great Idea explanations—"Economics" and "History"—suffered from two grave defects, which cast serious doubt on them as satisfactory prisms through which to read the Revolution of 1989.

Neither the economists' universe nor Fukuyama's had much room in it for the reality of evil. And yet the twentieth century has amply confirmed the ancient claim that evil is inherently a part of the human condition and will always find an organized social expression. That Nazism and communism failed does not mean that some other institutional carrier of human wickedness will not emerge to challenge and threaten the possibility of a humane social order. Indeed the opposite is far more likely to be the case. The relative success of the cause of freedom in the century of Auschwitz-Birkenau and the Gulag does not mean that the warning in 1 Peter 5.8 ("Be sober, be watchful. Your adversary the devil prowls around like a roaring lion, seeking someone to devour.") has lost its public or political salience.

Then there was Fukuyama's close identification of "history" with "politics." That, alas, was the idea that drove the people who created most of the trouble in the twentieth century, the people against whom the West marshaled the "daring, courage, imagination, and idealism" that Fukuyama celebrated.[23] But "history" is surely more than politics, as the Revolution of 1989—built on the foundations of what the "dissidents" called "independent culture"—dramatically demonstrated. "History" is literature, music, and dance; "history" is painting, sculpture, and architecture; "history" is theology and ethics and religious ritual; "history" is the warp and woof of relationships between men and women, young and old, parents and children, teachers and students, the powerful and the powerless.

And yes, "history" is politics. But history is not just politics. Those who thought it was made an abattoir of the twentieth century, and made a mockery of "politics" in the great tradition of the West as that was first formed in Jerusalem, Athens, and Rome. Theirs was a radically secularized form of the great human hope for what Judaism and Christianity have described as the "messianic age." But the distinction between a sacred and a secular horizon for "the end of history" is crucial. The Jewish and Christian expectation of the coming kingdom is, in the final analysis, a transcendent hope. And that tether to the transcendent serves as a powerful reminder that the affairs of this world are always marked by irony, pathos, and tragedy—which was Reinhold Niebuhr's way of saying, by the human propensity for sin.

Thus the transcendent hope for an "end of history" in the consummation of history has a powerful worldly effect: it keeps politics in line, and sets a barrier against the perennial human temptation to absolutize the political. In doing so, it makes possible a
politics of consent instead of a politics of coercion. The revolutionaries of 1989 understood that, in their several distinctive
ways. And that dimension of the revolution—the transcendent
dimension—is what is missing from the Fukuyama proposition
and from the answer that reads, "It was all a matter of delayed
modernization."

The Heart of the Matter

For so complex a historical event as the Revolution of 1989, there
is, of course, no simple or unilinear explanation. And, as with
many cataclysms of world-historical consequence, it was fraught
with close calls; as the Duke of Wellington said of Waterloo, it
was a damn near-run thing. Had Mikhail Gorbachev not been
general secretary of the central committee of the Soviet communist party, and then president of the USSR, the revolution would
probably not have happened like it did, or perhaps even when it
did. Had Jimmy Carter been reelected president of the United
States in 1980 (or had John Hinckley successfully joined the unsavory company of Booth, Guiteau, Czolgosz, and Lee Harvey
Oswald), things would have been different in U.S./Soviet relations: with certain, if certainly unknowable, consequences for
what became the Revolution of 1989. What would have happened if conservatives and emigré activists had blocked the
Helsinki Final Act? Human rights activism would have continued
in central and eastern Europe. But absent the lifeline to the West
provided by the Helsinki monitoring groups east and west of the
iron curtain, and absent the international pressures on repressive
governments created by the Helsinki review conferences, it seems
unlikely that the human rights movement in the Warsaw Pact
countries would have achieved critical mass by the second half of
the 1980s.

All of these contingencies—Gorbachev, Reagan, CSCE—were
important factors in shaping the Revolution of 1989. Nor ought
we discount as another key pressure the fact that the 1980s saw a
worldwide revolt against authoritarian and totalitarian regimes: a

revolt made possible in part by the widespread diffusion of communications technologies such as the transistor radio, the photocopier, the personal computer, the videocassette recorder, and the telefax. The word was around: things didn't have to be the way they were. It was, in truth, a kind of springtime of nations.[24]

The standard, realist, diplomatic, Hegelian, and economic accounts are also unsatisfactory—together, much less individually—because they do not give us compelling reasons for our being so profoundly moved by the events of June through December 1989. Why did we thrill to the Polish people's electoral rejection of communism in June 1989, what Timothy Garton Ash described as "the glorious work of deletion" (for the Polish communists, blundering to the end, had arranged the ballots such that unwanted candidates—which meant their candidates—had to be crossed out)?[25] Why did grown men and women in the West weep when the Berlin Wall was breached? Or when Václav Havel, Alexander Dubček, and Father Václav Malý (spokesman for Cardinal František Tomášek) addressed the massed crowds keeping candlelight vigil in Prague's Wenceslas Square? Or when the same crowds chanted, "Havel to the Castle!"—and then installed him there as president of Czechoslovakia? Why did anyone attuned to the extraordinary drama of these events finish 1989 with the conviction, at once humbling and exhilarating, that humanity had been given a second chance?

Because the Revolution of 1989 was, at its heart, a triumphant revolution of the human spirit: an expression of the final revolution, and of the transcendent nature of human aspiration.

Western analysts have often missed this connective thread through the tapestry of the Revolution of 1989 because the West has too often forgotten that politics is a function of culture, and that at the heart of culture is religion. But we can neither account for the revolution itself, nor for the intensity of our response to it, unless we think through this linkage more carefully.

The content of that linkage between politics and culture and between culture and religion, in the Revolution of 1989, will be filled in later. For now, let it stand as a proposition (albeit a proposition whose roots go back to the origins of the great political tradition of the West), a proposition that is the positive side of this reading of "1989."

The negative side of the coin is this: some western political leaders and some western analysts (both of the left and the right) were slow to grasp the meaning of the Revolution of 1989 because they had forgotten (and in some cases, never knew) the nature of Marxism-Leninism and the totalitarian states that were its historical embodiment. The West (or most of it, at any rate) understood communism and the Warsaw Pact as a military threat, and it understood how to check that threat: by massive conventional and nuclear deterrence. But over the forty years of the Cold War, many in the West paid ever less attention to Marxism-Leninism as a doctrine with a social ethic (so to speak) and the means of control necessary to enforce it. The West had, in short and to borrow from a debate of the late 1970s, forgotten the difference in kind (and not simply in degree) between authoritarianism and totalitarianism: between caudillos and commissars, between Bismarck and Honecker, Nicholas II and Yuri Andropov, Piłsudski and Gomułka. And having forgotten that, the West had not understood that any reversal of the Yalta imperial system—another embodiment of communist doctrine, for all its superficial resemblances to czarist ambitions of the past— would only come through a revolution that challenged Marxism-Leninism at the most basic level: as a doctrine and an ethic.

That is what the Revolution of 1989 did. That is why it worked. And that is why we thrilled to it: because the revolution, and the heroes who embodied it, broke through the hard shell of our power realism, our empiricism, and even our cynicism, to remind us that there is a difference between good and evil; that these categories are not irrelevant to politics (even to international politics); and that the human spirit can, indeed, overcome, from time to time.

There is, then, no way to comprehend the nature or to savor the accomplishment of the Revolution of 1989 without revisiting the ancien régime it toppled: the Marxist-Leninist system and the culture it created.

TWO

Calling Good and Evil by Name: The Communist Lie Confronted

On January 1, 1990, two days after the Velvet Revolution reached its exhilarating apogee with his election as president of Czechoslovakia, Václav Havel gave the traditional New Year's Day address to his countrymen over Czech and Slovak radio and television. What he had to say was not what they had been accustomed to hearing on these occasions:

> My dear fellow citizens: For forty years you have heard from my predecessors on this day different variations of the same theme: how our country flourished, how many million tons of steel we produced, how happy we all were, how we trusted our government, and what bright perspectives were unfolding in front of us.
>
> I assume you did not propose me for this office so that I, too, would lie to you.[1]

The hard truth of the matter was that Czechoslovakia was in terrible shape. It produced things that no one abroad wanted to buy, while basic commodities were unavailable at home. The "workers' state" exploited the workers and wasted the country's meager energy resources. The educational system was in tatters. Adult life expectancy was the lowest in Europe. The air, the water, and the soil were catastrophically polluted.

But as bad as this physical and economic damage was, repairing it was not the chief problem facing Czechs and Slovaks, according to their new president:

> The worst thing is that we live in a contaminated moral environment. We fell morally ill because we became used to saying something different from what we thought. We learned not to believe in anything, to ignore each other, to care only about ourselves. Concepts such as love, friendship, compassion, humility, or for-

giveness lost their depth and dimensions, and for many of us they represented only psychological peculiarities, or they resembled gone-astray greetings from ancient times, a little ridiculous in the era of computers and spaceships. . . .

When I talk about contaminated moral atmosphere . . . I am talking about all of us. We had all become used to the totalitarian system and accepted it as an unchangeable fact and thus helped to perpetuate it. In other words, we are all—though naturally to different extents—responsible for the operation of the totalitarian machinery; none of us is just its victim: we are all also its co-creators.

Why do I say this? It would be very unreasonable to understand the sad legacy of the last forty years as something alien, which some distant relative bequeathed to us. On the contrary, we have to accept this legacy as a sin we committed against ourselves. If we accept it as such, we will understand that it is up to us all, and up to us only, to do something about it. . . .

If we realize this, then all the horrors that the new Czechoslovak democracy inherited will cease to appear so terrible. If we realize this, hope will return to our hearts.[2]

In certain western circles, President Havel would doubtless have been charged with "blaming the victim," or some such, for giving this extraordinary speech. In fact, though, Havel's 1990 New Year's address was of a piece with the most penetrating analyses of the communist system that had been written in this century: by Koestler, Silone, Orwell, and Malraux among the novelists, and by Solzhenitsyn, Arendt, Kołakowski, and Miłosz among the chroniclers and philosophers. These men and women had understood—in many cases, through hard personal experience—that what Havel termed the "contaminated moral environment" was indeed the heart of the totalitarian darkness. Not as an accident but as a necessary by-product of itself, communism created a mental and moral slum that had to be cleared before there could be any hope of political reconstruction. Arendt knew this as a matter of theory; Havel and his colleagues in the Velvet Revolution knew it as a matter of fact.

As did many of their compatriots in the Revolution of 1989 throughout central and eastern Europe. Indeed, one of the most striking things about the "dissident" literature produced in the Warsaw Pact countries during the late 1970s and the 1980s was the breadth of conviction on this point: that moral regeneration, amounting to moral and cultural revolution, was the essential precondition to any attempt to throw off the political shackles of the Yalta imperial system. For that system embodied, not merely the foreign imposition of political-military power, but an alternative construction of human reality. Communism was not simply a different way of organizing a state. It was an alien worldview, one that represented a heretical break with the main political tradition of Europe. And yet, precisely because it was a worldview, communism could deploy quasi-moral ideological legitimations to buttress the Yalta imperial system and justify its irreversibility and expansion. Unlike other forms of modern dictatorship, communism had the formal elements of a religion: it had a doctrine, an ethic, and a ritual. And it was at this level, or so the "dissidents" of the 1970s and 1980s believed, that the contest with communism was most fully joined.[3]

American and western European political scientists and journalists tend to find all of this a bit abstract, or "ideological." And no doubt empirically measurable factors such as deteriorating economic performance helped set the stage for the Revolution of 1989. But there is no escaping the fact that the principal theorists of the revolution in the countries directly involved—Bronisław Geremek, Jacek Kuroń, Tadeusz Mazowiecki, Adam Michnik, and Józef Tischner in Poland, Miklós Haraszti, János Kis, György Konrad, and Viktor Orbán in Hungary, Havel and his colleagues in Czechoslovakia, a group that includes Christians, Jews, and agnostics, classic liberals, social democrats, and neo-conservatives—were agreed that a deeper analysis of their situation was the key to its possible transformation. They were agreed, in other words, that a moral-cultural revolution was the human precondition to any possible political revolution, given the realities of the communist system.

By which they meant, first and foremost, the moral realities.

Signs Among the Onions

For those with no direct experience of it, the moral degradation of life under communism was hard enough to imagine, particularly in the days when senior western statesmen lamented, in fin de siècle tones, the inevitability of America's playing Athens to an ascendant Soviet Union's Sparta.[4] It is even more difficult to comprehend now, when communism is a spent force in world affairs. But since we cannot grasp the crucial moral dynamics of the Revolution of 1989 without confronting the full truth about communism, Václav Havel's parable of the greengrocer, which was one of the most effective evocations of the ethos of the communist state, is well worth revisiting:

> The manager of a fruit and vegetable shop places in his window, among the onions and carrots, the slogan, "Workers of the world, Unite!" Why does he do it? What is he trying to communicate to the world? Is he genuinely enthusiastic about the idea of unity among the workers of the world? Is his enthusiasm so great that he feels an irrepressible impulse to acquaint the public with his ideals? Has he really given more than a moment's thought to how such a unification might occur and what it would mean?
>
> I think it can safely be assumed that the overwhelming majority of shopkeepers never think about the slogans they put in their windows, nor do they use them to express their real opinions. That poster was delivered to our greengrocer from the enterprise headquarters along with the onions and carrots. He put them all into the window simply because it has been done that way for years, because everyone does it, and because that is the way it has to be. If he were to refuse, there could be trouble. He could be reproached for not having the proper "decoration" in his window; someone might even accuse him of disloyalty. He does it because these things must be done if one is to get along in life. It is one of the thousands of details that guarantee him a relatively tranquil life "in harmony with society," as they say.[5]

The greengrocer's sign was, objectively, a bit of ideological window dressing. But did that mean the sign was of no serious consequence? Quite the contrary, according to Havel. The sign was about acquiescence. It said nothing comprehensible about the workers, the world, or their unification. But it said something very important about the greengrocer. The sign said, "I, the greengrocer XY, live here and I know what I must do. I behave in the manner expected of me. I can be depended upon and am beyond reproach. I am obedient and therefore I have the right to be left in peace."[6]

The sign, in other words, was a small but real act of surrender to the communist system. Its public message was, "Do not disturb." But the sign contained a subtext, too: and the message of the subtext, to the greengrocer and to the readers of the sign among the onions, was, "I am afraid and therefore unquestioningly obedient."[7] That was what the sign really meant. The greengrocer may not have liked putting the sign in the window. He may even have felt ashamed of himself from time to time for putting such arrant nonsense on display. But he did it. And each time he did it, he said, leave me alone; I am afraid, and because of that you can count on me to obey.

Since Mikhail Gorbachev opened previously closed aspects of life in Warsaw Pact countries to western scrutiny, and particularly since the Revolution of 1989, people in the West have gotten a more detailed sense of how grim life could be east of the iron curtain: poor food, foul air, bad cars, inadequate medical care, claustrophobic housing, polluted rivers, dead forests, and so forth. We have also been reminded (if further clarification were needed after the publication of, say, *The Gulag Archipelago*) of the repressiveness of the communist system and the brutality with which social, political, and cultural conformity were enforced. But the system's failures in terms of the production and distribution of consumer goods do not measure the depth of the failure of the communist project. That, as the "dissidents" and the victims of repression knew in their bones, could only be measured in moral terms. Multiply by the hundreds of thousands the seemingly minor concession of Havel's fictional greengrocer and the fear that it embodied, and one begins to get a sense of the daily routine of self-degradation that was life in the communist state: that was life in the culture of the lie.

The Web of Mendacity

According to Havel, the key to understanding—and resisting—the communist system was to recognize that it was a *structure of mendacity*: a "world of appearances trying to pass for reality."[8] The falseness of life under communism was not a reflection of the fact that human beings are sinners and thus lie from time to time. That was certainly true, but that fact did not explain the greengrocer and his sign (much less the labor camps and prisons). Rather, the falseness or corruption of life in the communist state was an expression of the system itself, in its rationale, its intention, and its structure. The web of mendacity had a horrible and inexorable logic to it:

> Because the regime is captive to its own lies, it must falsify everything. It falsifies the past. It falsifies the present, and it falsifies the future. It falsifies statistics. It pretends not to possess an omnipotent and unprincipled police apparatus. It pretends to respect human rights. It pretends to persecute no one. It pretends to fear nothing. It pretends to pretend nothing.[9]

The corruptions of the culture of the lie metastasized at five levels, each of which would have a devastating effect on the moral environment of central and eastern Europe: the personal, the relational, the legal, the historical, and the linguistic.

The first level of corruption touched individuals in their interior lives. Communism was different from other forms of dictatorship because, according to Havel, it amounted to a "secularized religion."[10] It offered a "ready answer to any question whatsoever," and it had to be accepted in toto: one could not sign on to merely this or that part of the package.[11] This had a certain attractiveness, at the beginning, for confused modern man: a minimum of confidence in the structure of the world and in one's place in it is essential for any human being to function. But later, one paid "dearly for this low-rent home." Why? Because the rent involved the regular handing over of one's conscience, which is to say, one's self, to the authorities, to the system. And the system was a total system. The political authority was, concurrently, the moral authority and the metaphysical authority. It assured the acquiescent individual that he, as part of the system, was "in harmony with the human order and the order of the universe." But the price tag was "the consignment of reason and conscience" into hands other than one's own.[12]

Communism thus required the worship of a false god, and the coin of tribute was the abdication of personal conscience. But, as the parable of the greengrocer so aptly illustrates, this abdication was not a once-and-for-all proposition, but rather a daily ritual of self-abasement. It did not involve, on most days, a major public gesture. But it did involve a daily decision to acquiesce in those small things (like the sign in the shop window) that, over time, deaden the soul by suffocating it within a scabby carapace of untruths. Every day the system evoked, in small ways, fear. And every day people decided to give in to the fear, and to burn that modest pinch of the incense of acquiescence that the system required.

When one puts this degrading process together with the gray drabness of life under communism, a terrible equation descriptive of life within the communist culture of the lie begins to come into focus: boredom plus fear plus an ineradicable feeling of uncleanliness eventually yields a kind of moral schizophrenia.[13] One lived a double life: lies (even so banal a lie as the sign in a greengrocer's window purporting to demonstrate the shopkeeper's allegiance to the ideological ruffles and flourishes of the regime) became the common coin of public discourse. Lying became the "normal" way that one behaved. And yet one could not, unless one was a moral cretin, deny the facts of one's mendacity, or of one's complicity in the system's mendacity: thus the feeling of personal contamination that led, quite logically enough, to feelings of hopelessness and powerlessness. That, of course, was just fine with the regime, because a hopeless people that believes itself to be without alternatives is likely to remain an acquiescent people. And so, as Havel put it in 1978, "individuals confirm the system, fulfill the system, make the system, *are* the system" at a basic moral level.[14]

But the "contaminated moral environment" of the communist state involved far more than personal corruptions: the corruption of the interior life led, inexorably, to the corruption of relationships. In the ordinary, day-to-day business of life, one could only assume that others, too, were lying. So whom could one trust? With whom could one share whatever measure of private space— space for being truthful—that one had managed to carve out for oneself? Under communism, individuals of conscience tended to divide the populace into "we" and "they": "we" being those who had created a private space of truthfulness in which to live at least part of their lives, a space to be shared with like-minded others; "they" being those who were utterly enmeshed in the system's web of mendacity. But how could one know, with any certainty, who "we" and "they" were? Perhaps better, how could one know how much "we" there was left in society?[15]

Many people in the West were familiar with (if insufficiently exercised about) the large-scale corruptions of the communist system on this matter of relationships: the secret police apparatus with its networks of informers, thugs, and suborned witnesses; the fakery of official trade unions; the rigged campaigns and elections; the bribery that was required if one wanted to acquire certain consumer goods (or even an apartment); the pervasive black marketeering; the attempt to penetrate and manipulate the Church through regime-instigated associations like the "Pacem in Terris" priests' organization in Czechoslovakia and the Pax movement in Poland; the planting of spies in seminaries; the punishment of children (in terms of admission to schools, for example) for the political activities of their parents. All of this led to what can only be described as a situation of public moral squalor, in which any gracefulness of life and manners was systematically eroded.

But because the devil, like God, is often in the details, the corruption of relationships in the communist state was perhaps even more poignantly illustrated by smaller acts of mendacity and seduction that usually escaped western notice. Poland may stand as representative of the general trend. In the late 1950s, for example, the Gomułka regime encouraged "free sex" in summer youth camps, and stocked youth hostels with alcohol during religious pilgrimages and fairs.[16] In 1966, the government arranged a twenty-five-gun artillery barrage to drown out Cardinal Stefan Wyszyński's sermon in Poznań during a celebration of the millennium of Polish Christianity.[17] (These "infrastructure" tactics, as we might call them, continued to be refined over the years. Even after the rise of Solidarity, the Polish government tried to build an expressway that would cut the Jasna Góra monastery off from the town of Częstochowa; traffic noise, the regime assumed, would interfere with services in the basilica that housed the Black Madonna.[18]) But no tactic was too petty for a regime that embodied the culture of the lie in its attempt to poison any independent human relationships: in 1964, the Polish secret police tried to recruit Cardinal Wyszyński's barber as an informant.[19]

The manipulations of the formal legal system and the extrajudicial repression of dissent just noted were, of course, bad enough. But the corruption of the law in the communist state went even deeper than that. At one level, of course, "socialist legality" meant that the law was what the vanguard party said the law was; and that the law could be changed to suit the advantage of the vanguard was all too well known to "dissidents."

But the totalitarian system differed from classic dictatorships in that it fretted about maintaining the appearance of legality. A classic dictatorship, an authoritarian regime if you will, has no need to hide its illegality: indeed, the public display of its extralegal muscle is a crucial part of its strategy of political control. But the communist state, Havel reminds us, wanted to control culture and society as well as politics: caesaro-papism without God, Christ, or the Church. Thus it was "utterly obsessed with the need to bind everything in a single order."[20]

The result of this obsession with what might be called an "unnatural" natural law was the further degradation of statutory law into sclerotic bureaucratic regulation: and not simply bureaucracy for its own sake, but bureaucracy in aid of the "complex manipulation of life" that was the essence of the system. Nor did this corruption touch only the lives of the politically engaged: "From the cook in the restaurant who, without hard-to-get permission from the bureaucratic apparatus, cannot cook something special for his customers, to the singer who cannot perform his new song at a concert without bureaucratic approval, everyone, in all aspects of their life, is caught in this regulatory tangle of red tape."[21]

And so in the culture of the lie, law became, not an expression of common moral conviction, but another instrument for the state's manipulation (and degradation) of society. A regime obsessively maintaining the facade of legality was in fact operating in a state of lawlessness, as the Solidarity theologian Józef Tischner put it.[22] Appearance and reality were, again, disjunct. Behind the scenes, suborned witnesses and regime stooges did their dirty work. Up front, so to speak, everything was done according to the book. Moreover, this schizophrenic legal situation compounded the schizophrenic moral situation of individuals and further polluted the world of human relationships: the appearance of legality provided an excuse for those who simply wanted to be left alone. Yes, it was a shame that so-and-so was convicted; and it was probably unjust; but it was done according to the law.

Thus the law became a wedge with which to widen the fissure between surface appearances and the real world: to deepen the slough of mendacity in the culture of the lie.

And then there was the corruption of history. In the totalitarian culture of the lie, history was an instrumental discipline. Like music, art, and literature, history was "correct" if it served the ideological and social-control purposes of the regime. History was an exercise in "false consciousness" if it challenged regime orthodoxies. Lenin described the "new" discipline and its intended results nicely: "Chaos and arbitrariness, which had heretofore dominated people's views on history and politics, gave way to an astonishingly uniform and harmonious scientific theory."[23]

Astonishingly uniform, indeed. Or as the Polish communist Stanisław Arnold put it (with an admirable lack of circumlocution) to the First Methodological Congress of Polish Historians in 1951, "The only scientific approach to historical problems is . . . to treat them as a most terrible ideological weapon directed against the rulers of Wall St."[24]

Thus life—real life—began in the countries of the Warsaw Pact in 1945 or thereabouts. Marshall Piłsudski's defeat of the Red Army at the Battle of Warsaw in 1920, and the relative successes of Czechoslovak democracy in the interwar period, were not matters of much consequence. The Yalta imperial system was presented as an alliance among equals, a partnership born from genuine peoples' revolutions against fascism and against more medieval forms of oppression (read: the Church). The West had reneged on Yalta; the Soviet Union always observed its treaty obligations scrupulously. The Soviet interventions in East Germany in 1953, in Hungary in 1956, and in Czechoslovakia in 1968 were "fraternal assistance"; the Soviet failure to cross the Vistula to fight alongside the Polish Home Army in the 1944 Warsaw Uprising (a deliberate policy decision by Stalin that resulted in the utter devastation of the city) was the result of "supply problems." The "arms race" was caused by the western "military-industrial complex"; the Soviet Union and its allies, surrounded by aggressive enemies, maintained a purely defensive military posture.[25]

The falsification and manipulation of history for ideological ends is an evil in its own right, of course. But it was a particularly devastating tactic in central and eastern Europe, and especially in Poland. For during the period of its partition (1795–1918), the Polish nation had been kept alive in and by its historical memory: by stories and traditions passed down by word of mouth from parents to children, and by poets and novelists like Adam Mickiewicz and Henryk Sienkiewicz. To deliberately and mendaciously strip away that historical memory was to commit a social and cultural lobotomy on a patient in a straitjacket.[26] And to replace the historic memory embodied in say, Kraków's Wawel Cathedral, the burial place of kings, queens, and poets, with the claptrap of that "astonishingly uniform and harmonious scientific theory" celebrated by Lenin led to yet a further deterioration of the public moral environment: for communist historiography "promised to banish the concepts of guilt and individual responsibility, and to explain the horrors of the recent past as the necessary trials of the nation's progress towards a better future."[27]

The fifth corruption was, of course, the corruption of language. For all its power, Orwell's image of "Newspeak" somehow fails to convey the full awfulness of the semantic debasement that characterized life in the communist societies of central and eastern Europe. In fact, though, it was the ideological corruption of language that bound together the web of mendacity in the Marxist-Leninist culture of the lie. For the abuse of language was a powerful and ubiquitous instrument for eroding personal conscience, degrading one's relationships, perverting the law, and falsifying history: social control by the pervasive use of the euphemism.

Government by vanguard was styled the "people's republic." What people experienced as their degradation was called their "liberation." Manipulative state power was defended as the "public control of power," and the arbitrary exercise of power was "observing the legal code." The state repressed culture and talked of "cultural development." The expansion of Soviet imperial influence was "support for the oppressed of the earth." No free speech was in fact "the highest form of freedom." Tolerance was "repressive."[28]

And so forth and so on, like some kind of horrible and all-pervasive political Muzak from which one could never escape, save only in the quiet of one's soul.

From Complicity to Resistance

The net result of this quintet of corruptions was described by Havel as a "vast ocean of . . . manipulated life.[29] But Havel's genius lay not simply in his elegant characterization of "the system," but in his understanding that "the system" was not solely to blame for the devastation of the moral environment.

The system depended on acquiescence. Which is to say, it depended on demoralization: not simply in the psychological sense of the term, but in the more fundamental human and ethical sense.[30] For all its claims to historical inevitability, to being the embodiment of The Way Things Are, the totalitarian system and its culture of the lie depended on complicity. The system was sustained, not just by the terrible power of the secret police and the whole internal security *apparat*, but by a critical mass of people who were willing to accept appearance as reality, to sign off on "the given rules of the game." And thus complicit individuals became players in the game themselves, made it "possible for the game to go on," made it possible for the game "to exist in the first place."[31]

To repeat: this was not blaming the victim. This was the hard truth of the matter. Particularly during the Brezhnevite "era of stagnation" that followed the 1968 invasion of Czechoslovakia, too many people in the Warsaw Pact countries had decided that life without honor was preferable to resistance.[32] Too many people were content, if in a surly and privately rebellious fashion, to live publicly within the culture of the lie. The fault line in the totalitarian state was not, at the most basic level, between rulers and ruled, but *within each person*: "for everyone in his or her own way [was] both a victim and a supporter of the system."[33]

And that is why the revolution had to begin, not with politics, but with culture: which is to say, with the individual and his or her recovery of conscience and a sense of self. There could be no effective political revolution in the Yalta imperial system without a prior revolution of the spirit.

Repairing the damage caused to the moral environment by the culture of the lie, and beginning to rebuild the foundations of a society worthy of human beings, required one thing above all else: it required individuals committed to what Havel called "living within the truth," to what Pope John Paul II described as "calling good and evil by name."[34] It required a "fifth column" of people who were "tired of being tired"; who would revolt against manipulation; who would straighten their backbones and "live in greater dignity as an individual"; and who, by doing so, would carve out "a territory full of modest expressions of human volition."[35]

Timothy Garton Ash coined a phrase that deftly captured the essence of this kind of morally grounded existential revolt: it was all a matter of living according to "the principle of As If." You may be in prison; you may be in a mandatory meeting of an official union; you may be dealing with the secret police, or a stupid boss who owes his position to being a party hack, or a soporific teacher who is peddling an ideological line—in all these circumstances, "try to live *as if* you live in a free country."[36] Refuse to live the double life. Bridge the gap between appearance and reality. Don't lie, and don't accept the lies of others. "Expand the space available for [independent] life."[37]

The beginning of the end for the system would come, in other words, not when the system reformed itself from within, for that was impossible: there could be no "communism with a human face," as the reformers of 1968 had hoped. No, the beginning of the end would come when enough people withdrew consent and refused complicity. This was the secret, so to speak, that the authorities had known all along. And what the "dissidents" who created the Revolution of 1989 had discerned was that here, on this matter of consent and complicity, was the system's most acute point of vulnerability:

> . . . The crust presented by the life of lies is made of strange stuff. As long as it seals off hermetically the entire society, it appears to be made of stone. But the moment someone breaks through in one place, when one person cries out, "The emperor is naked!"—when a single person breaks the rules of the game, thus exposing it as a game—everything suddenly appears in another light and the whole crust seems then to be made of a tissue on the point of tearing and disintegrating uncontrollably.[38]

Those who broke through the crust rightly insisted that there was something a bit off-putting about their being described as "dissidents." The opposition that they mounted—in the Church, in Charter 77, in the early days of Solidarity and during the martial law period in Poland—was in the first instance social and cultural, and only later political. The thinker who wrote what he wanted and was content to have it published only in *samizdat* (underground journals), the scholars who organized private seminars and tutorials after being dismissed from state-run faculties, the clergy who lived a free religious life without official approbation, the artists who created what they pleased, and those who defended all of these independent spirits: these were not people immediately concerned about the seizure of political power.[39] They cared far more about culture and society than about the state.

Moreover, "dissent" implies that that which is being dissented against has some sort of legitimacy. And this was precisely what those called "dissidents" insisted was *not* the case. "The system" was not simply an alternative politics with which they disagreed, and against which they proposed a different slate of candidates, as it were; it was something wholly and radically different. It was a "complex, profound, and long-term violation of society," or, given the harsh realities of complicity, "the self-violation of society." Political opposition to the system and its culture of the lie, on the pattern of the revolts of 1953, 1956, and 1968, was not only unrealistic, given the power realities; more to the point, it was "utterly inadequate, for it would never come near to touching the root of the matter."[40]

The only adequate response to the culture of the lie was pre-political. It was living in the truth. It was calling good and evil by name. It was letting loose "the special radioactive power of the truthful word."[41]

Revolutionary Morality, Reconsidered

The "pre-revolution" that preceded the Revolution of 1989—the lengthy, arduous process of revolutionary social regeneration that made possible the events of June through December 1989—was thus the work of a "fifth column" of independent men and women who had internalized, and were prepared to live out the consequences of, four norms that confronted the culture of the lie at the most fundamental level of resistance. Those four norms were truth, responsibility, solidarity, and nonviolence.

The commitment to "living in the truth" was a determination to resist relativism and to assert the objectivity of the moral order. Living according to appearances rather than according to reality was degrading and demeaning. The culture of the lie must be rejected, root and branch. Ideas counted; so did words; neither should be debased by ideological cant. Good values had good consequences; corrupt values led to corrupt societies. There were moral absolutes; they could be known; and they ought to be observed. Some things were off the board.[42]

The norm of responsibility was an existential extension of the norm of truth. Havel liked to quote his mentor, the philosopher Jan Patočka, who died in 1977 after a brutal police interrogation into his work as a Charter 77 spokesman: "The most interesting thing about responsibility is that we carry it with us everywhere."[43] It was foolish and morally degrading to "blame the system." Until one had made the commitment to living in the truth, to calling good and evil by name, one *was* the system in microcosm: both victim and supporter. And the truth had to be lived here and now, not on those rare occasions when one was allowed to visit a free society, and not in the easier circumstances of a life in exile. Living in the truth was not for dilettantes and trimmers. We are here, in this place, and under these circumstances, for a reason: "the Lord has set us down" here, Havel insisted, and we cannot "lie our way" out of the situation by avoiding it. One would never live responsibly—one would never live according to universal values—if one could not bring oneself to live responsibly here-and-now, even surrounded by the culture of the lie.[44]

Václav Benda, a Czech Catholic intellectual and another Charter 77 spokesman, summed up the norm of responsibility and helped define the politics of cultural renewal and social regeneration in these terms:

> To acquit oneself in this period, which is more burdensome than cruel, it is . . . not enough merely to look out for one's own soul and believe that Truth—the Truth which in a particular place and time took on human form and walked among people and assumed their suffering—is no more than a *position* which has to be *maintained*. . . . If, however, the chief form of the present political evil is a restrictive heaviness that all citizens carry on their shoulders and at the same time *within* them, then the only possibility is to shake that evil off, escape its power and to seek truth. Under such circumstances, every genuine struggle for one's soul becomes an openly political act, and a creative act at that, because it is no longer merely "defining oneself" against something else (there is nothing to define oneself against), but rather a jettisoning of ballast and opening oneself up to what is new and unknown.[45]

If living in truth meant living responsibly—living as if one's actions really counted—then it also meant living in solidarity with others: and that meant a willingness to sacrifice oneself for others if the circumstances demanded it. There could be no true, much less effective, resistance against the web of mendacity without the rebuilding of an ethic of solidarity.

"Solidarity" has, of course, been one of the key themes in the social teaching of Pope John Paul II, and this stress has surely been influenced by the pope's pastoral experience as archbishop of Kraków. For one of the more insidious social effects of the totalitarian system, and one of the grotesque ironies of "collectivism," was its atomization of life. One even sensed this in the characteristic architecture of "the system." In the steel town of Nowa Huta adjacent to Kraków, a town built as a model of the workers' paradise, there are great apartment blocks, eight or nine stories high, containing as many as 450 flats. And yet there is no way to pass laterally from one flat to another down the long axis of a building. If you want to visit a neighbor outside your contained module of two or three flats, you go down your elevator, leave the building, walk down the pavement, reenter the building, and go up your neighbor's elevator or stairs. The apartment blocks of Nowa Huta (for all that they contain some handsome flats) have often been described as human filing cabinets: and they were designed so that the files were rigorously separated. They embodied the atomization that the totalitarian system enforced by the culture of the lie and its corrosive effect on human relationships.

The only answer to this mass social fragmentation was to breach the walls that divided people through "the rehabilitation of values like trust, openness, responsibility, solidarity, love."[46] And this would involve, not so much the creation of organizations, as the recreation of *communities*. People had to come to know, again, the possibility of mutual and voluntary association. And as part of that rediscovery they had to relearn, as Jan Patočka said in his political last testament, that "there are some things worth suffering for."[47] Havel, a nonpracticing Catholic playwright, and Adam Michnik, a secular Jewish intellectual and activist, were wholly agreed with the Polish pope on this point: one moral building block of the revolution would be the rediscovery and reappropriation of the ancient Christian value of *sacrifice*.[48] In sum, and to take a symbolic reference point: Solidarity-the-movement could only be built on the sure foundation of solidarity-the-virtue.

WHY NON-VIOLENCE

The Communist Lie Confronted 53

Then there was nonviolence. In political terms, perhaps the most singular thing about the Revolution of 1989 was its nonviolence: a rejection of the Jacobin tradition in which "revolutionary" was synonymous with "executioner." Chesterton got the violent rot at the heart of the modern revolutionary impulse just right: "Men have tried to turn 'revolutionise' from a transitive to an intransitive verb."[49] The Revolution of 1989 would, conversely, be built on the conviction that revolutions were self-limiting enterprises, undertaken by and for human subjects who were not to be degraded into objects.

Moreover, and for those with a taste for the ironies of history, the triumphant nonviolence of the revolution was a splendid existential counterpoise to the Marxist claim that social conflict could only be resolved through class warfare and violent struggle. John Paul II, in 1991, did not hesitate to drive this point home, almost remorselessly:

> . . . The protests which led to the collapse of Marxism tenaciously insisted on trying every avenue of negotiation, dialogue, and witness to the truth, appealing to the conscience of the adversary and seeking to awaken in him a sense of shared human dignity.
>
> It seemed that the European order resulting from the Second World War and sanctioned by the Yalta Agreements could only be overturned by another war. Instead, it [was] overcome by the nonviolent commitment of people who, while always refusing to yield to the force of power, succeeded time after time in finding effective ways of bearing witness to the truth. This disarmed the adversary, since violence always needs to justify itself through deceit, and to appear, however falsely, to be defending a right or responding to a threat posed by others.[50]

From whence did this commitment to nonviolence spring? It certainly had its tactical elements: as the Polish historian and Solidarity adviser Bronisław Geremek freely admitted, "the route of violence seemed ineffective . . . because the communist regime was able to marshall more force than civil society."[51] Put less elegantly, the bad guys had all the guns, and the good guys knew it. The good guys also knew about the futility of armed resistance in 1953 (East Germany), in 1956 (Hungary), and in 1968 (Czechoslovakia), and they remembered how the Polish government had shot down rebellious workers at the Gdańsk shipyards in 1970. Moreover, they knew, and on the basis of bitter experience, that they could expect no help of consequence from the West in the event of an armed revolt against communism.[52]

But the nonviolence of the Revolution of 1989 was rooted in richer soil than that of political pragmatism. It was, at bottom, another expression of living in the truth, of living responsibly, and of living in solidarity even at the cost of sacrifice: the nonviolence of the revolution was "a statement about how things should be." Or as Adam Michnik insisted during the dark days of martial law in Poland, "those who start by storming bastilles will end up building their own."[53] The revolutionaries of 1989 wanted to break with lawlessness and to create a "normal society," by which they meant a law-governed democracy. Nonviolence seemed to them the morally appropriate means to that end.

The nonviolence of the revolution was also informed by a strategic judgment, which in turn was an application of the "dissidents'" penetrating analysis of the culture of the lie. Here, the central and eastern European intellectuals had learned from Aleksandr Solzhenitsyn, perhaps the premier analyst of the relationship between violence and the lie. For in his 1970 Nobel lecture, Solzhenitsyn had argued prophetically that "once the lie has been dispersed, the nakedness of violence will be revealed in all its repulsiveness, and then violence, become decrepit, will come crashing down."[54] It was, as we have seen, an analysis that would be wholly congenial to the first Slavic pope who, during his 1983 pilgrimage to Poland during the martial law period (which the Polish regime referred to as the "state of war") urged his fellow Poles time and again to "vanquish evil with good."[55]

Taken together, these four defining norms of the Revolution of 1989—truth, responsibility, solidarity, and nonviolence—involved a reconstitution of politics according to the classic tradition of the West: the tradition that begins with Aristotle and teaches that politics is an extension of ethics. As Timothy Garton Ash put it, politics was not, on this model, and in the first instance, a matter of right or left. It was a matter of right and wrong.[56] Father Józef Tischner described the same phenomenon with a wonderful image: Solidarity was "a huge forest planted by awakened consciences."[57] And so, in truth, was the Revolution of 1989 throughout central and eastern Europe.

Breaking the Fever of Fear

Because the captivity of these captive nations was cultural and social as well as political, liberation from captivity had to take place, first, in the sphere of culture and society. Individuals committed to living in the truth would do so by creating the institutions of an independent culture that would, in turn, form the basis of *civil society*: the theme that linked the revolutionaries of 1989 across the borders of nations and political philosophies.[58]

Resistance to the web of mendacity through the informal institutions of independent culture took a host of forms. There was *samizdat* (underground) publishing: of political tracts (among the most influential of which, and precisely on this question of civil society, were Havel's aforementioned 1978 masterpiece, "The Power of the Powerless," and Michnik's 1985 "Letter from the Gdańsk Prison"[59]), but also of classic literature and contemporary poetry and fiction. There was Poland's "Flying University": which Bronisław Geremek, one of its instructors, described later as "an underground university teaching sociology, law, politics, and history, and focused above all on the pursuit of truth."[60] There were music groups and jazz clubs.[61] There was underground and independent drama, much of which flourished (particularly in Poland during the "state of war") in churches. And there were groups that stood on the boundary between "society" and "politics," among whom pride of place should arguably be given to the Polish KOR, originally the "Workers' Defense Committee," but renamed in 1977 the "Social Self-Defense Committee-KOR."[62] The name, of course, said it all: if communism was indeed a massive and systematic violation or self-violation of society, then the only antidote was "social self-defense."

The recreation of "civil society" in the morally occupied countries of central and eastern Europe thus took place through the creation and defense of the "parallel structures" of an independent culture within which people could live in the truth.[63] These parallel structures were the embodiment of the commitment to call good and evil by name. But the fact of these structures does not explain their creation or their staying power in the face of regime oppression. How did people who had become accustomed to acquiescence break the fever of the fear that sustained the totalitarian system? Why did social self-defense work in the 1980s when it had failed before? How did civil society achieve critical mass in central and eastern Europe by the end of that decade?

The groundwork had been laid, of course, throughout the Cold War. But as one talked to central and eastern Europeans—leaders but also ordinary citizens—in the aftermath of the Revolution of 1989, one had to be impressed by the frequency with which one heard an explanation that went something like this:

Poland showed the way. The rise of Solidarity, which was a massive and undeniable expression of the workers' rejection of the putative workers' state (and the totalitarian system it maintained), was the key to the revolution throughout the Warsaw Pact. For the Solidarity revolution, in its first, glorious triumph at the Gdańsk shipyards and by its tenacious grip on life during the "state of war," proved that social self-defense could be effective and inspired hundreds of thousands of others to "live in the truth." Intellectuals and laborers could work in tandem. The forces of repression could be resisted nonviolently, if one was willing to make the sacrifice. The authorities could be compelled to bargain. The West could be energized, and precisely by witnessing the power of the powerless. The revolution had many points of origin. Still, and for the Revolution of 1989, Solidarity was the nonviolent equivalent of the "shot heard 'round the world."

And what explains the dramatic, unexpected, and extraordinarily rapid rise of Solidarity? Why "Solidarity," and why in Poland? Again, there are many parts to an answer: the strong position of the Church and its identification, in the popular mind, with the national identity; the festering memory of the 1970 Gdańsk shipyard massacre; the precedent created by the brave pioneers in the Committee of Social Self-Defense-KOR; the charisma of Lech Wałęsa in combination with the tactical savvy of Geremek, Kuroń, Michnik, and Mazowiecki. There is no shortage of causal factors.

But, again, people who were there have a simple, straightforward answer to the question, What broke the fever of the fear, and when, in Poland? With virtual unanimity, they answer: the fever was broken by the first pilgrimage of John Paul II to his homeland in June 1979. That was when the issue of who "we" were, and who "they" were, was decisively clarified. Whether the venue was Warsaw, Kraków, or Częstochowa, to be surrounded by hundreds of thousands of like-minded people who, in their passionate affirmation of the pope were demonstrating that they, too, had nothing but contempt for the system and for the culture of the lie, instantly showed who "we" were. "We" were society; "they" were but a crust. "We" had real authority, if we could break the fever of the fear; "they" had only the tools of coercion. There were millions of "us"; "they" were a pitiful minority of the wholly co-opted.

It is almost impossible for a westerner to imagine the extraordinary electricity of those nine days in June 1979. But they were the days of solidarity; and out of that solidarity came Solidarity. And from Solidarity, after another ten hard years of struggle, came the Revolution of 1989.

How was it that an institution, the Roman Catholic Church, that had for centuries been identified with the established order and the status quo, became the trigger for the revolution? And what difference, in the answer to that question, did the fact of Karol Wojtyła as pope make?

THREE

Catholics and Commissars:
1917–1978

On June 10, 1988, Cardinal Agostino Casaroli, the secretary of state
of the Holy See, addressed a glittering celebration in Moscow's
Bolshoi Theater marking the millennium of Christianity among the
eastern Slavs. The cardinal brought the personal greetings of Pope
John Paul II to Patriarch Pimen and his Holy Synod, and offered
congratulations to the government of Mikhail Gorbachev for its
new appreciation of the role of Christian believers in the process of
perestroika. Three days later, on June 13, Gorbachev met with
Cardinal Casaroli and his entourage and was presented with a private letter from John Paul II, which the pope had given Casaroli in
the hope that Gorbachev would receive it. On June 16, Msgr.
Audrys Bačkis, a member of the Vatican delegation to Moscow and
undersecretary of the Vatican's foreign ministry, told Vatican Radio
that Mr. Gorbachev had responded positively to the pope's suggestion that "regular contacts" (meaning diplomatic relations) be
established between the Kremlin and the Holy See, as indeed they
were following Gorbachev's 1989 visit to Rome.

These stunning events—which could scarcely have been imagined at the beginning of the 1980s, when the long arm of the
Kremlin appeared to have reached into St. Peter's Square during
the assassination attempt on John Paul II—marked the apogee of
the Holy See's formal relations with the late "Union of Soviet
Socialist Republics." To many observers, they reinforced the
image of the flexible and accommodating Mikhail Gorbachev,
willing to meet his former adversaries halfway. To those who
championed the *Ostpolitik* of the late Pope Paul VI and its
attempts to forge a less confrontational relationship with the
communist countries of central and eastern Europe, the celebration at the Bolshoi Theater was the crowning achievement of

Cardinal Casaroli, who had been the diplomatic architect and agent of that *Ostpolitik*.[1] Four years later, however, it seemed more likely that Gorbachev's new friendliness toward the Holy See was the act of a man eager to grasp any lifeline to the West amidst the crumbling foundations of his own empire. And while it was clear that the Catholic Church had had something to do with the unraveling of Stalin's *imperium*, it was not at all certain that that "something" was the *Ostpolitik* initiated by Paul VI.

Opening Gambits

The confrontation between communism and Catholicism was one of the great ideological and institutional struggles of the twentieth century. The Church had, of course, a lot of experience with tyrannies: from Caligula to Bonaparte, Catholicism had wrestled with (and, it must be said, sometimes accommodated itself to) dictators across a wide band of ideological conviction. But the Bolshevik Revolution was the first modern revolution that made militant atheism and a virtual war against religion its official state policy. Paul Johnson caught the essence of the Bolshevik attitude, as embodied in the founding father, in these terms:

> Religion was important to [Lenin] in the sense that he hated it. Unlike Marx, who despised it and treated it as marginal, Lenin saw it as a powerful and ubiquitous enemy. . . . "There can be nothing more abominable," he wrote, "than religion." From the start, the state he created set up . . . an enormous academic propaganda machine against religion. . . . Lenin had no real feelings about corrupt priests, because they were easily beaten. The men he really feared and hated, and later persecuted, were the saints. The purer the religion, the more dangerous. . . . The clergy most in need of suppression were not those committed to the defense of exploitation but those who expressed their solidarity with the proletariat and the peasants. It was as though he recognized in the true man of God the same zeal and spirit which animated himself, and wished to expropriate it and enlist it in his own cause. No man personifies better the replacement of the religious impulse by the will to power.[2]

Little wonder, then, that Lenin's wife, Krupskaya, insisted that the antireligious articles in the Soviet criminal code be placed between the articles proscribing prostitution and pornography.

The first quasi-diplomatic contact between the Holy See and the new Soviet regime came in 1919, when Pope Benedict XV's secretary of state, Cardinal Pietro Gasparri, sent a telegram to Lenin on behalf of persecuted Christian believers, to which Commissar for Foreign Affairs Georgiy Vassiliyevich Chicherin responded. The exchange was a harbinger of things to come:

> To Lenin, Moscow. We have heard from reliable sources that your followers are persecuting servants of God, particularly those belonging to the Russian religion called Orthodox. The Holy Father Benedict XV beseeches you to give strict orders that clergy of every religion be respected. Humanity and religion will be indebted to you. (Signed) Cardinal Gasparri.

> To Cardinal Gasparri, Rome. In receipt of your telegram of March 3, I am in a position to assure you that the reliable sources you mention are misleading you. After the separation of church and state was realized in Russia, religion has been regarded here as a private affair. It is absolutely wrong to speak of persecution of servants of religion. . . . You inform us that the head of the Roman Catholic Church beseeches us to alter our attitude toward the Orthodox clergy; such a sign of solidarity reaches us in the very moment when open and decisive action by the power of the people has exposed the betrayals with which the clergy deceived the masses, by basing its influence on lies. The gilded and bejeweled graves which contain what the clergy has called indestructible holy relics were opened, and there where relics of Tikhon of Sadonsk, Saint Mitrofan of Voronezh, and others were supposed to be, were found dust-covered and mouldy bones, padding, materials and even ladies' stockings. . . . The voice of humanity that our revolution is fighting for is not respected by those who consider themselves your followers; not a word has been heard from your mouth in favor of that voice. (Signed) People's Commissar for Foreign Affairs Chicherin.[3]

Not a particularly warm beginning, that. And yet both the Church and the commissars found reason to continue contacts in the years immediately following the Russian civil war.

The Soviets were interested in famine relief, and in whatever international credibility they might gain by even informal contacts with the Holy See. The Vatican had serious concerns on three fronts: it was bound in conscience to speak out on behalf of persecuted believers; it had to try to make provision for the continuity of sacramental life through a validly consecrated episcopate and a validly ordained presbyterate; and it had property interests, not so much in the financial sense, but because legally held church property gave the Church a physical toehold in the Bolshevik state.

And thus an initial, modest accommodation was reached in 1922, when the communist regime allowed "agents of the Holy See" to enter the Soviet Union "to devote themselves to the relief of the people by distributing foodstuffs to the hungry."[4] Later that year, Commissar Chicherin (now styled "Foreign Minister") and Archbishop Giuseppe Pizzardo, undersecretary of state of the Holy See, met at the Rapallo Conference. Still later, in 1924, 1925, and 1927, the papal nuncio in Berlin, Archbishop Eugenio Pacelli (later Pope Pius XII), met for secret negotiations with Soviet officials under the auspices of the Weimar government.

At the last of these meetings, in October 1927, Pacelli gave the Soviet ambassador in Berlin the Holy See's bottom-line proposal for a modus vivendi: the Vatican would take account of Soviet political objections to candidates for the episcopate, on the reciprocal understanding that the final choice of bishops remained with the Holy See. The proposal never received a reply. And thus Pope Pius XI told Cardinal Gasparri, in December 1927, "As long as the persecution continues in Russia, we can no longer negotiate with the Soviets."[5]

But while the search for a modus vivendi took place through the Berlin negotiations, Pius XI also tried to make unilateral provisions for the continuation of the Church's life in the Soviet Union should the negotiations fail: for a modus non moriendi, a "way of not dying." These efforts centered around the mysterious figure of Michel D'Herbigny. D'Herbigny, who was secretly consecrated a bishop by Archbishop Pacelli in 1926 in the chapel of the papal nunciature in Berlin, was a French Jesuit and academic specialist on the Russian religious philosopher and theologian Vladimir Solovieff, himself a prophet of the reunion of eastern and western Christianity who had been reconciled to Rome in 1896. D'Herbigny gained the confidence of Pius XI, who first appointed him president of the Papal Institute for Eastern Studies in Rome, and later as rector of the Russicum, the papal Russian College near the Basilica of St. Mary Major.[6]

In 1926, and without telling D'Herbigny of the negotiations Pacelli was conducting in Berlin, Pius XI sent the Frenchman to the Soviet Union in order to consecrate bishops secretly. These bishops were, perhaps inevitably, discovered by the Soviet secret police, and the underground hierarchy Pius XI tried to create in the USSR was wiped out (at least insofar as we are aware today).[7] The clandestine quest for a modus non moriendi proved as elusive as the diplomatic search for a modus vivendi through private negotiations. And that failure eventually struck at Michel D'Herbigny, who remained a controversial figure to the end of his days. Perhaps the victim of his own romanticism, perhaps the victim of curial intrigues, he eventually fell from Pius XI's favor and was exiled to Jesuit novitiates in Belgium and France, where he died in 1957.[8]

An influential student of Vatican *Ostpolitik*, the German journalist Hansjakob Stehle, has criticized Pius XI for this "dual strategy" of negotiation through Eugenio Pacelli, on the one hand, and clandestine activity through Michel D'Herbigny, on the other. In his *Eastern Politics of the Vatican*, Stehle is particularly disdainful of what he regards as the pope's duplicity: openly negotiating through Pacelli on the legal appointment of bishops while clandestinely dispatching D'Herbigny to consecrate a secret hierarchy; keeping Pacelli fully informed of D'Herbigny's activities while leaving D'Herbigny ignorant of the Berlin negotiations.

Perhaps Pius XI was naive in thinking that D'Herbigny could successfully install a secret hierarchy in so ruthlessly controlled a police state as the USSR. Perhaps Pius, influenced by D'Herbigny's missionary enthusiasms and his almost mystical regard for Solovieff, imagined a great rapprochement between Rome and the Russian people, given what the Holy See regarded as their betrayal by the Orthodox patriarchate of Moscow (which had taken an oath of loyalty to the Soviet regime in 1927). Pius XI's Soviet strategy did seem to be pulled in several directions simultaneously.

But Stehle's suggestion of duplicity seems badly misplaced. The pope surely believed himself to be under a grave obligation to provide for the continuity of the hierarchy (and thus the continuity of sacramental life) in the event that Pacelli's negotiations failed—and the behavior of the Soviet regime between 1917 and 1927 gave little ground for confidence in the likely success of the Berlin conversations. Nor is there any reason to think that the Soviet regime was moved to break off the Berlin negotiations because it was somehow offended by the D'Herbigny missions.

Stalin, then fully in control of the Soviet state and internal security apparatus and as bitter a foe of religion as Lenin had been, had his own reasons for refusing to make even a minimal accommodation with the Church.

Stehle's sharp criticism of the "dual strategy" is in fact another example of how some western analysts fail to account sufficiently for the distinctive character and ethic, so to speak, of Marxism-Leninism. The notion that Stalin—instigator of the Ukrainian terror famine and the Moscow purge trials—would have been offput by papal "duplicity" in running a clandestine operation at the same time as a formal negotiation is really rather ludicrous: it ascribes to the Soviet dictator a moral sensibility that was wholly absent from his other activities.[9] In his own ideological (and, some would say, pathological) frame of reference, Stalin regarded the Church as duplicitous by its very nature. Had a modest accommodation (on the basis of Pacelli's 1927 proposals) been reached, it would have been because Stalin perceived such an arrangement to be in the interests of his regime (as he would later judge a rapprochement with Orthodoxy during the "Great Patriotic War" of 1941–1945 to be in his interest). The activities of Michel D'Herbigny would not have made any difference, in that case. And they almost certainly were not to blame for Soviet rejectionism toward the Holy See in the late 1920s.[10]

The Confrontation Intensified

These initial attempts at negotiation were followed by a period of intense ideological confrontation between the Vatican and the commissars. In 1937, Pius XI issued the encyclical *Divini Redemptoris* and condemned communism as a "false messianic idea" in which a "pseudo-ideal of justice" is carried by a "deceptive mysticism" about the human condition and its worldly amelioration. The pope proscribed any cooperation between Catholics and communists, and called for a "vast campaign of the Church against world communism" under the patronage of St. Joseph, patron of workers.[11]

The confrontation sharpened even further in the post–World War II years, as Stalin imposed the Yalta imperial system on the nations of central and eastern Europe. The establishment of communist regimes in Poland, Hungary, Czechoslovakia, Romania,

Bulgaria, Albania, Yugoslavia, and the Soviet-occupied section of Germany was followed, in all cases, by a brutal persecution of the Church. The degree and scope of persecution differed from place to place; but Catholicism was clearly faced with the most severe wave of repression it had suffered since the persecution of Diocletian in the early fourth century.

The Church's resistance to the postwar Stalinist attack in central and eastern Europe was symbolically incarnated in five "martyr cardinals": the Hungarian József Mindszenty, the Pole Stefan Wyszyński, the Croatian Alojzije Stepinac, the Czech Josef Beran, and the Ukrainian Jósyf Slipyj. Each of these men suffered imprisonment and house arrest; Mindszenty and Stepinac suffered the further ignominy of public show trials; Mindszenty, Beran, and Slipyj died in exile in Rome; Stepinac died in internal exile in his native village. Yet all of them were, and remain posthumously, controversial figures (although Wyszyński less so than the others).[12] Mindszenty and Beran, it is said, shared Wyszyński's splendid stubbornness but lacked his tactical sophistication and thus left their churches in worse shape than might have been necessary.[13] Stepinac is accused of complicity in the atrocities committed by Croatian partisans during the fierce Yugoslav civil war that coincided with World War II and continued until the consolidation of Tito's power. Mindszenty is charged with attempting to impede the *Ostpolitik* of Pope Paul VI, with its search for a new modus vivendi, in the late 1960s and early 1970s.[14] Slipyj's quest for a Greek Catholic patriarchate of Ukraine was perceived in some Roman circles as a major impediment to ecumenical relations with Russian Orthodoxy, and a further complication in Vatican diplomacy with the Kremlin. None of these arguments can be settled here. What can be said is simply this: Stalin's attempt to eradicate living Catholicism in central and eastern Europe failed, and while the ultimate decision to resist lay within the conscience of each individual Catholic in the region, credit should surely be given to the leadership and witness of the "martyr cardinals" and their associates in the resistant hierarchy and clergy.

The resistant Church had a strong advocate in Pope Pius XII, who succeeded Pius XI in 1939 on the eve of World War II. In addition to his philosophical and theological convictions on the subject, Pius XII's personal experience with communism did not dispose him to any sort of rapprochement with Marxism-Leninism: he had been nuncio in Munich when communists seized power in that city during the crack-up of the Hohenzollern monarchy and he had, as we have seen, been Pius XI's chief agent in the fruitless search for a minimal accommodation with the Bolshevik regime in Moscow. These experiences, plus his fear of the spread of communism in western Europe (and particularly in Italy), plus his knowledge of the persecuted Church in central and eastern Europe, led Pius XII to denounce communism with what some regarded as relentless regularity, to revive the practice of the clandestine ordination of bishops, and to use the ultimate ecclesiastical sanction of excommunication against members of the communist party and even the party's more tepid supporters (in the West as well as the East). Pius XII also linked anticommunism to Marian piety; it has even been suggested that the pope's definition of the dogma of the Assumption in 1950 was influenced by his concern to place the Church and the world more firmly under Our Lady's protection in the face of communist persecution. But Pius XII was a diplomat as well as a pastor, and his pontificate saw the high-water mark of Vatican identification with the West in the forty-five-year struggle of the Cold War: the famous "Pacelli/Spellman alliance," as it was frequently dubbed.

During the crucial post–World War II period of his papal ministry, Pius XII's two closest aides were the Italian curialists Domenico Tardini and Giovanni Battista Montini. Tardini shared Pius's view that no acceptable accommodation with communism was possible, going so far as to criticize Cardinal Wyszyński's 1950 working agreement with the Polish communist regime as an untoward and potentially disastrous concession.[15] Montini was a gentler personality with a somewhat different cast of mind. His pastoral experience with the Italian Catholic student movement in the 1930s, his friendships with prominent Italian Christian Democratic politicians, and his high regard for the social and political thought of the French Catholic philosopher Jacques Maritain led him to believe that the *anathema* approach to the problem of the Church and modern public life was neither pastorally appropriate nor politically effective. And on the specific question of the Church and communism, by the end of the Stalin era (i.e., in 1953) Montini had begun to question, according to Stehle, "whether the 70 million Catholics in the East were still being served by the weapon of excommunication" and the general atmosphere of dramatic confrontation that had characterized Pius XII's approach since the Second World War.[16] Montini's 1954 appointment as archbishop of Milan (without the traditional cardinal's red hat) is sometimes ascribed to his futile advocacy, within the Vatican, of a modest Italian Christian Democratic "opening to the left." Whether it also had something to do with what could have been perceived (or at least described) by his adversaries as his disaffection from the confrontation-driven policy of Pius XII and Tardini cannot be known with any certainty today. In any event, Montini's departure from the Vatican ensured that the last years of Pius XII would see a continuation of an approach that was encapsulated in 1957 in one of Pius's most forceful anticommunist statements, a statement that also reaffirmed the Holy See's alignment with the geopolitics of the West:

> We, as head of the Church, have avoided, just as in earlier cases, calling Christianity to a *crusade*. We can, however, demand complete understanding for the fact that, where religion is a living heritage from their forefathers, people view as a crusade the struggle that was unjustly forced upon them by the enemy. . . . We are convinced that even today, the only way we can and will save the peace against a foe who is determined to impose upon all peoples in one way or another a particular and unbearable way of life, is by the strong and unanimous union of all who love truth and goodness.[17]

John XXIII and the Spirit of Dialogue

Angelo Giuseppe Roncalli, who succeeded Pius XII in 1958 under the name of John XXIII, had, like his predecessor, spent long years in the diplomatic service of the Holy See. But his experience had been different from Eugenio Pacelli's. As apostolic visitor to Bulgaria and later apostolic delegate to Turkey and Greece, Roncalli was continually faced with situations in which Catholicism was a decidedly minority confession. Later, as nuncio to France in the aftermath of the German occupation, Roncalli had to walk a very fine line among the various French political-ecclesiastical factions, and between Gallic sensibilities and Roman instructions. Experience and, as the world came to know, personality thus led Roncalli to adopt a different modus operandi than Pius XII on his election to the See of Peter. Subsequent mythologies notwithstanding, Roncalli was a conservative in his doctrinal views and his personal spirituality. But he was far more comfortable with dialogue than with confrontation—and the result would be a new tack in the Holy See's approach to the problems of the Church under communist regimes.

Pope John's great project was the Second Vatican Council, and the question of participation in the Council by Roman Catholic bishops from behind the iron curtain and by representatives of the Orthodox churches in communist countries was never far from the pope's agenda of concerns. By creating the Vatican Secretariat for Christian Unity in 1960, John XXIII established an institution capable of reopening a conversation with Russian Orthodoxy's Moscow patriarchate—and thus with the Soviet government, without whose approbation the patriarchate never acted—that skirted the problems posed by official diplomatic contacts.[18] In 1961, the pope received, and responded cordially, to greetings from Soviet premier Khrushchev on the occasion of the pontiff's eightieth birthday.[19] In 1962, during the Cuban missile crisis, the pope appealed publicly for peace in a way that distinguished the Holy See from its Pacelli-era Cold War identification with the West; Khrushchev may even have used the pope's plea (which was published in *Pravda*) as one face-saving device behind which Soviet missiles were removed from Cuba.[20]

This papal diplomatic initiative came hard on the heels of John XXIII's famous opening speech to the inaugural meeting of the Second Vatican Council, at which the pope chastised those "prophets of gloom . . . [who] in these modern times can see nothing but prevarication and ruin." John had a different, even optimistic, view: "In the present order of things, Divine Providence is leading us to a new order of human relations which, by men's own efforts and even beyond their very expectations, are directed toward the fulfillment of God's superior and inscrutable designs." Moreover, in correcting erroneous opinion, the "Spouse of Christ" in the new, Johannine dispensation would prefer "to make use of the medicine of mercy rather than that of severity," for the Church believed that "she meets the needs of the present day by demonstrating the validity of her teachings rather than by condemnations."[21]

The Johannine approach, with its preference for dialogue rather than confrontation, continued in the pope's most important substantive contribution to the reorientation of the Church's *Ostpolitik*, the 1963 encyclical *Pacem in Terris*. Here, John XXIII decisively broke with the tactics of Pius XI and Pius XII, by stressing that the Church would henceforth "make a clear distinction between false philosophical teachings regarding the nature, origin, and destiny of the universe and of man, and movements which have a direct bearing on either economic and social questions, or cultural matters or on the organization of the state, even if these movements owe their origin and tenets to these false doctrines." The latter could not change; but "the movements" could, and it was in the prospect of such change in communism-the-movement that the Church would place its hopes for the future. Besides, the pope wrote, "who can deny that those movements . . . contain elements that are positive and deserving of approval?"[22]

What accounts for this dramatic shift from the "crusade" of Pius XI and the confrontation/excommunication strategy of Pius XII to John XXIII's hope for the evolution of what would come to be called "socialism with a human face"? The death of Stalin, Khrushchev's denunciation of Stalinism at the 20th Party Congress in 1956, and the Kremlin's seeming openness to a less confrontational relationship with the Holy See all played a role. The pope's ecumenical concerns about Russian Orthodoxy also dictated a change in the style of the Holy See's approach to the Soviet Union and its satellites. But one should not discount, in weighing these and other factors, the impact of the Cuban missile crisis. According to many reports, John XXIII was deeply shocked by how close the world seemed to have come to a nuclear war during those thirteen days in October 1962. Nuclear weapons meant that the world was, in a sense, condemned to peace. The *anathema* approach, on this analysis, would only exacerbate tensions. The choice for the "medicine of mercy" rather than "that of severity" followed.

John XXIII died in June 1963, just weeks after the public release of *Pacem in Terris*, and was succeeded by Giovanni Battista Montini, whom John had rehabilitated and made his first cardinal in 1958. As previously noted, Montini had already concluded in the mid-1950s that the *anathema* strategy of Pius XI and Pius XII had lost its utility, and it was thus no surprise that, as Pope Paul VI, Montini would extend and amplify the new Johannine approach to the Church's relationship with communist regimes. But first there was the Council to be completed.

Vatican II and the Catholic Human Rights Revolution

There were two Council documents directly relevant to the strategy and tactics of the Church's approach to communism: the "Pastoral Constitution on the Church in the Modern World" (*Gaudium et Spes*) and the "Declaration on Religious Freedom" (*Dignitatis Humanae*). The latter would have the greater long-term impact, although it was "The Church in the Modern World" that Catholics eager to lessen the tensions between (communist) East and (putatively Christian) West took as their magna carta.

Gaudium et Spes was the most "Johannine" of the conciliar texts, famous for its eloquent affirmation of the Church's solidarity with the human family: "The joy and hope, the grief and anguish of the men of our time, especially of those who are poor or afflicted in any way, are the joy and hope, the grief and anguish of the followers of Christ as well. Nothing that is genuinely human fails to find an echo in their hearts."[23] Its openness to many of the intellectual and cultural accomplishments of modernity; its pastoral tone in discussing the problems of belief and the phenomenon of contemporary atheism; its warnings against the dangers of the deterrence system—all of these elements contributed to an ecclesiastical atmosphere far more attuned to the search for reasonable accommodation than to sharp confrontation. Thus *Gaudium et Spes* became the charter for official Roman Catholic participation in one of the distinctive enterprises of the 1960s, the "Christian-Marxist dialogue." Vatican participation in that conversation would take place at the most senior levels, through the new Secretariat for Non-Believers created by Paul VI in 1965 and led for almost twenty years by the archbishop of Vienna, Cardinal Franz König. What was inconceivable under Pius XI and Pius XII—Catholic participation in the search for possible areas of cooperation between Catholics and communists based on a mutually respectful philosophical and even theological dialogue—became the policy of the Holy See under Paul VI.[24]

Great hopes were invested in the "Christian-Marxist dialogue." But it was another Council document, the "Declaration on Religious Freedom," that would provide a firmer theological and moral foundation for the Catholic human rights revolution—and its support for democracy against authoritarian and totalitarian regimes—in the 1980s. The Declaration was the great American achievement at the Council, and the man who made the most significant American contribution to its drafting, the Jesuit John Courtney Murray, can be considered a kind of courtesy grandfather to the Revolution of 1989. In the 1940s and 1950s, from his spartan study at the old Woodstock College in the Maryland countryside, Murray rolled an intellectual pebble down an ecclesiastical mountainside: and that pebble—with, of course, many others—led over time to a political avalanche in central and eastern Europe.

The pebble was Murray's reorientation of Catholic thinking about religious freedom.

The problem, when Murray first began work on it, had nothing to do with central and eastern Europe, of course: it had to do with the United States, and with the official Catholic appraisal of the First Amendment's separation of church and state. Murray's defense of the American arrangement as "articles of peace" congruent with the main trajectory of Catholic thinking about the proper relationship between the Church and the public order was highly controversial in the 1950s.[25] But the American bishops, led by Cardinal Francis Spellman of New York, were determined to raise the issue of religious freedom at Vatican II. And their interest in defending the American arrangement happily intersected with the interests of bishops from central and eastern Europe who wanted the Council to endorse the right of religious freedom in the face of continuing communist persecution. Murray, who was not invited to the Council's first session in 1962, was brought to the second, third, and fourth sessions as Spellman's personal *peritus* (theological expert), and played a major role in shaping the Council's Declaration on Religious Freedom, which the Council fathers adopted in 1965 at the end of the fourth session. Its central affirmation is worth citing at length:

> This Vatican Synod declares that the human person has a right to religious freedom. This freedom means that all men are to be immune from coercion on the part of individuals or of social

groups and of any human power, in such wise that in matters religious no one is to be forced to act in a manner contrary to his own beliefs, whether privately or publicly, whether alone or in association with others, within due limits.

The Synod further declares that the right to religious freedom has its foundation in the very dignity of the human person, as this dignity is known through the revealed Word of God and by reason itself. This right of the human person to religious freedom is to be recognized in the constitutional law whereby society is governed. Thus it is to become a civil right.[26]

The Declaration on Religious Freedom had a decisive impact on the subsequent history of the Church's approach to politics, in four ways.

First, it confirmed that Catholicism entered the debate over the right-ordering of society as *defensor hominis*: as the "defender of man," the defender of the human person who, made in the image and likeness of God, with intelligence and free will, was the bearer of rights and obligations that were his "by nature," prior to his status as a citizen or a subject of state authority. The Council taught, in other words, that within every human person was a *sanctum sanctorum*, a holy of holies, into which the coercive power of the state could not tread. Thus the Church's first interest in the realm of society and politics was to defend that human sanctuary of conscience against all who would abuse it for the ends of power.

The Declaration on Religious Freedom was, therefore, and in the second place, a profound challenge to totalitarianism. It is often said that the Second Vatican Council issued no condemnation of communism per se. And yet it is hard to imagine a more thoroughly (indeed, radically) antitotalitarian statement than *Dignitatis Humanae*. The Declaration struck at the roots of the totalitarian enterprise: as a worldview, as an anthropology, and as a system for the organization of social and political life. In the Declaration on Religious Freedom, the Second Vatican Council made its own the answer of the Polish bishops to the coercive claims of the communist state: "*Non possumus*"—"We cannot accept. . . ." Nor could the Church be accused of making a political claim that was rooted solely in an idiosyncratic religious conviction: according to the Council fathers, the right of religious freedom could be known "by reason itself." All men, and all states, were thus bound by it.

And so the Declaration inevitably raised, in the third place, the question of political structures. By saying that the human person had a fundamental right to religious freedom, the Council fathers implicitly condemned, as a moral monstrosity, any political system which denied that freedom as a matter of state policy. Put more positively, the Declaration on Religious Freedom raised the question of where, in the modern world, one found political systems that acknowledged in principle and defended in practice the inalienable right of religious freedom. The question, raised, was shortly answered: religious freedom was most securely protected, under modern conditions, in democratic states. Thus the Declaration on Religious Freedom was, fourthly, the intellectual and moral bridge between Catholic doctrine and the Church's postconciliar advocacy on behalf of the democratic revolution against authoritarian and totalitarian states. Indeed, one could find in the document itself a declaration that the Church believed itself obliged to work actively on behalf of religious freedom for all men; as the Council fathers put it, "the Church is . . . being faithful to the truth of the Gospel, and is following the way of Christ and the apostles, when she recognizes, and gives support to, the principle of religious freedom as befitting the dignity of man and as being in accord with divine revelation."[27] Thus the Church would not be content with affirming an abstract principle. Knowing her own failings on this question in the past, the Church would yet take up the responsibility of active work in the world so that the principle of religious freedom became a reality in the lives of men and nations.

In sum, the Declaration on Religious Freedom gave Roman Catholicism a powerful instrument of leverage in the wider struggle for human freedom in the modern world. Because she affirmed religious freedom as the right of all (and indeed, as John Paul II would later insist, as the first of human rights and the foundation of any meaningful scheme of such rights), the Church could no longer be accused of acting merely for its own institutional advantage. *Dignitatis Humanae* made the Church politically "disinterested," in the sense of partisan politics: the Church was not merely another faction in society, but was rather the *defensor hominis*, the defender of the rights of man. (Viewed from another angle, *Dignitatis Humanae* corrected what Reinhold Niebuhr once called "the root error of Catholicism in the political order," which was "to regard the Church as, on the one hand, a transhistorical institution and, on the other hand, as a political force which must be protected and whose interests, including its political interests, must always be paramount."[28]) And that principled disentanglement of the Church from the partisanship of faction gave the Church enormous political power at the most basic level of politics: the definition of a social and political order commensurate with human dignity.

A New *Ostpolitik*: The Quest for a Reasonable Accommodation

That Vatican II's Johannine "spirit of dialogue" should have affected the *Ostpolitik* of the Holy See should have come as no surprise. Indeed, a new pattern of Vatican activity vis-à-vis communist regimes was evident even as the Council met. Negotiations with the communist government of Yugoslavia began in 1964, and a partial agreement between the Holy See and the Hungarian government was signed that same year—the first such agreement between the Vatican and a communist state since the agreement on Soviet famine relief in 1922.[29] In 1965, Paul VI met Soviet foreign minister Gromyko at the United Nations in New York, where the pope made his plea for "Never again war; war never again!"

The pace only intensified in the next decade. In 1966, four months after the Council had completed its work, Gromyko came to Rome and was received in private audience by the pope, while Vatican diplomats undertook negotiations in Prague and Bucharest. (That same year, the Warsaw regime denied Paul VI a visa to attend the celebrations of the millennium of Polish Christianity.) In 1970, the Vatican established formal diplomatic relations with Yugoslavia, and a year later Tito made a state visit to the Holy See. Later in 1971, Cardinal Mindszenty left Budapest for Rome. (Cardinal Slipyj was sent to Rome from the Gulag in 1963, the Soviet authorities only allowing him to see his episcopal see of L'viv from the train window. Cardinal Beran had gone to Rome from Prague at Paul VI's request in 1965. Cardinal Stepinac had died in 1960. Thus Cardinal Wyszyński was, by the early 1970s, the last of the "martyr cardinals" still exercising his episcopal office in situ.) Negotiations with Czechoslovakia continued through 1972 and 1973, and it was in the latter year that the Holy See began its work at the Conference on Security and Cooperation in Europe at Helsinki. Vatican diplomats were in active conversation with East German, Polish, Czechoslovakian, Bulgarian, Romanian, Hungarian, Yugoslavian, and Soviet officials throughout the mid-1970s, and by the end of his pontificate in 1978, Paul VI had received in private audience, in addition to Tito and a host of Warsaw Pact foreign ministers and prime ministers, Soviet president Podgorny, Romanian president Ceauşescu, Bulgarian president Zhivkov, Hungarian party leader Kádár, and Polish party leader Gierek.

The vigorous *Ostpolitik* of Paul VI, with its emphasis on a "step-by-step" approach and its moderation at the level of public rhetoric, had its successes and its failures. Its greatest success, for all that it is rarely (if ever) acknowledged as such, was the Holy See's crucial support for the "Basket Three" human rights provisions of the Helsinki Final Act: whose seminal role in creating conditions for the possibility of the Revolution of 1989 was noted in Chapter 1. Its greatest frustration, even failure, was in Czechoslovakia, where the position of the Church remained terribly difficult under an incorrigibly repressive regime. In situations like Czechoslovakia, Paul VI operated on the Italian principle of *salvare il salvabile,* "saving what could be saved." Thus Paul's goal, in the hardest cases, was not altogether different from Pius XI's and Pius XII's quest for a modus non moriendi: to salvage the sacramental life of the Church without fatally compromising the linkage between the Holy See and the national episcopate in question. The difference, and the source of considerable controversy, was the modus operandi of the *Ostpolitik* of Paul VI: the open dialogue with party leaders; the replacement of men like Beran and Mindszenty (who symbolically represented the resistance strategy of anticommunist activists); the muting of overt criticisms of eastern bloc human rights performances (on the Pius XI and Pius XII models) for the sake of maintaining negotiations.

The new ecclesiastical atmosphere created by *Pacem in Terris* and the Second Vatican Council accounts in part for the transformation of Vatican *Ostpolitik* under Paul VI. Like John XXIII, Pope Paul believed that the confrontational strategy and tactics of Pius XI and Pius XII were not only dysfunctional diplomatically; they were inappropriate ecclesiologically. This was not the way the "Spouse of Christ" should present herself to the world.

JUSTIFICATION FOR POPE PAUL'S STRATEGY

But on the publicly available evidence, one might reasonably conclude that the *Ostpolitik* of Paul VI was also based on a set of historical judgments: that Marxism-Leninism retained ideological vitality and thus had historical staying power; that the Yalta imperial system was a relatively permanent fact of the international scene with which the Church would have to deal well into the twenty-first century (and perhaps beyond); that nuclear war was a real and present danger whose avoidance was the first order of business in East/West relations; that reform communism was a possibility; and that there might even be, at the end of a long process of change on both sides of the East/West divide, a convergence between a softening communism and an increasingly social-democratic West.

The *Ostpolitik* of the Holy See from the mid-1960s through the late 1970s did not, in other words, anticipate even the remote possibility of the Revolution of 1989. (Neither, to be fair, did either the local churches in central and eastern Europe or the governments of western countries. Nor did those western European liberals whose reading of the signs of the times was one external influence on Vatican diplomacy.) Pope Paul's purpose was to achieve a modus non moriendi that might, over time, evolve into a genuine modus vivendi. It was an honorable hope. But it was a hope that would be fulfilled by means other than those anticipated in the *Ostpolitik* of Paul VI.

FOUR

The Wojtyła Difference

His motto, *Totus tuus* ("All yours"), reflects his dedication to the Blessed Virgin Mary who stands beneath the cross of the Christ on the shield of his papal coat of arms. But the distinctive ministry of Karol Wojtyła, the pope who came to Rome armed with a heroic hope, might also be captured by another Latin phrase: *Nolite timere*, "Be not afraid!", the words spoken by Jesus to his apostles during the storm on the Sea of Galilee (Mark 6.50). Three times during his first great sermon on October 22, 1978, at his solemn installation as bishop of Rome, John Paul II repeated that call to conscience and courage: "Be not afraid!" The message rang true because it was drawn from a deep well of personal experience and conviction. As the French journalist André Frossard put it, reflecting on the drama of the occasion:

> That October day when he appeared for the first time on the steps of St. Peter's, with a big crucifix planted in front of him like a two-handed sword, and his first words [in Italian], *"Non abbiate paura!"* ("Be not afraid!") echoed over the square, everyone realized then and there that something had happened in heaven: after the man of good will who had opened the Council, after the deeply spiritual man who had closed it, and after an interlude as gentle and fleeting as the flight of a dove, God was sending us a witness.[1]

Since the focus here is on Pope John Paul II's public ministry and its effects on world politics in general and the Revolution of 1989 in particular, it should be emphasized at the outset that, from the day of his election, this pope has made clear his determination to act first and foremost as a *pastor*. He defines his ministry, within the Church and as the Church's representative to the world, in the terms of Jesus' commission to Peter: his task is to strengthen the brethren (see Luke 22.32). This evangelical work has had a great impact on the affairs of men and nations. But it would be a fundamental mistake to read John Paul II as a "political pope": a pope who is primarily a diplomat. He is, surely, the most geopolitically astute pope of the twentieth century. But as a matter of intensely felt personal vocation as well as of institutional self-understanding, he is essentially a pastor: a pastor who believes that a Church taking itself seriously *as Church*, as the Body of Christ in the world, can by that very fact change the face of politics among nations.

Whose Humanism?

On one interpretation John Paul II is a very complex, unpredictable character, "conservative" doctrinally but "liberal" in his economic and political views. And it is true that this pope defies the regnant stereotypes by which the mass media characterize religious leaders. But on closer scrutiny it appears that John Paul II does not so much occupy an idiosyncratic place along the conservative/liberal spectrum as he defines a path that transcends that continuum. Moreover, what is often taken as the pope's complexity is in fact a highly sophisticated simplicity.

It is a *Christological* simplicity, for the teaching of John Paul II—on core issues of Catholic belief, as well as on the Church's vision of a just human society—consists in complex variations on a single, great theme: that "Christ is not only a revelation *of God* and his salvific will for all mankind . . . but also a revelation *of man*, of what man was intended to be at creation and is by reason of the Incarnation of the Son of God and by reason of the Crucifixion, Resurrection, and Ascension of the God-Man Jesus Christ."[2] Christ reveals to man, not only the face of the Father, but the full meaning of humanness. Christ is "the existentially adequate response to the desire in every human heart for goodness, truth, and life."[3]

Thus, in John Paul's scheme of things, the person most dependent on God, the person most open to God's summons to communion in the life and love of the Trinity, is the person who is most fully human. Communion with God, made possible through Jesus Christ, is not a zero-sum game; dependence on God increases human freedom. Therefore, those who try to exclude Christ from history are acting against man, against humanness.

"Open the doors to Christ!" the pope urged the world at his inauguration. Nor should this challenge—this demand—be understood primarily as an institutional concern (the pope acting as chief executive officer of Roman Catholic Church, Inc.). No, John Paul II is sure that the death of God is the death of man, and that man alive in Christ is man most fully alive. According to the Polish pope, today's defective—not to say demonic—humanisms are best countered by a thoroughly Christian humanism.

And here is where the evangelical proclamation of John Paul II touched the worlds of politics in the late twentieth century, and particularly the politics of those nations caught in the communist culture of the lie. Karol Wojtyła of Kraków knew all about the web of mendacity and the inhumanity it had spawned when he was elected to the chair of Peter. He also knew that the system had to be confronted at its roots: at the baseline where the argument, "Whose humanism?" was directly engaged. The best antidote to the silent fear that made the greengrocer burn his joss stick of obeisance by putting communist slogans amidst the carrots and the onions in his shop window was the clarion call, "Be not afraid!" And the most effective challenge to the regimes which inculcated that fear was not political, but evangelical: "Open the doors to Christ!" The pope would be *defensor hominis*, the defender of man, precisely by acting as the vicar of *redemptor hominis*, the redeemer of man (as John Paul entitled his inaugural encyclical).[4] And this defense would address, "not . . . the 'abstract' man, but the real, 'concrete,' 'historical' man . . . for each [man] is included in the mystery of the Redemption and with each one Christ has identified himself forever through this mystery."[5] To the eyes of the world, this may look suspiciously like a complex, or perhaps even devious, two-track strategy: "doctrinal conservatism" and a "liberal" defense of human rights. John Paul II insists that it is all of one piece.

A Man for This Season

His election as pope on October 16, 1978, was a great surprise. So was the fact that he quickly emerged as perhaps the world's foremost defender of basic human rights. But those who explored his intellectual and pastoral career prior to his becoming pope discovered a remarkable logic—which believers could only see as providential—in the path that took Karol Józef Wojtyła from Poland to Rome, and from Rome to the world.

He was born on May 18, 1920, in Wadowice, about thirty miles southwest of Kraków. His father, Karol, was a retired officer of the Austro-Hungarian army. His mother, the former Emilia Kaczorowska, who was ill throughout his childhood, died before young Karol had made his first communion; his older brother, Edmond, a doctor, died of scarlet fever in a hospital in which he was serving when Karol was twelve. A good student and an active athlete (especially devout tourists in Wadowice can visit the soccer pitch on which "Lolek," the future pope, played goalie), Karol graduated from the local municipal high school and, with his widower father, moved to Kraków where in 1938 he enrolled as an undergraduate in the ancient Jagiellonian University. There, over the entrance to the Aula of the university's Collegium Maius (once home to Copernicus), he found the Latin motto, *Plus ratio quam vis*: "Reason rather than force."

His matriculation in philosophy and Polish philology was drastically interrupted in 1939 by the German occupation of Poland at the beginning of World War II. The university was shut down and its professors shipped off to the Sachsenhausen concentration camp where the great majority later died.[6] Young Wojtyła was first assigned to manual labor in a stone quarry, and later to the Solway sodium factory. His father died in February 1941, and twenty-year-old Karol Wojtyła was alone, in a country under Nazi occupation.

It was during this period, when he was working by day as a common laborer and participating at night in various underground religious, literary, and theatrical activities, that his priestly vocation crystallized.[7] His high school teachers had thought of him in these terms, but Karol was not easily persuaded: "Toward the end of my years at the lycée the people around me thought that I would choose the priesthood. As for me, I did not give it a thought. I was quite sure that I would remain a layman. Committed, to be sure, determined without any doubt to participate in the life of the Church; but as a priest, certainly not."[8] Gradually, however, he came to the conviction, not so much that he should choose the priesthood, but that he had been chosen by God for it, and that to refuse the offer would be unthinkable. An influential figure in the maturation of this decision, and on the young man's concept of the priesthood as vocation rather than career, was the lay mystic Jan Tyranowski, in whose "Living Rosary" prayer group Wojtyła participated. John Paul II would later describe this simple tailor as a "real master of [the] spiritual life" who exemplified "a new world that I did not yet know": the world of a "life given entirely to God alone."[9] Thus in October 1942 Karol Wojtyła joined the clandestine seminary organized by Cardinal Adam Sapieha, the archbishop of Kraków, who would be a model and mentor to the young seminarian he ordained in 1946. (Sapieha, the scion of a noble Polish-Lithuanian family, was a man of dignity and great personal courage. Hans Frank, the Nazi *Gauleiter* who had set up shop at the heart of Polish nationalism, Wawel Castle, hard by Kraków's cathedral, kept pressing for an invitation to dinner at the archbishop's residence. Sapieha finally issued the invitation, and then served Frank a meal of dry bread and weak tea, explaining that this was the diet on which the archbishop's people were trying to survive. The statue of a tormented and prayerful Cardinal Sapieha, outside the metropolitan curia in Kraków, identifies him as the "archbishop of the long, dark night of occupation.")

It was during this period that four of Karol Wojtyła's interests intensified in ways that would shape his ministry as bishop of Rome some thirty years later.

The first two of these interests were in Polish language and literature, and in the theater. Polish literature was one of the cultural means by which Polish national identity was maintained between the third partition of 1795 and the resurrection of Poland as an independent state in 1918. But the future pope was also absorbed in the study of the Polish language, which would serve him well in his later confrontation with the banalities and mendacities of communist newspeak. Timothy Garton Ash was struck by this during the pope's first pastoral visit to Poland in June 1979, after which the British historian remarked on the pope's "beautiful, sonorous Polish, so unlike the calcified official language of communist Poland," and the pope's eloquent evocation of his nation's cultural history, to which the crowds responded, "We want God, we want God. . . ."[10]

The future pope's skills as preacher and teacher were also amplified by his youthful experience as an actor and a novice playwright. Karol Wojtyła took the drama very seriously, and prior to entering Sapieha's illegal seminary, thought of it as at least a part of his future career. The underground "Rhapsodic Theater" which he helped form during the Nazi occupation had to conduct its business clandestinely, without the usual stage materials and props. But that experience of theater-as-poetry enhanced what Sir John Gielgud once referred to as the pope's "perfect" sense of delivery and timing.[11]

Karol Wojtyła also made his first serious exploration of philosophy, the discipline in which he later made his most significant academic contributions, during this period. John Paul's reconstruction of the impact of his initial encounter with a manual of metaphysics given him during his days in the clandestine seminary is worth noting:

> Straightaway I found myself up against an obstacle. My literary training, centered around the humanities, had not prepared me at all for the scholastic theses and formulas with which the manual was filled. I had to cut a path through a thick undergrowth of concepts, analyses, and axioms without even being able to identify the ground over which I was moving. After two months of hacking through this vegetation I came to a clearing, to the discovery of the deep reasons for what until then I had only lived and felt. When I passed the examination I told my examiner that . . . the new vision of the world which I had acquired in my struggle with that metaphysics manual was more valuable than the mark which I had obtained. I was not exaggerating. What intuition and sensibility had until then taught me about the world found solid confirmation.[12]

What was this "new vision of the world"? Technically, the future pope had absorbed the realist philosophical precepts of Thomistic metaphysics and epistemology. More personally, one can say that, early on in his intellectual career, Karol Wojtyła came to a *unitive* vision of the human person and the human experience. The reality of "the world," and the relationship of the world as "object" to the human person as knowing "subject," were defensible and illuminating positions for Wojtyła, not the stumbling blocks they would be for intellectuals influenced by British empiricism and its Kantian successors. From the beginning, Wojtyła's philosophical activity was characterized, not by the relativism and skepticism that undergird so much modern philosophy, but by a conviction that things fit together, human things and the things of this world, according to an order discernible by rational reflection on their nature. The Thomistic certainties of that obscure metaphysics manual would be tempered and refined by Wojtyła's later encounter with existentialism and phenomenology, by his bracing intellectual duel with theoretical Marxism, and by his doctoral work on the moral philosopher Max Scheler. And the mature thought of John Paul II, as pope, has been far more intensely theological than philosophical. But the unitive vision of reality and the conviction that that unity was not an accident, gained from that first hard encounter with philosophy, would endure.

The result would be a philosophical stance that the pope's intellectual biographer, George Huntston Williams of Harvard, has characterized as a "reconception of individualism," or "responsible personalism."[13] Its fundamental anthropological (indeed, metaphysical) premise was that the human person was an active *subject*, a free intellectual and moral agent, whose subjectivity could not be impugned without committing a crime against humanity. The humanity of the human subject could not be reduced to race (the Nazi heresy); nor could it be understood as the expression of "objective" historical forces to which it had to accommodate itself (the Marxist-Leninist heresy). Karol Wojtyła might well have come to these convictions on the basis of experience. But what he had once intuited through experience was confirmed and deepened by his first steps in philosophy. And it is here—in this insistence on the inviolability of the human person, in the demand that man not be reduced to an object by any earthly power—that we find one source of the pope's teaching on basic human rights: including, preeminently, the right of religious freedom or freedom of conscience. Karol Wojtyła's introduction to philosophy thus helped equip him to challenge Marxism-Leninism precisely on the basis of a truer humanism.

The fourth element of Wojtyła's intellectual personality that emerged at this early period was his mysticism. The deaths of his parents and his brother, the occupation and its brutalities, and a severe accident Wojtyła suffered before he entered the clandestine seminary (struck down on the road by a German truck, his skull was fractured and when he was found unconscious in the street the next morning, it was feared that the injury might be life threatening) raised questions of belief and unbelief, vocation and fate, very directly indeed. The lay worker/mystic Jan Tyranowski helped Wojtyła probe those questions in prayer. Tyranowski also made the initial link between spirituality and the life of the mind for his disciple, by lending Wojtyła books on St. John of the Cross. In the late 1940s, when sent by Cardinal Sapieha to Rome for graduate studies in theology, Father Wojtyła taught himself Spanish so he could write his doctoral dissertation on the great Spanish mystic: which was, according to the pope's later recollections, far more than a dry exercise in academic hoop jumping. Rather, it was "the revelation of a universe," the "shock" of which "was comparable to the one I felt . . . in the depths of my metaphysical forest."[14]

These early intellectual influences—Polish language and literature, the theater, philosophy, and mysticism—and the young Father Wojtyła's early pastoral experience (teaching children their catechism, instructing young couples before their marriage, hiking in his beloved Tatra mountains with youth groups) worked together to produce a distinctive character: a modern intellectual who was neither a skeptical modernist nor an abstract egghead;[15] a priest and pastor who had had a normal adolescence (unlike many of his papal predecessors who had entered the seminary at age eleven or twelve); an active sportsman; and a man skilled in the deployment of language as a medium of truth. Karol Wojtyła was also a disciplined thinker whose moral philosophy focused on the human person as a unique moral agent, and stressed that freedom entailed responsibility and that politics was an extension of ethics.[16] Linking all these qualities and attributes was the fact that Wojtyła was a deeply prayerful man who had learned from his widower father that there was no contradiction between manliness and prayerfulness.[17] His prayer in turn reflected his intellectuality and his mysticism: prayer, and particularly meditation on the Scriptures, was for Karol Wojtyła "a quite distinct mode of knowledge—not so much a question of *knowing* God as of *making his acquaintance*."[18]

John Paul II's is, in sum, an exceptionally unified personality: intellectually centered on the concept of the inviolable dignity and worth of the human person; committed as philosopher and theologian to human freedom, understood in Lord Acton's famous phrase as "having the right to do what we ought;" convinced that history has to be understood as a whole, and not merely as a sequence of random episodes; a man of great personal presence, physically as well as intellectually and spiritually active; an experienced churchman, dedicated to his role as pastor and willing to conceive that role broadly; a Christian believer to the depth of his being. All of these convictions and qualities are variations on the one theme that is Karol Wojtyła.

Yet John Paul II came to Rome personally acquainted with the darker side of the human condition and with the evils of modern totalitarian systems. He was an orphan before he reached his majority. He had lived one step removed from the status of a slave laborer under backbreaking physical conditions. He had spent his entire adult life under the authority, if such it can be called, of Nazis and communists. He had confronted, daily, the culture of the lie and its corrosive effects on individuals and on human relationships. He had listened and counseled for thousands of hours in the confessional. There was no Panglossian optimism in his worldview.

But there was faith: faith in God, and because of that, faith in man and faith in history. When he came to Rome in October 1978, Karol Wojtyła had long been convinced that the history of the modern world had to be read against a larger, transcendent horizon. The paradox was that it was precisely from that vantage point that the present, with its mix of dangers and possibilities, came into clearer focus.

Out of that clarity would come a distinctive Vatican *Ostpolitik* with world-historical consequences.[19]

"Breathing Space"

Officials of the Holy See naturally stress the continuity of Vatican diplomacy over time, and tend to downplay the role of the Holy See's diplomats in resolving disputes within nations, between nations, or between the Church and a particular government.[20] This is entirely understandable, given the Church's nature, its evangelical mission, and its conception of itself as a community unified in purpose over time. The self-imposed modesty of the Holy See's secretariat of state also makes good practical sense: claiming credit for some accomplishment now may make life more difficult in the future. Moreover, in recent years, efforts to distinguish elements of the *Ostpolitik* of John Paul II from the *Ostpolitik* of Pope Paul VI and Cardinal Agostino Casaroli have been resisted on more personal grounds. Paul's *Ostpolitik* had its passionate critics (even, perhaps especially, among otherwise very loyal Catholics), and the focus of that criticism was usually Cardinal Casaroli. Thus attempts to distinguish the "Wojtyła difference" are sometimes rebuffed, in Vatican circles and elsewhere, as being a more subtle form of attack on the person, intentions, and diplomacy of Cardinal Casaroli.[21]

Agostino Casaroli was a dedicated churchman who served four popes with great distinction as a close adviser. Nor need it follow that acknowledging the distinctive character of John Paul II's *Ostpolitik* implies a harsh judgment on Casaroli, or drives one inexorably to the conclusion that John Paul II rejected the work that the cardinal had done under the direction of Paul VI. John Paul II, after all, named Casaroli his secretary of state, presumably in the conviction that the cardinal would be as faithful a servant of his policies as he was of Pope Paul's.

Yet the public record, and an analysis of the *Ostpolitik* of the Holy See in central and eastern Europe from the late 1960s through 1978, suggest that that diplomacy was based in part on two judgments which John Paul II did not share and which are, in any event, surely open to respectful scrutiny.

First, in the *Ostpolitik* of Paul VI, the Yalta imperial system was viewed primarily in diplomatic terms as a historical and geopolitical fact: perhaps things ought to have worked out better, in the endgame of the Second World War, but the postwar division of Europe was a given. The *why* of the Yalta system—what it said about the Marxist-Leninist project, and what it said about the West—was not regarded as of particularly great significance for the diplomacy of the Holy See. The division and the system were facts, and Paul VI, who spent over thirty years in the Vatican diplomatic service, was convinced that they were facts that had to be recognized as at least a starting point for strategy. The status quo had to be acknowledged if it were to be dealt with, and the Church's situation improved, over time. Stability was the precondition to reform.

The second judgment informing the *Ostpolitik* of Paul VI was an analytic extension of the first. Paul VI and his closest associates believed that the communist regimes of central and eastern

Europe would last for many years: not because they enjoyed popular legitimacy, but because of the omnipresence of the Soviet Union as the imperial hegemon committed to the maintenance of Stalin's external empire. Paul VI took the imposition of Soviet power after World War II, and the reaction of the Soviet Union to the East German, Hungarian, and Czechoslovak revolts, seriously. Perhaps these regimes might modify themselves over time. But their fate as satellites of the USSR seemed sealed for the foreseeable future.

It was on these two premises—"Yalta" was to be dealt with as a fact, and the regimes in the Warsaw Pact were as permanent as things get in this world—that the *Ostpolitik* of Paul VI was created, and then executed by Cardinal Casaroli and his associates. Pius XII's confrontation strategy was rejected (as it had been under John XXIII), and a "step-by-step" approach was substituted in its place. The diplomacy of Paul VI and Casaroli would take things in a measured way, and would calibrate its dealings with communist regimes on the basis of their relative openness (or lack thereof). First, small steps (even, say, opening an official exploratory conversation with a communist government) would be followed by later negotiations. Moreover, the *Ostpolitik* would be conducted on something like a state-to-state basis, between officials of the Holy See and officials of the government in question, rather than through the local national hierarchy as intermediary (Cardinal Wyszyński would have none of this in Poland, and successfully interposed himself as the gatekeeper of the dialogue); beneath this preference for a state-to-state approach may have lain the judgment that reform in the communist world would come from above.[22] These initiatives in central and eastern Europe would be complemented by disentangling the Holy See from the vestiges of the old Pacelli/Spellman alliance. The Church's traditionally stern, even condemnatory, rhetoric about communism, its violations of basic human rights, and its attempts to manipulate the Church (e.g., through the "Pacem in Terris" movement of regime–co-opted priests in Czechoslovakia) would be tempered. There would be more vocal criticism of certain western policies (e.g., in the Second Indochina War). And the Holy See would be much more assertive on behalf of social justice in Latin America and in the new nations of the Third World.[23]

The goal of this step-by-step approach was what one Vatican

official, himself an agent of the *Ostpolitik* of Paul VI, described subsequently as "freedom for the Church to survive" the gray, chill winter of communist control, or what Cardinal Casaroli frequently described as "breathing space" for the Church. There were doctrinal and disciplinary boundaries which the Holy See would not violate. Pope Paul VI could not and would not concede the Church's final authority on the nomination of bishops; this was an unresolvable sticking point with the Czechoslovakian regime and the result was that the majority of bishoprics in Bohemia, Moravia, and Slovakia were left unfilled. So it would be wrong to think of Pope Paul's eastern diplomacy as weakly concessionary, even supine. But on the basis of the currently available documentary record and in terms of the actual unfolding of events, it does seem that the *Ostpolitik* of Paul VI involved, strategically, a limited set of goals. Pope Paul was not so much seeking a modus vivendi, a way of living (perhaps even somewhat satisfactorily), with communist regimes; he was trying to effect a modus non moriendi—a tolerable relationship with these regimes—so that the Church, even in a diminished or hard-pressed condition, would not die.

What would that modus non moriendi have looked like? In the minds of those who designed and implemented the *Ostpolitik* of Paul VI, the Church would have achieved something of real significance in the countries of central and eastern Europe if it could nominate bishops without state interference; if its bishops could deal freely with their priests; and if the Church could conduct programs of religious education without excessive legal harassment.[24] That, it was thought, would constitute a great victory.

A Changed Game

The *Ostpolitik* of the Holy See changed dramatically and decisively on October 16, 1978, when the College of Cardinals elected Karol Józef Wojtyła of Kraków as the Bishop of Rome. Elements of continuity would remain, in terms of both tactics and personnel. But the *Ostpolitik* changed, because the cards on the table, and indeed the game itself, were changed by the election of John Paul II.[25]

First, the fact that the 263rd successor of Peter was the first

Slavic pope, and a son of Poland to boot, ensured that international attention would be refocused on central and eastern Europe. Under these circumstances, the West could not achieve a lasting accommodation with the Soviet Union, a true détente, without a significant amelioration of the situation of the people of the Warsaw Pact countries. The maneuvering room of the Soviet Union and its satellites was also constrained, for John Paul II, the pope from the eastern bloc, would bring the harsh glare of international scrutiny to bear on anything like the 1968 invasion of Czechoslovakia, and would make sure that the spotlight was kept on "high" until a morally satisfactory alternative was achieved. Furthermore, the locus of the confrontation between freedom and totalitarianism would shift: for the Polish pope could take the battle onto communism's home court, so to speak. The communists simply couldn't keep him out—at least out of Poland—without major international public relations problems.

The game also changed in more subtle ways. The election of a Pole to the papacy—and the public celebrations this provoked in central and eastern Europe, but especially in Poland—were sharp blows to communist claims about the building of "new socialist man." For whatever else Karol Wojtyła was, he was most assuredly not "new socialist man." The reaction to the election of this Polish sign of contradiction to the chair of Peter had to be debilitating to those charged with maintaining the ideological facade of the culture of the lie.

The game was also changed because one of its principal actors, the Slav pope, having lived under communism and challenged its intellectual, moral, and operational claims for thirty years, knew that the system's maximum point of vulnerability was on the question of acquiescence. The system endured, and seemed monolithic and impermeable, because of the fear. And the fear endured because of the acquiescence: because enough people were not yet ready to say "No" to the fear, and thus to the system. But now there came a solution to the dilemma brilliantly described by Václav Havel: How do we get a situation in which enough people are willing to straighten their spines and live in greater dignity?[26] The solution was this: enough people will say "No" when enough people are convinced that their lives should be built on the foundation of a higher and more compelling "Yes." The road to that "Yes" could be scouted by a great "witness," as André Frossard aptly put it. The new fact of that witness—a witness to a "Yes" that resonated far more eloquently in the historically Christian cultures of central and eastern than communist newspeak—changed the game in a decisive way.

So one ought to have expected that the election of a pope from the East would have made a difference over time in the *Ostpolitik* of the Holy See, because the Holy See (like the governments of central and eastern Europe) was now dealing with a new situation. But the impact of this new factor—the Polish pope—was magnified by Karol Wojtyła's distinctive combination of personal experience and intellectual and moral conviction.

Training for Moral Combat

Karol Wojtyła's life as archbishop of Kraków provided a crucial experiential base and a set of themes for his papal *Ostpolitik*.

There was the experience of Kraków itself: an ancient city whose history lives on its streets and in its buildings, and in a trumpeter's broken summons to the citizenry, sounded every hour on the hour from the tower of the Marian Church in the market square: a tradition of civic memory, and a subtle call to the defense of *Polonia semper fidelis*, that dates to the thirteenth century.[27] Unlike Warsaw, which was devastated by the Nazis in the Second World War, Kraków survived largely intact, the only major Polish city to do so. Here Karol Wojtyła lived, for exactly forty years, as student, laborer, curate, teacher, and archbishop, amidst the historic continuity of Kraków itself, Kraków with Poland, and Kraków with Europe. And it was in being a Krakówian, according to the distinguished Polish editor Jerzy Turowicz, that Karol Wojtyła became a European—not an east European, or a central European, but a European:

> Though he may be head of the Universal Church, citizen of the world, and European, John Paul II has not in the least stopped being a Pole and a Cracovian. On the contrary. No one can be a European in the abstract. It is membership of one of the nations living in Europe and having one's roots in one of the national cultures whose diversity and richness make up the common European heritage, that makes one a European. European culture is not merely the mechanical sum of those cultures nor some sort of com-

mon denominator, but a living organism growing in time through the fertile interaction of its national elements. If Shakespeare belongs to the common European (and not only European!) cultural heritage, it is not only because his works contain general human values, but precisely because they are so very English. To recapitulate, European culture has nothing to do with leveling, uniformity, the rubbing away of differences, but rather with the embodiment of what is universal in the specific cultures of nations.

Therefore, John Paul II is a European thanks to being a Cracovian.[28]

In other words, it is precisely because he was a Krakówian— the inheritor of a great local and national culture that was one embodiment of the concepts of "Europe" and "European"—that John Paul II could challenge the false universalism and uniformity of Marxism-Leninism and its project of creating "new socialist man."

To be a Krakówian means to love Wawel Hill, with its castle and cathedral, and Karol Wojtyła was very much a son of Wawel: the Wawel of poets, priests, and monarchs, the Wawel where Polish identity and Christian identity are thickly intertwined, as in the Latin inscription over the gateway to the castle, *Si Deus Nobiscum Quis Contra Nos* ("If God is with us, who can be against us?"). Wawel was the site of his cathedral church for fourteen years. But Wojtyła's Wawel connection goes back farther and has a more personally definitive character than that. For it was to the crypt of St. Leonard in Wawel Cathedral, hard by the tombs of Polish kings, queens, and heroes, that the newly ordained Father Wojtyła came, on the Feast of All Souls, 1946, to offer his first three Masses for the repose of the souls of his parents and his brother. From the beginning of his priesthood, personal history and Wawel—and all that Wawel meant as the symbolic center of Polish culture and history—were intimately linked in Karol Wojtyła.[29]

So conscious a student of Polish history and culture must also have reflected, after his appointment as archbishop, on the witness of his first predecessor in the see of Kraków, St. Stanisław, whose remains rest in a silver casket suspended over a great altar in the nave of Wawel Cathedral. Stanisław, killed in 1079 by King Bolesław the Bold, was a martyr, a defender of the rights of the Church, and a victim of one of the first confrontations between the Church and state authority in Poland. The line of bishops between Stanisław and Adam Sapieha had its less glorious characters, from time to time. But the special moral texture of the Kraków episcopate was fixed early on. It surely amplified the sense of vocational obligation felt by Karol Wojtyła, archbishop of Kraków.

Wojtyła lived that vocation as archbishop in many ways: in a steady stream of writings (in his own name and, in the case of his poetry and drama, under a series of pseudonyms); in his work with the Kraków branch of the Clubs of the Catholic Intelligentsia, which did so much to heal the rift between the Church and Polish intellectuals (a process that would pay rich dividends in the Revolution of 1989); by his outdoor activism;[30] by his constant interest in young people, his parish visitations, and his work as a university professor. But perhaps the symbolic centerpiece of Wojtyła's experience as archbishop of Kraków was the building of the Ark Church in Nowa Huta.

The Kraków suburb of Nowa Huta, home of the Lenin Steelworks that have wreaked such enormous environmental damage on the Kraków region, was intended by Poland's communist regime to be a model workers' city, rationally planned to provide for all man's needs, rationally understood. Needless to say, these needs did not include a church. For almost a quarter of a century the people of Nowa Huta, supported by their archbishop, struggled with the authorities to build a church in their "model town." The church was finally completed in 1977, after ten years of work. The result is a fine piece of contemporary church design and decoration: for Cardinal Wojtyła was not about to have just any church in Nowa Huta. He wanted a church that would reflect the great battle his people had fought for the right to build it. And that is what Wojtyła got, in the church of the Ark of Our Lady, Queen of Poland.

The church was built entirely by voluntary labor. Its exterior walls are decorated with two million shells, taken from the riverbeds of Poland. Outside and in, the structure is intended to suggest the Church as the ark in which Our Lady is saving her people amidst the storms of communist rule. There is no crucifix per se, but rather an enormous steel corpus of the crucified Christ, built in the Lenin Steelworks by the workers, suspended in sacrifice over the church's gently sloping great nave. To the right, in the sanctuary, is the ikon of the Black Madonna of Częstochowa; to the left is the altar of repose and its globe-shaped tabernacle, in the center of which is embedded a piece of moon rock, a gift to Wojtyła from an American astronaut. The Ark Church—the very fact that it exists, and the beauty of its conception and execution—was a stunning achievement: it, and Wawel Cathedral, might be considered the two symbolic poles between which the electric current of Karol Wojtyła's ministry as archbishop of Kraków flowed. That current gave a distinctive charge to Wojtyła's ministry as bishop of Rome and to his *Ostpolitik*.

Going on Offense: The *Ostpolitik* of John Paul II

As archbishop of Kraków, then, Karol Wojtyła learned from hard, if stimulating, experience how to deal with communism: and not just to resist its repressions, but to challenge it morally, culturally, and historically on the basis of a deeper humanism. He deftly rebuffed all efforts by the authorities to drive a wedge between himself and the primate, Cardinal Wyszyński.[31] He kept close to his people through, among other efforts, a five-year-long, archdiocesan-wide process of prayer and reflection on the texts of the Second Vatican Council. He had regular, personal, and intense contacts with intellectuals and was instrumental in closing the historic breach between the intellectuals and the Church which the communists had tried to exploit since the early days of the oxymoronic Polish People's Republic. A literary man in his own right, Karol Wojtyła knew what to say to communism, and he knew how to say it.

Wojtyła thus became pope having accumulated a vast store of useful experience that could be brought to bear on the *Ostpolitik* of the Holy See. And that he intended to put this experience to good use need not be doubted. Indeed, according to one of his close collaborators, the first thing the new pope did after his election was ask to see the archives on the *Ostpolitik* of Paul VI.

Nor did the new pontiff wait very long to exploit the techniques for dealing with communists he had developed over thirty years, but which could now be deployed on a much vaster stage. In fact he began with the ceremony of his installation. Polish national television (then under strict communist control) had agreed to broadcast four hours of the installation Mass from Rome. John Paul, knowing that the Polish authorities hoped that the Mass would not last quite that long, so that regime propagandists could put the government's spin on Wojtyła's election at the end of the broadcast while exploiting the visual backdrop of St. Peter's Square, called in the papal master of ceremonies and told him that the ceremony had to last four hours: however the MC did it, it had to last four hours. Thus, as many will remember, there was a seemingly interminable procession of the cardinals to the newly installed pope's throne, each of whom got more than a perfunctory embrace from John Paul II. And at the end of four hours, there was the Polish pope, cross held high, exhorting the crowd, "Be not afraid!" It was a media masterstroke, made possible by the experience of a very savvy John Paul II.[32]

The new pope was much more than an accomplished stage director, of course. John Paul II also reoriented the themes and dynamics of the *Ostpolitik* of the Holy See. The new, primary theme of the public catechesis of the pope—the pope's address to "all men and women of good will"—would be human rights, and the right of religious freedom as the key to any meaningful scheme of rights would be stressed time and again. On the very night he was elected, addressing the crowds in St. Peter's Square, he identified the "road of the Church" with the "road of history." He raised the question of human dignity as the foundation of a just polity in his first meeting with the diplomats accredited to the Holy See, on October 20, 1978.[33] He spoke relentlessly and passionately about human rights on his first pilgrimage home to Poland in June 1979 (about which, much more later). Human rights were the chief theme of his address to the General Assembly of the United Nations in October 1979, and were a constant reference point in his meetings with new diplomats when they presented their credentials in the early days of his pontificate.[34] The Holy See pressed vigorously for compliance with the human rights provisions of the Helsinki Final Act at the CSCE Review Conference in Madrid, the pope making a personal appeal to the delegates in explicit terms: "Religious freedom guaranteed by law will serve to assure tranquillity and the common welfare of every country and of every society."[35] John Paul also linked human rights, human culture, and the pursuit of peace in his address to UNESCO at its Paris headquarters in 1980.[36]

This persistent emphasis on human rights as the centerpiece of the Church's address to the world of politics—and thus as the core of the Church's *Ostpolitik*—was not in contradistinction to Cardinal Casaroli's step-by-step diplomacy. John Paul II had no principled aversion to pursuing what was possible, step-by-step, in quasi state-to-state relations, by the methods pioneered by Paul VI and Casaroli. But John Paul was determined to put an end to some festering problems, such as the activities of the "Pacem in Terris" priests in Czechoslovakia.[37] Perhaps even more to the point, he was determined to locate step-by-step diplomacy in the context of a dynamic, aggressive, and comprehensive *evangelical* campaign, in which he would take a highly visible role.

The pope would act and speak, not as one politician making demands on another, but as the *defensor hominis* who spoke and acted on behalf of man, on behalf of humanity. In doing so, the pope would be "strengthening the brethren" throughout the world, while concurrently giving some tactical space to hard-pressed fellow bishops who could then defend their human rights activism as an *imitatio Petri*, a following of the pope's lead. The campaign would also be sharpened substantively: human freedom would be defended, not as a concession to be sought from governments (which would imply that governments had claims which trumped the basic human rights of persons), but as a moral demand to be insisted upon (the implication being that governments that denied the basic human rights of their people lacked moral legitimacy).

Finally, John Paul was determined to pursue a politically disinterested campaign, in several senses. The Church's proclamation of basic human rights would be, first and foremost, a defense of man, rather than a defense of the Church's institutional prerogatives (although these would not be ignored or minimized). Second, the Church would challenge the human rights records of countries like Chile, South Korea, and the Philippines as well as the countries of the communist world: as a matter of consistency and principle, which in turn took the campaign beyond the Cold War context. Third, it would be a campaign in which the legitimate prerogatives of governments were recognized: subject, of course, to their respect for basic human rights. Finally, and with particular reference to the countries of central and eastern Europe, John Paul's personal campaign would be fought simultaneously on the three crucial fronts of ethics, culture, and history. It would be built on an anthropology that stressed the nature of the human person as a responsible moral agent. The pope would persistently remind all Europeans of their common cultural roots in Christian civilization. And John Paul would work to revivify the central and eastern European churches' sense of their own history by linking the human rights struggles of the present to popular piety and to the great figures of the Church's past. Indeed, in describing his desire to return home to Poland, in an audience held for Poles in Rome on the day after his installation as pope, John Paul said that he wanted to "go back for the 900th anniversary of St. Stanisław."[38] No Pole could have missed the reference or its implications.

In sum, it would be a campaign in which the Church would, evangelically, take the offensive. On the basis of thirty years' experience, John Paul knew that that was doing the right, as well as the prudent, thing.

Questions of Conviction

This human rights campaign, and the post-1978 *Ostpolitik* of the Holy See, also embodied four personal convictions that Karol Wojtyła brought to the papacy.

The first of these had to do with Yalta: and "Yalta" as a symbol as well as a discrete moment in history. "Yalta," for Wojtyła, was fundamentally a moral catastrophe. At Yalta, Poland lost World War II—for the second time. Betrayed by the Molotov-Ribbentrop pact of 1939, Poland lost again at Yalta, when the West consigned the Poles to the tender mercies of Stalin. But "Yalta" stood for more than the already unbearable fact that Poland, a putative victor of World War II, was in truth a double loser. "Yalta" was the triumph of a false and antihuman realism over the moral pledges that had been made to Poland (and, by extension, to all the other victims of Hitler's aggression) by the western Allies. "Yalta" stood for the (temporary) victory of violence over principle. "Yalta" was where the forces of freedom, confronted by another totalitarian power, blinked: because they did not grasp the full moral import of the devil's bargain they had made with their Soviet ally and the system he enforced. As John Paul put it in 1991, the Second World

War, "which should have re-established freedom and restored the rights of nations, ended without having attained these goals"— indeed, it ended with "the spread of communist totalitarianism over more than half of Europe and over other parts of the world."[39]

If "Yalta" was a grave injustice, a moral abomination, then the Yalta imperial system had to be dealt with, in the first instance, at that level. Taking the Yalta system simply (if regretfully) as a diplomatic fact just made matters worse: worse for the people of the captive nations and worse for the world, for no peace worthy of the name could be built on a foundation of fundamental injustice.

"Yalta," then, was central to the morally driven geopolitical vision of John Paul II.[40] It was a defining event of the late twentieth century, because it starkly embodied the clash of humanisms—the false humanism of communism, and the true humanism that ought to have informed the policy of the West—that the pope perceived at the center of world politics. The moral squalor of the Yalta imperial system had to be addressed as such. And that was best done, not by name calling, but by the Church's bold, persistent, and principled insistence on the rights of man *as man*.

Does the fact that "Yalta" was central to John Paul's thinking about the history of the Cold War world suggest that he believed, at the time of his election, in the near-term possibility of what an earlier generation had called "rollback"? That seems unlikely. But it is not impossible, and in fact quite plausible, that in the wake of his pilgrimage to Poland in June 1979 and the extraordinary outpouring of popular affection it provoked, John Paul came to the view that the communist system was in something approaching terminal condition. Such speculations aside, what does seem clear is that the pope believed the Church had an obligation to challenge the moral legitimacy of the Yalta imperial system: not head on politically, as Pius XI would have done and Pius XII tried to do, but through the medium of the Church's evangelical campaign on behalf of basic human rights, in which the Polish pope would take the leading role. John Paul also believed, as a matter of both principle and prudence, that the challenge to the Yalta imperial system had to be nonviolent: and he would urge this on his audiences time and again. Finally, the pope, who is very much a Slav with a Slav's respect for other Slavic cultures, understood how the Yalta imperial system was also a moral disaster for the Slavic people of the hegemonic power, the Soviet Union. Thus he could address the Soviet Union, under the new conditions created by Mikhail Gorbachev's glasnost, from within the family, so to speak, rather than as an outsider seeking to whittle down the influence of the Soviet Union in world affairs.

Secondly, Karol Wojtyła came to Rome in 1978 a convinced "European," determined to help end the artificial (and violently imposed, and violently maintained) division of the continent into "western Europe" and "eastern Europe." In this he was a true son of Poland, for the Poles have never regarded themselves as "eastern Europeans" (a phrase of Stalinist provenance), but rather as "Europeans," period, and indeed as one of the historic points of cultural contact between the Europe that grew out of Rome and Aachen, and the Europe that grew out of Byzantium, Kiev, and Moscow. Just as Wojtyła the philosopher believed that the division of "politics" and "morality" was aberrant, Wojtyła the man of culture believed that the division of Europe into eastern and western blocs, itself the result of an amoral political decision, was unnatural.

John Paul signaled his interest in the cultural, which is to say, moral, reunification of Europe in several ways. He regularly spoke about "Europe" as a "body that breathes with two lungs." In 1980 he made the apostles to the Slavs, Sts. Cyril and Methodius, co-patrons of Europe (with St. Benedict), and devoted his fourth encyclical, *Slavorum Apostoli*, to a reflection on their Christian witness and its meaning for the Europe of the late twentieth century. Thus the *Ostpolitik* of the Holy See, under John Paul II, was conducted in the conviction that the Church, whose historic role in the formation of European culture the pope cherished, ought to speak, again, "for Europe": not as a "western" institution reaching out across a natural divide, but as a bearer of the great tradition of European humanism and culture that included within one home Erasmus, Copernicus, and Dostoevsky.

John Paul is also, of course, a Polish European. And while this did not, as Jerzy Turowicz insisted, make him into a narrow nationalist (but in fact into a true European, and a true internationalist), the pope's Polish convictions and sensibility played an important role in his distinctive *Ostpolitik*.

For example, John Paul the Polish intellectual is not embarrassed, but is in fact deeply influenced, by the popular piety of his countrymen. His devotion to the Black Madonna of Częstochowa has already been mentioned: it was under her protection, Karol Wojtyła believed (along with millions of Poles), that their nation had survived when their country was lost—lost in the three partitions, lost under Nazi occupation and dismemberment, lost under the artificial imposition of communism and the reduction of Poland to an appendage of the USSR. Then there was St. Stanisław: the first bishop of Kraków and a Christian martyr, to be sure, but also the symbolic embodiment of the conviction that resistance to government oppression is of the essence of the episcopate and the Church. Popular devotion to St. Stanisław was, without any hint of cynicism, a subtle form of political protest.

Wojtyła was also not embarrassed by his countrymen's image of their country (which dates back to the Polish Enlightenment) as "crucified Poland," the nation whose sufferings will have redemptive value for the whole world. Nor was Wojtyła disturbed, as other intellectuals might have been, by the traditional Polish understanding of Poland as the *antemurale Christianitatis*, the "rampart of Christendom."[41] Wojtyła was not off-put, but in fact accepted, the notion of "Christendom," and did not regard it (as western intellectuals often did) as having overtones of "cultural imposition." The former archbishop of Kraków, who celebrated Mass at Wawel on so many occasions, surrounded by the monuments of heroes like Jan Sobieski, victor against the Ottomans at the Battle of Vienna in 1683, did not regard the image of the "rampart" as romantic national braggadocio.

In his *Ostpolitik*, therefore, John Paul II could draw on a deep reservoir of popular piety and folk imagery, precisely because he did not dismiss these as premodern fantasies. Having experienced the power of that piety in his own life and in his ministry as priest and bishop, and having achieved, in his theological work as well as in his evangelical style, a synthesis between traditional elements of Polish religiosity and his own intellectual sophistication, Karol Wojtyła as pope had a powerful armamentarium of moral weapons to deploy with an audience that was composed of both the intelligentsia and the common people of his country. When he invoked the Black Madonna during the June 1979 pilgrimage, for example, he was speaking, and being heard, on four levels—religious, moral, historical-cultural, and national—simultaneously.

Some western reporters, tone deaf to the polyphony, imagined this as some kind of benign Khomeinism: an analogy which the secular Jewish historian and activist Adam Michnik thought was about as great a misconception as could be imagined. What the pope had done in June 1979, said Michnik, was to teach a great "lesson in dignity."[42] That was the personalist heart of his *Ostpolitik*. And that heart beat to the rhythms of popular piety, even as the mind that disciplined the heart was defending the rights of man in terms drawn explicitly from contemporary philosophy.

Wojtyła's millennialism also shaped his distinctive *Ostpolitik*. Here we are into deep waters indeed. Still, references to the impending dawn of the third millennium of the Christian era, the two thousandth anniversary of the birth of Christ (who, it must always be remembered, is both the revelation of God to man and man to himself), have been a distinctive part of the catechesis of John Paul II. That anniversary, according to the pope's Christological humanism, ought to be the occasion for a great renewal of the human spirit, based on a rededication to "the truth about man." What better arena to press that case than in the captive nations of central and eastern Europe, where the most insidious antihumanism of the age held sway?

John Paul II is not a millenarian of the wild-eyed sort usually associated with the term. His witness, informed by the mystical dimensions of his spirituality, is nonetheless a disciplined witness. Moreover, the pope has had an extensive experience with the "use," so to speak, of great anniversaries as instruments for personal and social renewal. He was deeply involved in one of Cardinal Wyszyński's initiatives, the nine-year-long Great Novena that preceded the celebration of the millennium of Polish Christianity in 1966 (and that helped revivify the Polish Church so that it could later play the crucial role it did in the Revolution of 1989). In the years prior to his election as pope, he had made effective pastoral use of the impending nine hundredth anniversary of the martyrdom of St. Stanisław to initiate the Synod of Kraków and the archdiocesan-wide study of the documents of Vatican II (a typical combination of the contemporary and the traditional). Thus it should have come as no surprise that, in Rome, John Paul gave regular attention to the turn of the third Christian millennium as a sign of the times to which the Church had to attend in its evangelical ministry and its public witness. This theme also reflected the pope's conviction that Providence was guiding his own life: a conviction that intensified after the assassination attempt in 1981 in which, as he later put it, "One hand fired, and another one guided the bullet."[43]

Each of these themes—"Yalta," Europe, Poland, popular piety, the impending millennium—helped to reshape the *Ostpolitik* of the Holy See. Under John Paul, the status quo in central and eastern Europe would not be taken as a given in Vatican diplomacy, for the status quo was inherently unjust and no morally acceptable outcome could issue from it. The new *Ostpolitik* would not abandon the negotiating fora created by Pope Paul and Cardinal Casaroli. But those negotiations would be amplified by a more assertive public address to the enduring and grave problems of human rights in the captive nations. The need for change, rather than the fact of the status quo, would be the starting point for the Church's approach to these issues, and Church leaders in central and eastern Europe would be expected to be strong advocates of freedom. Nor would the Church assume that reform in the communist world could only come from the top down. Indeed, the *Ostpolitik* of John Paul II seemed to assume precisely the opposite: that only a revivified civil society could create the kind of sturdy, nonviolent resistance that might bring the walls of oppression tumbling down—without mass violence and without a global conflagration.

John Paul II accepted his election to the see of Peter in the same spirit in which Albert Einstein once asserted that "God does not play dice with the universe." Karol Wojtyła, who had already booked his return flight to Kraków when he entered the second conclave of 1978, was convinced, in the course of that experience and on the basis of a mature faith, that it was not an accident that the vicar of Christ had been called from Poland at this moment in human history. To suggest that he could have thought otherwise is to have missed the entire trajectory of his life.

Did John Paul II receive the pallium of the Bishop of Rome on October 22, 1978, convinced that he was God's chosen instrument for dismantling the Yalta imperial system? The answer to the question, put that way, is almost certainly, "No." Why? Because John Paul would not have conceived his ministry primarily, or even secondarily, in those terms. What we can discern from the public record, read against the background of his life, is a deep conviction that the election of a Slavic and Polish pope was an expression of God's purposes in history; that his primary task was to "strengthen the brethren"; and that doing that would involve a persistent defense of basic human rights, especially the right of religious freedom.

But John Paul also seemed to sense that, precisely by being a vigorous pastor, he could have an impact on the politics of nations. He understood communism, and communists, from the inside. He had measured its vulnerabilities in the crucial sphere of the human spirit. He was determined to lead, out of a deep sense of vocational responsibility and a deep conviction that God had put him where he was precisely so that he could say, again and again, "Be not afraid!"

So he would lead. His leadership would put the *Ostpolitik* of the Holy See into the more comprehensive context of his world-wide campaign for human rights. He would be a disciplined witness; but he would not avoid the hard questions and the confrontations. He would insist on nonviolence; but he would also insist on the truth. The truth, he believed, would set men free in the deepest sense of human freedom.

Thus he would be, in his own way, a revolutionary. But the revolution to which he called his people would be the final revolution, the revolution of the spirit. As for the rest, the business of the politics of freedom, God would take care of that, in God's good time.

That time was not long in coming.

FIVE

Poland: Igniting the Revolution

Men have been digging salt out of the earth at Wieliczka, a village 8 miles southeast of Kraków, from the Neolithic period (about 3500 B.C.) onward. Commercial mining has been underway continually in the Wieliczka pits since A.D. 1290; revenues from the mine underwrote one-third of medieval King Kazimierz the Great's royal expenditures.

Over the centuries some 180 miles of shafts have been dug on nine levels at the Wieliczka mine, the deepest of them more than 600 feet below the earth's surface. The mine has been open to tourists since 1935, and after descending on a lift down a shaft sunk in the seventeenth century, the visitor is surrounded by a fantastic wonderworld of stalactites and stalagmites, of working pits and elaborately decorated galleries, of saints' statues and jolly gnomes—all formed by or carved out of shimmering salt.

At the bottom level of the Wieliczka mine is the greatest of the excavation's several chapels: the chapel of Blessed Kinga (wife of a thirteenth-century prince of Kraków, Bolesław the Shameful). Six thousand cubic yards of salt were removed to create the space for a chapel over 30 yards long, with five great carved salt chandeliers and a magnificent salt altar dedicated to the Virgin Mary. The acoustics are such that the chapel is regularly used as a concert hall. But it is the light in this subterranean world that captures the imagination: for when the tapers burn down on the chandeliers in the Kinga Chapel, the impression one gets is of standing inside a diamond being lit by the rays of the sun.

Lodged deep within the soil so near to Kraków, its ornaments carved from native material and radiating light where one expects to find darkness, the chapel of Blessed Kinga in the mine at Wieliczka is an apt metaphor for Catholicism in Poland. The land above the mine pits is flat: a natural invasion route from west or east, on which many a marauder has marched and laid waste to the substance of the nation and to its people. The country has sometimes been described as "the disputed bride," condemned to be fought over, continually, by her suitors.[1] Those "suitors" have even managed to wipe "Poland," the nation-state, off the map of Europe from time to time. But Poland, the nation, has lived.

It has lived, in large part, because of the faith that has been so closely identified with the nation. The Austrians may have been in Kraków and the Russians in Warsaw, but the Black Madonna, the Queen of Poland, reigned at the Jasna Góra monastery, the "Bright Mountain" in Częstochowa. And her statue graced the altar deep within the mine at Wieliczka. There beat the steady heart of Poland. It beat to the rhythm of a freedom that could be temporarily chained, but never finally denied.

The assertion of that freedom—the freedom of the final revolution—was the spark that lit the flame of the Revolution of 1989.

Saddling the Cow: Stalinist Poland, 1944–1956

The stubbornness of the Polish peasantry had something to do with it, but it was also Poland's intensely Catholic identity—and the inseparability of Catholicism from the ardent Polish sense of nationhood—that led Stalin to crack, famously, that introducing communism to Poland was like "fitting a cow with a saddle."[2] But Poland, the center of central Europe, was the geopolitical pivot of the continent and the keystone of the security cordon that Stalin was determined to build between himself and what was left of postwar Germany. However grotesquely inapt the fit, the Poles would have to be broken to the communist saddle.

That, at least, was Stalin's intention, and the consequent depredations were visited on a country already prostrate from the experience of the Second World War—the war that Poland lost twice. Six million Polish citizens (including 2.9 million Polish Jews), out of a prewar population of 35 million, died during the war: a mortality rate of 18 percent, or almost one in five.[3] The Polish Church did not escape the devastation wrought on the Polish nation: after their invasion in September 1939, the Nazis killed almost 2,000 priests (another 1,500 survived the concentration camps), 6 bishops, 850 monks, 300 nuns, and 113 seminarians.[4] Church property was destroyed from one end of the country to the other; some of the fiercest fighting during the Warsaw Uprising of August 1944 took place in St. John's Cathedral: hand-to-hand, pew-by-pew, and later down in the tangled warren of tombs in the crypt. Stalin and his Polish puppet, an old Comintern hand named Bolesław Bierut, tried to saddle the Polish cow by performing a kind of cultural lobotomy on the Polish nation.[5] The tactics of this crude operation, and the artifacts of Polish Stalinism, were captured by historian Norman Davies in these terms:

> Xenophobia was the official fashion. Any contact with the outside world was instantly denounced, creating a social atmosphere where political trials looked normal and innocent men and women could be arbitrarily sentenced as foreign spies. People were encouraged to live communally, and to think collectively. They no longer belonged to themselves as individuals, or to their families, but to their work-force, their shock-brigades, or their regiment. The Russian system of informers was introduced in factories and schools. . . . Conformism in dress and thought was encouraged. A specific form of megalomania took hold. All the public works of the day had to be colossal. Bigger was thought to be better. Quantitative production was the ultimate good. Statistics acquired a magical value. Workers were enslaved by their ever-increasing work norms. In art, Socialist Realism gained exclusive approval, with novels about tractor drivers, and paintings about concrete factories. However miserable and downtrodden the writers actually felt, they were ordered to exude optimism. In public architecture, a taste developed for marble, for soaring facades with heavy columns and vulgar pinnacles. The symbols of the age were provided by the Palace of Culture and Sciences in Warsaw, an unsolicited gift from the USSR, and the new town of Nowa Huta near Kraków, which boasted the largest steelworks in Poland together with acres of primitive workers' housing and no church.[6]

The Polish communists avoided a direct confrontation with the Polish Church in the eighteen months immediately after the war: among other reasons, because the fighting in Poland did not end on what the West celebrates as V-E Day, but continued in partisan form until the summer of 1947. Some churches were rebuilt, and the Catholic University at Lublin was reopened, as were a number of seminaries. But on September 12, 1945, the Polish government gave a dark glimpse into its future plans by unilaterally abrogating Poland's 1945 concordat with the Holy See, on the grounds that the Vatican maintained relations with the Polish government-in-exile in London and did not recognize Polish sovereignty over the "western territories" ceded to Poland at the end of World War II.

The direct assault on the Polish Church began in earnest in 1947, after Bierut's communists won an "election." A militant, aggressive, and officially sanctioned atheism was now added to the xenophobia and collectivism of Polish Stalinism. In 1949, the regime promulgated a "religious freedom" decree in order to assert state control over the Church. Priests and monks were arrested in droves. All ecclesiastical properties, with the exception of church buildings and their surrounding churchyards, were expropriated. The Church press was banned. Catholic schools were declared illegal. Catholic Action and other Catholic voluntary associations were shut down, and the state seized their institutions and properties. In their place, the Polish communists substituted "patriotic Catholic organizations" in order to undermine the authority of the hierarchy and to create a climate of malleable "Catholic opinion." (The most notorious of these was the "Pax" movement, which over time came to seem "almost more Stalinist than the Party."[7]) The government confiscated the 2,000 hospitals, nursing homes, and orphanages of the Church's charitable organization, "Caritas," retaining its name (and thus confusing those who thought it was linked to the international Catholic charity of the same title) while gutting its Catholic content.[8]

Poland's Stalinist rulers tried to control, and eventually to eliminate, the Church through a tripartite strategy: confrontation and direct attack when tactically feasible; cooptation when possible; and, withal, a slow strangulation of the Church's evangelical mission through relentless pressure on both Church leaders and the Catholic populace. It was a strategy that would prove cruelly effective in others of the captive nations of the Yalta imperial system. But in Poland it failed. Indeed, in Poland it backfired: for in 1966, on the millennium of its national founding and after twenty years of communism, Poland was more intensely and publicly Catholic than ever before. And twenty years after that, Poland, inspired by a Polish pope, led the nonviolent revolution that toppled Stalin's empire.

No small part of the credit for that second "miracle on the Vistula" must be given to Cardinal Stefan Wyszyński, the man celebrated in Poland today as the "primate of the millennium."

The "Interrex"

In the years between 1572 and 1795, the Roman Catholic primates of Poland, the archbishops metropolitan of Gniezno, served as "*interrex*"—as acting heads of state between the death of a Polish king and the election of his successor by the Polish nobility. Stefan Wyszyński was, in effect, the *interrex* of Poland for thirty years, a "substitute for the absent authority of the country's political rulers" from 1948 until 1978.[9]

Wyszyński was born in 1901, in the intensely Catholic region of Mazovia. After attending high school in Warsaw and seminary in Włocławek, during the days when Piłsudski's Poles stopped Tukhachevsky's Red Army at the 1920 "miracle on the Vistula," Wyszyński was ordained priest in 1924. He received his doctorate in canon law in 1929, although his primary academic interests were in sociology and Catholic social doctrine: a field he had an opportunity to explore in depth during a year's post-doctoral sabbatical in western Europe. On returning to Poland, and in addition to teaching in the Włocławek seminary and filling a number of diocesan posts, the young Father Wyszyński was active as a chaplain to Catholic youth movements and trade unionists; in 1932, he helped establish the Catholic Union of Young Workers. Wyszyński was always an anticommunist. But his social and economic views put him firmly on the left of the traditionally conservative Polish Church.

Father Wyszyński was a man on the run during the Nazi occupation of Poland: his prominence as a Catholic social theorist and labor activist made him a suspect in the eyes of the Gestapo. After surviving one Nazi arrest, Wyszyński served as a kind of roving chaplain, working in various villages and later in Warsaw (under the nom de guerre "Sister Cecilia," as in "Where is Sister Cecilia saying Mass today?"). At the war's end Wyszyński returned to Włocławek to take up the threads of his many pastoral activities with young people and workers and to help reopen the seminary, of which he was then named rector. But the Holy See had other plans for Wyszyński, who was named bishop of Lublin by Pope Pius XII in March 1946: a position Wyszyński wanted to decline, only to be told by the primate, Cardinal August Hlond, "One does not say no to the pope." Wyszyński left Włocławek on the day that five of his faculty colleagues returned from Dachau, and was consecrated bishop at the Jasna Góra monastery in Częstochowa on May 12, 1946.

Bishop Wyszyński's ministry in Lublin would not last long, however, for just over two years later, on November 12, 1948, Pius XII named him the successor to Cardinal Hlond as archbishop of Gniezno and Warsaw. At the age of forty-seven, Stefan Wyszyński was primate of Poland. And Poland, having been scourged for almost six years by Nazism, had now fallen under the jackboot of Stalin and his Polish epigones.[10]

Cardinal Wyszyński (who received the red hat in 1952) was a complex personality, whose categorization by some western commentators as a "rigid, anticommunist conservative" does little justice to the man, his pastoral vision, his strategic and tactical skills, his social and economic views, and his historical record. Wyszyński brought several convictions to the primate's throne in 1948. He believed that the Church had suffered a terrible shock during the war, and was not fully prepared to withstand a direct confrontation with the communist regime. He was convinced that the reestablishment of the Church's pastoral ministry in its full dimensions and the country's spiritual renewal (which he identified with a renewal of Marian piety) were his first responsibilities. A student and expositor of modern Catholic social teaching, he was committed to social and economic reform in Poland, while rejecting communist atheism and communist political brutality.

Cardinal Wyszyński's personal style was, in the words of one Polish Catholic observer years later, "fantastic . . . almost medieval."[11] And yet he deliberately reshaped the Polish priesthood by vigorously recruiting students from urban areas and giving them a much more rigorous intellectual training. At the same time, Primate Wyszyński could speak to, and touch, the heart of Polish religiosity by his constant appeals to the spirit of the nation and to the Black Madonna (whom he placed on his primatial coat of arms, but without a crown, because, as he remarked, Poland was too poor for her queen to wear a crown[12]). Wyszyński had lived through two world wars and was an astute observer of both history and geopolitics: and his great concern as a Polish patriot was to prevent, at all morally bearable costs, the extinction of his country by its hegemonic neighbor to the east. Finally, Cardinal Wyszyński's thirty-three years as primate were marked by a stubborn, unshakable, and (it should be said) ultimately vindicated conviction that he—better than the Vatican—knew what had to be done vis-à-vis Poland's communist rulers: and that what had to be done could only be done if the Church maintained a solid and disciplined front of unity.

Cardinal Wyszyński was not afraid of confrontation. Indeed, in later years he seemed to go out of his way to create confrontations when he thought that the moral atmosphere needed cleansing: and that his Church and its people needed reminding of just what kind of struggle they were in. But his first instinct as primate was to try and effect a minimal modus vivendi with the communist regime. Wyszyński, who wanted "martyrdom only as a last resort," believed that the Polish Church had "showed in Dachau and in the Warsaw Uprising that we have learned how to die for the Church and for Poland." The Church's first responsibility, in the late 1940s, was to show that it could still live.[13]

"Non Possumus"

Thus Wyszyński, with the support of the Polish episcopate, concluded a nineteen-point accord with the Polish regime in 1950—not a legal agreement but an attempt to set the ground rules of coexistence, so to speak. The regime recognized the Church's autonomy in matters of faith and internal organization, acknowledged the Church's religious links to the papacy, and agreed to permit monastic orders. Basic pastoral ministries—religious education in schools, hospital and prison chaplaincies, the Catholic University in Lublin, pilgrimages—were also conceded. The Church, in turn, recognized the communist regime as Poland's government, promised to help work for national reconstruction, and guaranteed that it would oppose "activities hostile to the Polish People's Republic."[14]

Wyszyński was criticized by officials of the Holy See for what they regarded as concessions to the regime. (Indeed, on this point, some in the Holy See and the Kremlin seem to have had the same view of the 1950 accords: that they were the first step toward the capitulation of the Polish Church.) But such criticism was of little ultimate consequence given the rapid flow of subsequent events, in which the regime's mendacity, and Wyszyński's distinctive combination of steely strategic resolve and tactical flexibility, revealed themselves. For no sooner had the regime signed the 1950 accord then it began to violate the religious freedom it had putatively proclaimed a year earlier.

The communist state created an "Office for Religious Affairs" to monitor and harass the Church's independent activity. An "Association of the Friends of Children" was established to provide instruction in the "spirit of socialism"; parents were pressured (by the threat of losing their jobs) to place their children in the Association's schools. The 1952 constitution of the Polish People's Republic decreed the separation of Church and state, by which it meant the subordination of the Church to the state. One by one, Catholic publications were squeezed (by manipulations of paper and other supplies, and by pressure on their employees) and then closed, as were all minor (preparatory) seminaries. Priests were again being arrested in large numbers, or being subjected to continual financial harassment with new taxes. Meanwhile the "patriotic priests" associations, often in league with "Pax," publicly attacked the more resistant bishops (one of whom, Czesław Kaczmarek of Kielce, was arrested in 1951 and sentenced to twelve years in prison after a classic Stalin-era show trial).[15] The "Pax" leader, Bolesław Piasecki, accused the Vatican of being under the influence of "German revanchists and the NATO alliance"—a sure sign of pressure from the USSR.[16]

The high (or low) point in this process of strangulation and repression came in May 1953, when the regime ordered the implementation of a decree giving the state the authority to appoint and remove both priests and bishops. Moreover, all clergy were to take a loyalty oath to the Polish People's Republic. The Roman Catholic Church, in other words, was to become a subsidiary of the Polish state: which meant, in this instance, the oxymoronic "Polish United Workers' Party."

The Polish episcopate now chose confrontation. Cardinal Wyszyński himself threw down the gauntlet in a sermon at St. John's Cathedral in Warsaw: "We teach that it is proper to render unto Caesar the things that are Caesar's and to God that which is God's. But when Caesar seats himself on the altar, we respond curtly: he may not."[17] Under Wyszyński's chairmanship, the bishops then met in Kraków and issued a historic memorandum

Karol Józef Wojtyła, Pope John Paul II: The pastor who preached, "Be not afraid!," he became the architect of the revolution of conscience that made possible the Revolution of 1989. *(Catholic News Service/Arturo Mari)*

ABOVE: The Second Vatican Council (1962–1965): Its "Declaration on Religious Freedom" was a profound critique of totalitarianism and the charter of the Catholic human rights revolution. *(CNS/Giordani)*
BELOW: Cardinal Stefan Wyszyński (1901–1981), primate of Poland: Revered as the "primate of the millennium," his personal authority, strategic vision, and tactical skill prepared the Church and the Polish nation for the Revolution of 1989. *(CNS/KNA)*

The newly elected Pope John Paul II greets Cardinal Stefan Wyszyński, October 1978. *(CNS/Arturo Mari)*

ABOVE: The Ark Church in Nowa Huta, the "model workers' town" adjacent to Kraków: The workers demanded the church that the regime thought was superfluous. *(CNS/KNA)* BELOW: The interior of the Ark Church: The Black Madonna, a piece of moon rock, and a crucified Christ forged by the Nowa Huta steel workers. *(George Weigel)*

ABOVE: John Paul II celebrates Mass in Warsaw's Victory Square, June 2, 1979: The crowds interrupted the pope's sermon with the chant, "We want God! We want God!" *(CNS/Chris Niedenthal)*   BELOW: The Jasna Góra monastery at Częstochowa, home of the Black Madonna, during John Paul II's return to his homeland in June 1979: The pope's pilgrimage, which Adam Michnik described as a "great lesson in dignity," decisively clarified how strong "we" were, and how weak "they" were. *(CNS/Chris Niedenthal)*

The Gdańsk shipyard gates, 1980: In the name of Solidarity, the workers rejected the workers' state, under the banner of the Black Madonna and the inspiration of Pope John Paul II. *(The Bettmann Archive)*

Lech Wałęsa: The Gdańsk electrician who leapt the fence at the Lenin Shipyards and successfully negotiated the birth of Solidarity, the communist world's first free trade union. *(CNS/KNA)*

ABOVE: Father Józef Tischner: The theologian who taught that Solidarity was "a huge forest planted by awakened consciences." *(CNS/KNA)*
BELOW LEFT: Tadeusz Mazowiecki: A leader of the Polish Catholic intelligentsia, and the first non-communist prime minister of Poland since World War II, his alliance with the Gdańsk shipyard workers was crucial to the rise of Solidarity. *(CNS/KNA)* BELOW RIGHT: Cardinal Franciszek Macharski, successor of Karol Wojtyła as archbishop of Kraków: The resistance Church was acting in the ancient role of *defensor civitatis,* the "defender of the city" against the invading barbarians. *(Czesław Czaplinski)*

Jerzy Turowicz of *Tygodnik Powszechny:* The editor whose columnist became pope, his work and his paper helped bridge the historic gap between the Church and Poland's secular intellectuals. *(George Weigel)*

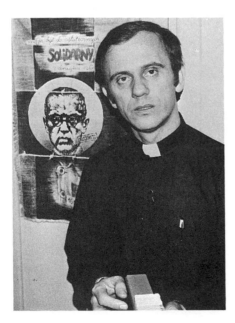

LEFT: Father Jerzy Popiełuszko (1947–1984): The martyr-priest of Solidarity, he continually challenged his people, "Which side will you take? The side of good or the side of evil? Truth or falsehood? Love or hatred?" *(CNS/KNA)*

Father Popiełuszko's church, St. Stanisław Kostka in Warsaw: The one place between East Berlin and Vladivostok where ten thousand people gathered regularly and publicly to challenge the Yalta imperial system. *(George Weigel)*

The grave of Father Jerzy Popiełuszko in the churchyard of St. Stanisław Kostka, Warsaw: "Solidarity's sanctuary," it was "a piece of free Poland." *(George Weigel)*

St. Maximilian Kolbe church in the Mistrzejowice district of Nowa Huta, consecrated by Pope John Paul II during his 1983 pilgrimage: Here, Father Kazimierz Jancarz, the chaplain of the Lenin Steelworks, led a ministry of resistance in which the Church "tried to give people back their memory." *(George Weigel)*

A resistance triptych in the Kolbe church, Nowa Huta: "Mother of Solidarity, pray for us." *(George Weigel)*

ABOVE: Cardinal František Tomášek, the octogenarian archbishop of Prague and primate of Bohemia: Throughout the 1980s, Czechoslovakia witnessed "this singular spectacle of the cardinal getting older and tougher at the same time." *(CNS photo from KNA, courtesy of National Catholic Register)* BELOW LEFT: Father Oto Mádr: A veteran of Czechoslovakia's communist prisons and labor camps, he survived to help craft the Church's ringing endorsement of the Velvet Revolution. *(George Weigel)* BELOW RIGHT: Father Václav Maly: As an underground priest, he brought the Gospel to his fellow stokers in the boiler room of a Prague hotel; as a key leader of Civic Forum, he served as master of ceremonies and chaplain at many of the great public rallies of the Velvet Revolution. *(George Weigel)*

ABOVE LEFT: Václav Benda: Czech Catholic philosopher and Charter 77 activist, he argued that resistance to communism through "living in the truth" implied a whole project of moral, cultural, and social regeneration. *(Martin Poš)* ABOVE RIGHT: Kamila Benda: The secret police ransacked her apartment fifteen times and the neighbors looked the other way; she helped keep the resistance alive in Prague and secretly brought communion to her imprisoned husband. BELOW: Ján Chryzostom Korec, S.J., during his days in the underground: Clandestinely ordained a bishop at age 27, he worked as an elevator repairman while serving as a leader of the resistance Church in Slovakia. Korec was named cardinal by Pope John Paul II in 1991.

ABOVE: Silvester Krčméry: The Slovak lay activist whose "treason" consisted in evangelizing young people and workers, and translating papal social encyclicals into Slovak. BELOW: The memorial in Prague to the victims of the *masakr*—the trigger for the Velvet Revolution. *(George Weigel)*

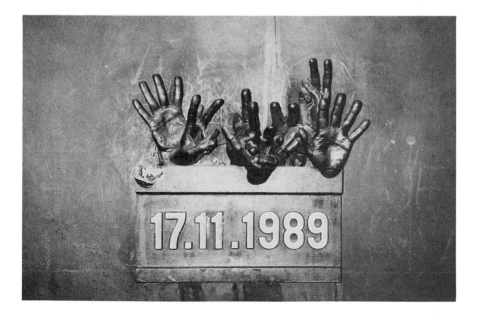

Václav Havel and Pope John Paul II: The playwright-president wondered aloud whether he believed in miracles, but confessed that he was witnessing a miracle when he welcomed the "apostle of love" to a free Czechoslovakia in 1990. *(CNS/Arturo Mari)*

defending the independence and integrity of the Church. The memorandum outlined the Church's attempt to reach a modus vivendi with the regime, and then stated bluntly that "internal peace" in Poland was solely dependent on "the government's forsaking its radical, destructive hatred towards Catholicism, and abandoning its aim of subjugating the Church and turning it into an instrument of the state." After reviewing the reasons why the decree on state appointment and removal of pastors and bishops would violate the nature of both Church and state, the bishops concluded: "We are not allowed to place the things of God on the altar of Caesar. *Non possumus!*"[18]

The bottom line had been reached, and on this point the bishops would not budge: better vacant bishoprics and pastorates than to "place the spiritual rule of souls in unworthy hands." The regime's response was to label the memorandum as high treason (or, in the preferred euphemism, "an attack on the constitution"). And thus on the night of September 25–26, 1953, Cardinal Wyszyński was arrested and interned: first, in a former monastery in northwest Poland (where he was denied medical assistance), and later, in a convent in the south of the country.[19]

Overcoming loneliness and physical discomforts, Wyszyński put his time as a prisoner to good use, writing several books and planning a great nationwide pastoral initiative. But the regime's attempts to bring the Church to heel became even more draconian. By the end of 1953, 8 bishops and 900 priests had been imprisoned. The faculties of theology were closed, further taxes were levied on church property and on priests, and harassment of parents who wanted religious instruction for their children intensified. In 1955, religious education in the schools was stopped. And by the end of that year, over 2,000 Catholic activists—bishops, priests, monks, nuns, and laity—were imprisoned.[20]

Then, in 1956, Poland's communist regime decided that it needed Stefan Wyszyński and the Roman Catholic Church after all.

The Years of the "Great Novena": 1956–1970

Faithful Stalinist that he was, Bolesław Bierut did not expect to hear what he heard when he went to Moscow for the twentieth congress of the communist party of the Soviet Union in February 1956. What he heard, of course, was Nikita Khrushchev's denunciation of Stalin's ideological deviations, crimes, and cult of personality. The shock was evidently too much; Bierut died in Moscow on March 12.

Khrushchev's twentieth party congress speech sent shock waves throughout the Yalta imperial system. On June 28, Polish workers called a general strike in Poznań, and 50,000 demonstrators marched through the streets under banners reading "Bread and Freedom" and "Russians Go Home." Marshall Konstantin Rokossovsky, the Red Army leader who was also Poland's defense minister, crushed the demonstration with tanks; more than seventy people were killed.

With social unrest stirring throughout the country, an enraged Khrushchev in Warsaw demanding a restoration of order, the Red Army poised to attack on Poland's eastern frontier, and the Soviet fleet patrolling off the Baltic shoreline at Gdańsk, the new party leader, Władysław Gomułka, asked Cardinal Wyszyński to return home to Warsaw and take up his post as primate again.[21] Wyszyński would not accept his release until Gomułka agreed to certain conditions: the 1953 decree on church appointments had to be repealed; a Mixed Commission consisting of government and episcopate representatives had to be recreated; Bishop Kaczmarek had to be released from prison, and the other bishops forced from their diocese were to be reinstated; the Catholic press had to be reactivated and the normal administrative procedures of the Church restored. Gomułka agreed, and the primate returned to Warsaw on October 28, 1956. By the end of the year, the 1953 decree had been nullified, the imprisoned bishops had been released, optional religious education was permitted in schools, hospital and prison chaplaincies were reestablished, and the Church's administration was restored in the "western territories" that had become part of Poland in 1945.[22] An innovation that would come to a dramatic fruition in the events of 1989— the formation of "Clubs of the Catholic Intelligentsia"—was approved by the regime, and a Catholic parliamentary group, *Znak*, was created.[23]

Tensions remained after the 1956 accord, but the Church developed new tactics and sharpened familiar ones to meet the regime's persistent efforts to strangle religious life, which recommenced shortly after the threat of Soviet intervention waned. When the Catholic press was shut down or cut off from vital paper supplies, *samizdat* publishing tried to fill the gap. The regime continued to tax the Church and its priests; parishioners responded with increased contributions. The regime denied building permits for new churches; prefabricated sections of churches were hidden in parishioners' homes and then suddenly assembled in the dead of night as a fait accompli for the authorities. When religious education was, once again, banned in the schools, the Church established thousands of catechetical centers throughout the country. Like the intellectuals' clubs, these would prove crucial for the future: if, as Father Józef Tischner later argued, Solidarity was a "huge forest planted by awakened consciences," it was in these catechetical centers, often unheated in the bitter Polish winter, that many of those consciences were first formed, and the final revolution gestated.[24]

Nor did Wyszyński disdain civil disobedience when he thought the circumstances required more direct confrontation with the regime. When the government forbade members of religious orders from teaching catechism, the decree was simply ignored. When the regime tried to license and pay religion teachers, the Church replied that priests were not permitted to receive compensation from the government. When the clergy's taxes were raised even more ruinously higher, the bishops told their priests not to pay.[25] But the regime did not shrink from certain forms of confrontation either: it was at this period that the Gomułka government adopted a permissive abortion law, in a direct attack on the Church's authority in the arena of sexual morality and family life.

On his return from three years' imprisonment, in other words, Cardinal Wyszyński did not come home to a "normal" Church-state situation, as normality would be understood in the West. But despite the constant harassment, he and his people had won some breathing room. And thus Wyszyński could now move ahead with the pastoral initiative he had planned during his internment: a "Great Novena," a nine-year program of national spiritual renewal, which was to culminate in 1966 with the rededication of the Polish nation to Mary, Queen of Poland, on the occasion of the millennium of Polish Christianity.

The Concept of the Great Novena

In the secularized West, and even among western Christians unaccustomed to massive public displays of piety, Wyszyński's "Great

Novena" may have seemed to be nothing more than a grandiose indulgence in folk religiosity. It was, in fact, an extraordinary act of national self-restoration, religious in conception but with unforeseen (but perhaps not wholly surprising) public consequences.

At one level, of course, the Great Novena was an expression of Wyszyński's deep Marian piety, painted on a very large canvas indeed. As his former colleague and biographer Andrzej Micewski puts it, Cardinal Wyszyński decided, during his imprisonment, "to defend the faith of the nation against militant atheism by means of the power of the Virgin Mary." Crushed under two totalitarianisms since 1939, "the nation and the Church would beg that the country be freed from unwanted, imposed political submission," through the intercession of the Holy Mother.[26]

But Wyszyński conceived the Great Novena at more than one level of analysis and expectation. The revival of popular (which in Poland meant Marian) piety was essential in the struggle with communism. And there can be no doubt that Wyszyński truly believed in the efficacy of the Virgin Mary's intercessory powers on behalf of Poland. But Cardinal Wyszyński was not just a simple country pastor. His goals for the Great Novena were larger and more complex, the result of his internment reflections on the nature of the communist adversary and the best means to defeat him.

Wyszyński knew, for example, that Poland's communist regime had tried to rewrite the nation's history, and would try to do so again in 1966, at the Polish millennium. Rewriting history was a moral offense against the intellect, of course. But it was also a lethal attack on Polish national identity. For it was precisely Polish memory, kept alive in poetry, literature, drama, and history, that had kept Poland-the-nation alive when Poland-the-state was carved up and extinguished.

The Great Novena would, then, challenge the communist attempt to separate the Polish people from their past in order to subjugate them in the present. It would do so by giving back to the people what was rightfully theirs and theirs alone: their historical memory. By its focus on the Black Madonna of Częstochowa, *Regina Poloniae*, the Great Novena would also, and unashamedly, invoke the image of Poland as the *antemurale Christianitatis*, the rampart of Christendom: not, this time, against invading Turks, but against a toxic cultural parasite that would, unchecked, destroy its host.

Thus the Great Novena would armor the people of Poland culturally as well as spiritually for the long struggle to maintain a measure of independence that Wyszyński foresaw. As the cardinal once put it in a sermon at the primatial cathedral in Gniezno, "It is my earnest desire that you take a hard look at the Past and the Present, and, having learned to love the history of this Christian nation, that you see the [present] reality of its Catholicity with open eyes."[27]

The Novena Unfolds

Wyszyński's Great Novena had three components, each intended to strengthen the spiritual and national life of Poland in preparation for the act of consecration that would take place in the millennium year of 1966. The Polish episcopate agreed that each of the nine years between 1957 and 1966 would have a theme (faith, the Ten Commandments, the family, the moral life, social justice, etc.), and that this theme would shape that year's preaching and teaching within Church institutions. Thus, over the nine-year period, the entire Polish nation would be thoroughly recatechized in the basic truths of the Catholic faith and in the Church's understanding of the moral life.

The Great Novena would also be a time of pilgrimage (another classic expression of Polish piety). In addition to encouraging regular pilgrimage visits to the country's major shrines, the primate himself would make a continuous pilgrimage throughout the country in the millennium year, province by province, meeting the people, preaching the themes of the Great Novena, and calling the nation to reconsecrate itself to the Queen of Poland in preparation for its second thousand years. But Wyszyński's national peregrinations in 1966 also became a kind of traveling referendum on the Polish communist regime: a referendum which the regime lost decisively in Gniezno and Częstochowa, in Kraków and Warsaw, in Katowice, Gdańsk, Wrocław, Lublin, and Toruń. "Everywhere he was greeted by tens and hundreds of thousands of people, by delegations of miners in uniform, by processions of men, women, and children, by girls in regional costume, by crowds upon crowds, standing in the rain or kneeling by the roadside. Never [had] anyone in the People's Republic enjoyed such a massive display of devotion."[28] And, of course, the devotion lavished on the Church was devotion denied to the regime which claimed to rule in the name of the people. If anything clarified Cardinal Wyszyński's role as Polish *interrex* during the country's communist years, it was the Great Novena.

But the greatest of all the pilgrimages of that nine-year period of national renewal was that undertaken by the Black Madonna herself.[29] This was the linchpin of the Great Novena and of the pastoral program Wyszyński conceived while interned: like the New Testament Mary visiting Elizabeth prior to the birth of their sons (see Luke 1.39–56), the Black Madonna would go on pilgrimage throughout Poland for nine years, diocese by diocese, church by church, stopping at every Catholic parish in the country: which would, on the occasion of her visitation, sponsor a day- or evening-long vigil of parish prayer and reconsecration.

Legend has it that the Black Madonna was painted from life by St. Luke on wood taken from the Holy Family's house in Nazareth: whatever its historical provenance, the painting is a splendid example of the Byzantine hierarchical style in which the Virgin's face combines sorrow, conviction, compassion, and steadfastness in equal proportions. And it is Mary's face that gives the ikon its most distinctive, and distinctively national, characteristic: when marauders tried to steal the painting in 1430, the picture grew so heavy (according to the legend) that the thieves could not carry it—and in frustration they slashed the face of the Holy Mother, which immediately began to bleed. After its restoration in Kraków, the ikon retained its gash (which remains visible to this day). In 1655, according to yet another tradition that secured the ikon's position in Polish history, it was the intercession of the Black Madonna that broke the Swedish siege of Częstochowa and saved Poland from conquest.

And yet to think of the Black Madonna as simply a historic painting is to miss its power. For an ikon is more than a painting: it not only represents, it re-presents, makes present again, those whom it images. As Father Mieczysław Maliński puts it, because the ikon is a "living person," the pilgrimage of the Black Madonna during the Great Novena was not a traveling picture show: it was an occasion for Poles to "meet with the Blessed Mother" in and through her picture. Thus the pilgrimage of the Black Madonna was not the journey of a painting; it was, to devout Poles, "a journey of the Blessed Mother in and through Poland." Through this very Polish image of the Mother of God, the Mother of God went door to door in Poland for nine years.

All of which may seem peculiar hocus-pocus to the skeptical mind, but to Poland's communist rulers, the pilgrimage of the Black Madonna was very serious business indeed. So serious, in fact, that, several years into the Great Novena, the authorities "arrested Mary," as Father Maliński describes it, took the ikon back to Częstochowa, put a guard on it, and told the Church that the ikon could not leave the Jasna Góra monastery. The Black Madonna was, so to speak, interned. But this did not stop Cardinal Wyszyński and the bishops: for they continued the Virgin's pilgrimage by sending the ikon's empty frame from parish to parish, where it was met with the same fervor the Black Madonna herself had received. And, according to Father Maliński, why not? "The people knew Our Lady was there."[30] And they were determined to spend some time with Mary, *Regina Poloniae*.

The Millennium Year

Cardinal Wyszyński's plans for the millennium of Polish Christianity and the reconsecration of the nation to the Holy Mother were obstructed throughout the Great Novena by the authorities, who proved true to form all the way to the end: Pope Paul VI, whom Wyszyński had invited to come to Częstochowa in 1966 to receive the nation's vows of reconsecration, was denied a visa by the Polish government. At the August 26 Mass celebrating the millennium, the 1 million Poles who had come to the Jasna Góra monastery could see the pope's portrait on an empty chair, "wreathed in red and white roses."[31]

The regime's recalcitrance had several sources. It was, in part, a backhanded compliment to the success of Wyszyński's pastoral program and to the Great Novena: given the numbers that had participated in these events over the past nine years, who knew what might have happened had the pope arrived in Częstochowa to mark the millennium of Polish Christianity? One might also speculate that the new post-Khrushchev masters of the Kremlin, then just beginning their own crackdown on dissent, were not enthusiastic about the idea of Paul VI coming to the heart of the Warsaw Pact.

But the Gomułka regime was also in a fury because, in a letter to the German bishops announcing the forthcoming millennium year, Cardinal Wyszyński, in the name of the Polish episcopate, had made a historic gesture of reconciliation to the "revanchists": "We forgive," read the letter to the Germans, "and we ask to be forgiven." It was not a wholly disinterested act; Cardinal Wyszyński surely knew that reconciliation between the churches in Germany and Poland was the ecclesiastical precondition to the regularization of (Polish) bishoprics in the western territories taken from Germany and ceded to Poland at the Tehran Conference during World War II. But to accuse Wyszyński of mere calculation in this matter is to misread the character of the man. Twenty years after the war, it was time for reconciliation. A sense of justice might have dictated that the first gesture come from those whose countrymen had done the invading. But Cardinal Wyszyński believed that justice was completed in charity, and thus he was willing to take the first step toward the old foe. It was not a gesture easy for a communist to comprehend—the authorities launched "a furious propaganda campaign . . . against the Polish bishops' letter," portrayed the bishops as patriotically "unreliable," and even threatened Wyszyński with arrest yet again.[32]

In addition to attacking Wyszyński personally (state security, *Sluzba Bezpieczentswa,* familiarly known as "the SB," forged and circulated a book of what were purported to be the cardinal's sermons[33]), the regime also did its best to co-opt the millennium. But it was hopeless. Every church in Poland displayed a banner reading "*Sacrum Poloniae Millenium,* 966–1966" ("Poland's Sacred Millennium"); the regime hung banners in the streets, "*Tysiącle-cie Państwa Polskiego*" ("A Thousand Years of the Polish State"). The church banners read "*Deo et Patriae*" ("For God and Country"); the regime responded with "*Socjalizm i Ojczyzna*" ("Socialism and Fatherland"). The churches proclaimed "*Naród z Kościołem*" ("The Nation is with the Church"); the regime tried "*Partia z Narodem*" ("The Party is with the Nation"). Finally, and perhaps most pathetically, to the Church's proud banner, "*Polonia Semper Fidelis*" ("Poland Ever-Faithful"), came the sorry response "*Socjalizm Gwarancja Pokoju i Granic*" ("The

Communist Regime is the Guarantee of Peace and Frontiers").[34] It was clear, from the banners, who had won the struggle for Poland's history—and thus for Poland's spirit.

Close observers of modern Polish history continue to regard Cardinal Wyszyński's Great Novena as a major turning point in the country's struggle against communism. For Dominican theologian Father Jacek Salij, a prominent dissident during the Solidarity period, the Great Novena existentially reinforced both the truth of the Church's claim to be the true bearer of Polish nationhood and the falseness of the regime's assertions about a "people's republic." In short, the Great Novena made it indisputably clear who stood with, and for, "the people," and who, so to speak, had the votes. Moreover, according to Father Salij, the Great Novena was an important exercise for a Church unused, after years of repression, to flexing its organizational muscles. That the entire Great Novena, and the millennium celebrations themselves, were organized and managed without any assistance whatsoever from the state—indeed, in the face of active state harassment—taught the Church and its people an important lesson about their own capabilities.[35] Bishop Józef Życiński, who was a boy at the beginning of the Great Novena, believes that Cardinal Wyszyński's initiative was essential in "maintaining the spiritual tension" in Polish society, at a moment when the dead weight of Stalinism might have proven stifling.[36] From a perhaps more neutral perspective, historian Norman Davies argues that the millennium celebrations were an important moment in Poland's rejection of the "shame which Stalinism had injected into everything connected with Poland's independent past," and thus to the recovery of her history: the lifeblood of her sense of nationhood.[37]

The Great Novena of Cardinal Stefan Wyszyński did not make the Revolution of 1989. But the Great Novena helped make the people who made the Revolution of 1989: and it did so by reminding them of the final revolution and its priority, even in worldly affairs.

Poland and Vatican II

The years of the Great Novena overlapped with the years of the Second Vatican Council. The complex Polish reception of the

Council is not our story here, but because so much has been written in the West about "conservative Polish Catholicism"—by which is usually meant a Catholicism that has rejected, or has not even been exposed to, the teachings of Vatican II—a few words are in order.

In Poland, it did not seem as if there had to be a choice between the Great Novena and the Council: indeed, men who celebrate the Great Novena also regard the Council as a crucial factor in the evolution of a Polish Catholicism capable of giving the kind of leadership it would during the decade-long overthrow of communism between 1979 and 1989. Father Mieczysław Maliński describes the Council as the "second great moment of rescue" of the Polish Church, and argues that the Council "had a greater impact in Poland than in any other country," in part because throughout the four sessions of the Council Poles maintained overnight vigils in their parish churches, praying for the success of the bishops' deliberations.[38]

Bishop Tadeusz Gocłowski of Gdańsk stresses the importance of two Council documents, the Pastoral Constitution on the Church in the Modern World (*Gaudium et Spes*) and the Declaration on Religious Freedom (*Dignitatis Humanae*), for the subsequent life of the Polish Church and for the struggle against communism. *Gaudium et Spes* identified the threat that "administrative atheism" (i.e., not the atheism of personal intellectual conviction, but state-sponsored and enforced atheism) posed to all human values. But the Council was not merely condemnatory; according to Gocłowski, the pastoral constitution also outlined a true Christian humanism in the fields of culture, the family, and the economy. Then there was *Dignitatis Humanae*, which not only taught that the human being is obliged to seek the truth, but that freedom of conscience is essential if that search is to come to a truly human fruition in faith. The humanism of *Gaudium et Spes* and the linkage of truth and freedom in *Dignitatis Humanae* were, in Bishop Gocłowski's judgment, essential themes in the Polish Church's subsequent confrontation with communism.[39]

Cardinal Franciszek Macharski of Kraków also stresses the importance of *Dignitatis Humanae*. The fundamental right of religious freedom makes everything else possible. It puts a basic check on coercive state power, because it declares the incompetence of the state of the deepest level of human being in the world. Moreover, by adopting *Dignitatis Humanae*, the Council created a situation in which the Church could "open its space" to all, believers and unbelievers, who were, as the cardinal put it, "honest to man." And this new openness would prove crucial in the years to come.[40]

Cardinal Wyszyński was, to be sure, nervous about the possibility that the Council's reforms would erode the unity of the Polish Church for which he had worked so hard, and which he believed essential to a successful resistance against a communist regime that had long tried to play divide and conquer. Thus the Polish Church might be strengthened by the introduction of Polish to its liturgy; but Wyszyński and the episcopate declined to introduce the Council-approved practice of ordaining married men as deacons, fearful (and not without reason) that this would create a new opportunity for the regime to penetrate the Church's official ministry. It is true that the cardinal was concerned about the sort of theological innovation (and dissent from authoritative teaching) that had created divisions in the churches of western Europe and North America. But it is also true that the cardinal disliked theological controversy precisely because he feared for the safety of the Church against the depredations of a regime that would exploit any possible opening to divide the bishops among themselves, the bishops from the priests, the clergy from the people, and the intellectuals from the Church. At a more personal level, Cardinal Wyszyński also resented the way in which devotion to Mary was downplayed, to the point of being scorned, in some "progressive" western theological and ecclesiastical circles.

But if Cardinal Wyszyński was cautious on the matter of the Council and its implementation, he was certainly not an obscurantist.[41] Moreover, the cardinal and the Polish Church had come through the Council, through the beginnings of a new Vatican *Ostpolitik* (in which Wyszyński successfully interposed himself as gatekeeper between the Holy See and Poland's communist authorities), and through the Great Novena/millennium celebrations in a remarkably strong condition, for which there was no analogue in any other communist country. The country's sense of its history had been revivified. Polish Catholicism was, clearly, the prime institutional bearer of the national identity. There had been no penetration of the Church, and the bishops had successfully resisted the regime's attempts to manipulate them. The bishops were united as a collegial body; the new archbishop of Kraków, Karol Wojtyła, had deftly resisted the regime's clumsy efforts to set him against the primate; and if there were tensions between the hierarchy and some of the more adventurous laity, these were kept well within the family, so to speak.

Ten years after his return from imprisonment, Cardinal Stefan Wyszyński presided over a Church that, for all it was continually harassed, enjoyed a greater measure of freedom than any other Catholic community in the Yalta imperial system.

Prelude to Revolution: 1970–1978

If the Church entered the 1970s in a strong position, the same could not be said for the Polish regime. A generation of bungling and mismanagement had put the Polish economy under severe strain. Needed reforms were delayed by communist party haggling and internal disputes, and by 1970 "drastic measures had to be introduced." But the Poles, after twenty years of sacrificing for the promise of industrialization and a prosperous future, were ill disposed to take the bitter medicine that the government intended to propose. An improvement in their standard of living, not further deprivation, was what the people demanded.[42]

With characteristic clumsiness, the Gomułka regime picked December 12, 1970, two weeks before the great religious and familial Christmas holiday, to announce major food and fuel price increases without any commensurate increase in wages. The workers at Gdańsk's Lenin Shipyards struck two days later and demonstrated against the prices increases in the city center of the Baltic seaport. The militia tried to break up the demonstration and only succeeded in instigating a violent confrontation. The eruption spread to the neighboring city of Gdynia the next day, and the regime authorized the use of the army to stop the demonstrators. The shooting began on December 16. According to official figures, which may be presumed to be low, 28 workers were killed, 1,200 were wounded, and 3,000 arrested in Gdańsk alone, with more deaths, shootings, and jailings to follow in the other cities along the Baltic coast until order was restored on December 18.[43]

Having violated the first principle of Polish political life—Pole

shall not kill Pole—Władysław Gomułka was ousted as first secretary of the Polish United Workers' Party on December 19, and
replaced by Edward Gierek, a younger technocrat who had been
party boss in Silesia. With the country on the verge of insurrection (and, we may assume, with the ever-present danger of Soviet
intervention in mind), Gierek promptly acknowledged that the
"working class was provoked beyond endurance," conceded that
the party had lost touch with the nation, and asked all citizens,
"believers and nonbelievers" alike, to work together in solving
the country's problems.[44]

Neither the threat of Soviet intervention nor Gierek's reference
to "believers" was lost on Cardinal Wyszyński who, in his
Christmas Eve sermon at Warsaw's Cathedral of St. John, deplored
the "almost unique" tragedy of Pole shooting Pole, and appealed
to all for calm:

> We beg of you, do not accuse. Show understanding, forgive, feel
> compassion, put your hands to the plow so that there can be more
> bread in our Motherland, and justly distribute the slice of bread
> first of all to the children of the nation, working mothers and
> fathers, because they have the first right to this bread which grows
> on Polish soil. . . . We are capable of, and we can afford, true
> democracy in Poland, because this has existed in the traditions of
> the Polish people since the times of the kings. We can afford to
> exact from our Christian spirit more active cooperation with the
> children of God in the whole nation.[45]

But the protests did not end, despite the cardinal's plea for
calm, until Gierek made dramatic personal appearances at the
end of January 1971 in the Szczecin and Gdańsk shipyards, and
the workers grudgingly returned to a normal schedule. After a
mid-February strike by the women of the Łódź textile mills
threatened to reignite the whole process again, the Gierek government finally withdrew the price increases.[46]

At the time, the accession of Gierek seemed to mark the beginning of a new day for Polish communism, and just possibly for
the Polish nation. In retrospect, however, the 1970 strikes in the
Tri-City on the Baltic were the beginning of the Polish communist
party's descent into senility and decrepitude—a process of decay
into which the party dragged the Polish economy. The problem
was not that the Gomułka regime had mismanaged the system;
the problem was that the system was economically insane. Prices

had no relationship to real-world values. Production and distribution decisions were made by bureaucrats, not by entrepreneurs or workers, or according to the laws of supply and demand. Polish agriculture, which had never been collectivized, continued to produce reasonably well; but since export decisions were made for political purposes and to meet the needs of other "fraternal socialist states," the best of Poland's meat, vegetables, and dairy products ended up outside the country or were priced beyond an ordinary person's means within it. The Gierek government borrowed huge amounts of money from the West, which were then squandered in attempts to shore up a fundamentally unsound system, while Poland's hard currency debt service rose exponentially.

The only answer to Poland's economic woes was to scrap the system: but that was impossible, for ideological reasons and because of the death grip of Brezhnev's USSR within the Warsaw Pact. And so the Gierek regime slogged along through the 1970s, as the economy slowly eroded and popular dissatisfaction once again reached the boiling point. The explosion came in June 1976 after another attempt to increase food prices. On June 24, the day the new prices were announced, the entire work force at the Ursus Tractor Factory in Warsaw went out on strike. In the town of Radom, the workers at the metalworks struck and then set fire to the local community party headquarters. Strikes and riots quickly spread throughout the country. The regime withdrew the price increases on June 25 and the strikes stopped. But then, in a fit of madness, the militia and the SB launched a campaign of reprisals in which thousands were arrested. Moreover, "many of those detained, especially in Ursus and Radom, were beaten and systematically tortured by the militia, the Security Service, and the prison wardens on a scale unprecedented since 1956."[47]

The Gierek regime was, clearly, coming unhinged. And as the economy eroded, so did the spirit of the people: a dull ache of sullenness, occasionally spilling over into anger and despair as at Ursus and Radom, was seeping across the land. A frightened party first secretary sent Primate Wyszyński seventy-five red roses to mark his seventy-fifth birthday on August 3, 1976. In September, the Polish bishops conference again appealed for a "common effort" to solve the country's problems, but also urged "the state authorities to cease its oppression of workers who took part in the anti-government protests. Workers who participated in the protests should have their rights and their social and professional positions restored. They should receive compensation for their losses. Those sentenced should be given amnesty."[48]

It seemed that a time of reckoning might be soon at hand.

Movements Old and New

During the 1970s, as the credibility of the Polish communist regime waned, the stature of the Church continued to wax. The country grew ever more thoroughly Catholic. By the late 1970s, 93 percent of the population had been baptized. The number of priests in Poland had doubled since 1945, to approximately 20,000. There were 6,300 seminarians studying in 46 seminaries. Children took religious instruction in some 21,000 catechetical centers.[49] On this solid foundation, a number of renewal movements which would help lay the moral-cultural foundations for the Revolution of 1989 came to maturity.

The "Oasis" summer camps, which had begun as a Christian family outdoors program, evolved into the "Light and Life" movement under the charismatic leadership of Father Franciszek Blachnicki. The movement aimed to create a "diaconate of liberty through truth" in Poland, demonstrating that the faith was not a matter of escape into otherworldliness but rather a way of making a distinctive Christian contribution to the renewal of Poland here and now. The movement was also a call to live "as if": to live "as if" one were in a free country, and "as if" fear were no longer the hallmark of social life. To Father Blachnicki, this meant a Polish theology of liberation, and he described it in terms that would provide a Polish Catholic counterpart to Václav Havel's "Power of the Powerless":

> To abide and persist in truth means to bear witness to the truth in one's life and to live according to the truth. To do so one must overcome the fear which keeps us from speaking and living the truth. We have to realize that only when we have the courage to bear witness to the truth, regardless of the consequences, will we become free men. For enslavement is caused not so much by outside factors such as violence but by fear. If the majority of Poles plucked up their courage to live by the truth and to unmask lies we would already be a free society: our enemies would be helpless.

They are powerful only if they can intimidate us into pretending that we believe in their lies, when we ourselves repeat them against our will and our beliefs. This situation cannot prevail forever, for man has been created to be free. It was this yearning for freedom which was at the core of the postwar revolts in Poland. . . .

A person finds the courage to bear witness to the truth when he is willing to make sacrifices for the truth, to the point of sacrificing one's life as Christ did. The mystery of the Cross is the key element of this Polish theology of liberation. In fact without it no theology of liberation can be constructed.

The question arises: How does one come by the readiness to suffer, to take up the cross? This leads to the still missing element of the theology of liberation. This element is trust in God, faith in the love of God who receives and rewards our readiness to sacrifice, springing from the love and trust of a child and through a new life in the resurrection. This trust of God in the hour of our death is also the attitude of Christ on the cross. Everyone must adopt this attitude in order to achieve inner freedom. . . . [50]

Over 300,000 Polish youngsters received a "Light and Life" spiritual formation from the mid-1970s through the late 1980s; by the latter date, over 40 percent of the country's vocations to the priesthood and religious life were coming out of the movement. The communist authorities paid their own special tribute to "Light and Life" by trying to infiltrate it and by harassing its program, despite the fact that the bishops put the movement under the protection of the hierarchy.[51]

It was also during the 1970s that the Kraków-based Catholic weekly, *Tygodnik Powszechny* ("Universal Weekly"), became widely recognized as Poland's best newspaper: the most reliable source of undoctored information, and the most stimulating forum for social commentary. Under the leadership of veteran lay editor Jerzy Turowicz, and with regular contributors like Cardinal Karol Wojtyła and Father Józef Tischner, *Tygodnik Powszechny* unmasked the ideological pretensions of the regime and sketched the contours of a truly democratic society with an intellectual integrity and depth that could not be approached by even the most sophisticated of the communist "opinion" journals, Mieczysław Rakowski's Warsaw-based *Polityka*.[52]

The regime constantly harassed *Tygodnik Powszechny*: editorially, through censorship, and functionally, by manipulating its circulation through the government's control over newsprint.[53]

(American magazine publishers talk about the "multiplier," the number of people who actually read one issue of a journal. *Tygodnik Powszechny* had a "multiplier" in the dozens, as its readers passed issues along through a network of intellectual dissent.) But there were also more direct threats and pressures on its editors and contributors, a fact that had led Cardinal Wyszyński, in late 1960, to appoint the recently consecrated Bishop Wojtyła, auxiliary of Kraków, as the "unofficial protector" of the newspaper's staff: an appointment confirmed by the entire episcopate at its January 1961 meeting.[54]

In addition to its services to free information and robust political and social commentary, *Tygodnik Powszechny* was also an important link in the chain of common concern built in the 1970s between the Church and non-Catholic intellectuals and activists: a chain that would ultimately prove its tensile strength during the rise of Solidarity.

Poland's antiregime intellectuals had stayed silently on the sidelines during the Baltic coast upheavals in 1970. But the Ursus and Radom strikes in 1976 led men like Jacek Kuroń, Bronisław Geremek, and Adam Michnik to form the Committee for the Defense of Workers (usually known by its Polish initials, KOR) which added a new factor—independent, intellectual dissidents— to the already volatile mix of Polish politics.[55] Indeed throughout the 1970s, as Timothy Garton Ash puts it, "there was a deliberate, difficult, and fruitful coming together of intellectuals from traditions that just twenty years before had been bitterly opposed: Jewish socialists sat down with Christian Democrats, former Stalinists with Home Army veterans, hardened ex-revisionists with inspissated Thomists."[56]

The rapprochement among the intellectuals, and between the intellectuals and the Church, was difficult because the lay Polish intelligentsia had a long tradition of liberal anticlericalism behind it. Moreover, the dialogue between Catholic and non-Catholic intellectuals in the Polish context inevitably meant confronting the difficult and painful history of anti-Semitism in Poland. But that the dialogue bore fruit was made plain by the witness of no less a central figure in the secular-intellectual opposition than Adam Michnik, himself of Jewish heritage, who in a seminal 1977 book (that could only be published in Paris), *The Church, the Left, and Dialogue*, told his traditionally anticlerical fellow secularists of the left, and in no uncertain terms, that things had changed: "For many years now, the Catholic Church in Poland has not been on the side of the powers-that-be, but has stood out in defense of the oppressed. The authentic enemy of the left is not the Church, but totalitarian power, and in this battle the Church plays a role which it is impossible to overestimate."[57]

The expatriate Polish philosopher Leszek Kołakowski, a former Marxist, agreed with Michnik. Kołakowski argued that, in the Church, the communist regime confronted an institution whose genuine authority revealed the hollowness of the claims of the "People's Republic." So what, wrote Kołakowski, if the regime could "smash thirty or so uncensored . . . journals and . . . gaol a few thousand active people? [It] is not possible with internal repressive instruments to destroy the most powerful crystallizing force of social consciousness to resist the Sovietization process and the most powerful source of moral authority, viz., the Catholic Church."[58]

Tygodnik Powszechny, according to Catholic journalist and former Solidarity activist Kazimierz Wóycicki, was "crucial" to this reconciliation because it amplified the image of a Church open to intellectual dialogue with all men of goodwill. Thus *Tygodnik Powszechny*, often in tandem with another maturing movement of the 1970s, the Clubs of the Catholic Intelligentsia (led in Warsaw by Tadeusz Mazowiecki, who also edited the Club's monthly journal, *Więź* ["Link"]), prevented a split in the anticommunist opposition that the regime could have exploited, and laid the groundwork of common conviction and cooperation that would make possible the worker-intellectual alliance at the Gdańsk shipyards in 1980—the alliance that became Solidarity.

The Rise of Solidarity: 1978–1981

On October 16, 1978, the conflict between what were known in Poland as "the society" and "the power" entered its decisive phase as the archbishop of Kraków, Cardinal Karol Wojtyła, was elected Bishop of Rome under the title John Paul II.

Americans of certain ages remember where they were when Pearl Harbor was attacked, when President Roosevelt died, when President Kennedy was assassinated. Poles remember where they were when John Paul II was elected. More to the point, they remember how they felt. Over a dozen years after that stunning surprise, Polish faces still light up in irrepressible happiness when Poles are asked, "What did it feel like when Cardinal Wojtyła was elected?"

Kazimierz Wóycicki of the newspaper *Życie Warszawy* remembered it as "a tremendous victory" (and deemed it superfluous to say for whom, and against what).[59] For *Tygodnik Powszechny* editor Jerzy Turowicz, it was "a great experience of hope." (And, doubtless, of satisfaction: how many other newspaper editors have one of their columnists elected pope?)[60] To Barbara Paluch, a teacher in Tarnów, it was a "fulfillment of [our] national dreams," and a moment when "people felt their dignity": a "Polish worker could be such a thing!"[61] Ferdinand Chrobok, who later lost his job as a forensic physician because of his Solidarity activities, remembers that day simply in terms of adjectives: "fantastic," "unbelievable," "stupendous."[62]

Historian Norman Davies once argued that "the essence of Poland's modern experience is humiliation."[63] *That* is what changed in the hearts of millions of Poles, on October 16, 1978.

The June 1979 Pilgrimage

Taking a cue from Cardinal Wyszyński's Great Novena and its celebration of the millennium of Polish Christianity, Cardinal Wojtyła had planned a similar process of pastoral renewal in Kraków, built on a prayerful study of the documents of the Second Vatican Council and culminating in a 1979 celebration of the 900th anniversary of the death of St. Stanisław, Wojtyła's first predecessor in the bishopric of Poland's ancient capital. Nor did Wojtyła think that his changed circumstances, as of October 16, 1978, should make a very great difference in his plans: in the early days of his pontificate, the new pope made it clear that he wanted to visit his homeland to participate in the anniversary celebrations he had set in motion six years before.

The Polish regime knew that it was impossible to keep so distinguished a son of Poland out of the country, but they balked at the date. In the communists' minds, Stanisław's resistance to the civil authority of his day had uncomfortable parallels to the current Polish situation. Thus the regime censored the following passage from John Paul's first Christmas letter back to his former archdiocese of Kraków, which was to have been published in *Tygodnik Powszechny*:

> In accordance with 900-year old tradition, St. Stanisław has become the patron of moral order in our country, of that moral order which is so needed in our times. . . . As bishop and shepherd of the Kraków Church, St. Stanisław defended his contemporary society from the evil which threatened it, and he did not hesitate to confront the ruler when defense of the moral order called for it. In this way he became a magnificent example of concern about people, which we have to compare with our indifference, our negligence and despondency, and our concern with our own interests.
>
> The welfare of the people and of society is indivisibly linked with concern for the moral order. Using modern language we can see in St. Stanisław an advocate of the most essential human rights, on which man's dignity, his morality, and true freedom depend.[64]

Jerzy Turowicz refused to print the letter in bowdlerized form; the full text was then read from all the pulpits of the archdiocese.[65] But the struggle between Church and regime over the pope's 1979 pilgrimage had begun. John Paul was not shy about pressing his claims; when the government stonewalled on an official invitation, the pope invited himself, telling the Polish authorities on January 11, 1979, "that he considered it his 'duty' to take part in the ceremonies" commemorating the martyrdom of St. Stanisław.[66] After further negotiations, a compromise was finally announced on March 2, 1979: the pope would not come for two days in May (i.e., for the Stanisław commemoration), but for nine days in June, during which he would visit six cities rather than just Warsaw and Kraków. In the course of the official announcement, the government-controlled Polish media warned against the "illusion" that the pope's impending visit would in any way change the principle of the party's vanguard role in society, or would alter what it termed the "strictly secular" character of the Polish People's Republic. But it was all so much hot air. The party may have thought it had won the battle over St. Stanisław. In fact it had lost the war for Poland.

For John Paul's triumphant nine days in June 1979 were the beginning of the end of the Yalta imperial system, not only in Poland, but throughout Stalin's empire. In Warsaw, Gniezno,

Opole, Częstochowa, Mogiła, and Kraków, John Paul began in earnest the process by which the communist system was finally dismantled from within. And he did it through thirty-two sermons in which he preached, not insurrection, but the final revolution: the revolution of the spirit in which conscience confronted the fear and acquiescence that kept "the society" in the grip of "the power."

The instruction began at the very outset of the pilgrimage, during the pope's meeting with Edward Gierek and other state functionaries at Warsaw's White House, the Belvedere Palace. After the Polish communist leader made the obligatory statement about the importance for Poland of its unbreakable alliance with the Soviet Union, John Paul replied that peace could only be built on the foundation of respect for basic human rights, which included the right of a nation to freedom and to the creation of its own culture. Nor would the pope let Gierek get away with the suggestion, bruited by Mieczysław Rakowski in a *Polityka* piece during the previsit maneuvering, that the Church's role in society was simply cultic:

> Given that [the temporal dimension of human life] is realized through people's membership of various communities, national and state, and is therefore at the same time political, economic, and cultural, the Church continually rediscovers its own mission in relationship to these sectors of human life and activity. By establishing a religious relationship with man, the Church consolidates him in his natural social bonds.[67]

Thus in the very first hours of his pilgrimage the pope frontally challenged the Marxist claim that religion was both the expression and the further cause of human alienation. On the contrary, said John Paul: the temporal mission of the Church, which was indivisible from its evangelical and sacramental mission, was to defend human rights, to help human beings live creatively, and to make men and women more devoted servants of each other, of their families, and of their society. For the execution of this mission the Church "does not desire privileges," but only the freedom that was hers by her nature[68]—the freedom which, the pope did not need to add, Poland had pledged herself to defend by signing the Universal Declaration of Human Rights.

John Paul forcefully proclaimed the Christological core of his message later that day, at a Mass celebrated before hundreds of thousands of Poles in Warsaw's Victory Square: "Christ cannot be excluded from man's history anywhere in the world, from any geographical latitude or longitude. Attempts to exclude Christ from man's history are directed against man. Without Christ it is impossible to understand the history of Poland."[69] Marxist "humanism" was in fact inhuman. Christ revealed to humankind the fullness of its humanity, which was achieved in union with the Creator who satisfied his divine fatherhood in the Son, and in the people the Son had called his own. Any attempt to block human access to the Father through the Son was, to be sure, an offense against God. But, the pope would insist from one end of Poland to the other, it was also a crime against humanity. The crowds agreed: the pope's Victory Square sermon was interrupted time and again by chants—"We want God, we want God, we want God in the family circle, we want God in books, in schools, we want God in government orders, we want God, we want God." To which the pope replied, accurately enough, "People are preaching with me."[70]

John Paul returned to this Christological theme at the Cistercian abbey in Mogila on June 9 (the closest he was allowed to Nowa Huta, the authorities being determined that he would not celebrate Mass in the Ark Church). And on this occasion, he sharpened the Christian critique of Marxism-Leninism even more pointedly: "Remember this: Christ will never agree to man being viewed only as a means of production, or agree to man viewing himself as such. He will not agree that man should be valued, measured, or evaluated only on this basis. Christ will never agree to that!"[71]

But the pope was not interested in a merely formulaic or inherited faith: that would be an insufficient response to the antihumanism of the communist enterprise. As he told his former students from Lublin, when he met them at Częstochowa on June 6, "Any man who chooses his ideology honestly and through his own conviction deserves respect." The real problem, particularly in communist lands, was that the lack of free choice had led to a deadening conformity. "The real danger for both sides—for the Church and for the other side, call it what you will—is the man who does not take a risk and accept a challenge, who does not listen to his deepest convictions, to his inner truth, but who only wants to fit somehow, to float in conformity, moving from left to right as the wind blows."[72]

At Gniezno, the historic cradle of Polish Christianity, the pope sent a message eastward. He reminded his listeners of the gradual expansion of Christianity among the Slavic peoples of central, eastern, and southern Europe, and of how Christian faith had been historically interwoven into the fabric of their emerging national cultures. Then, in an unmistakable reference to the problems of religious freedom throughout the Yalta imperial system, and referring to those Slavs who could not come to Gniezno, the pope said,

> I hope, dear brothers, that they can hear us. I hope that they can hear me, because I cannot imagine that any Polish or Slav ear, in any part of the world, would be unable to hear words spoken by a Polish pope, by a Slav! I hope that they can hear me because we live in an epoch where the freedom to exchange information is so precisely defined, as is the exchange of cultural values. Here [i.e., in religious freedom] we are reaching the very roots of those values.[73]

And, just to ensure that the message wasn't misinterpreted, the pope returned to this theme in Opole in lower Silesia on the third day of his pilgrimage, in words that spoke volumes, if subtly, about John Paul's contempt for the Yalta system and the ideology it embodied:

> As respect for the rights of every member of a community, a nation, or, for example, a family, is a condition for inner unity within each society or social body, so recognition of and respect for the rights of each nation is a condition for reconciliation among nations. This includes, first of all, the right to exist and the right to self-determination, then the right to one's own culture and to multidirectional development.[74]

Thirteen million Poles heard John Paul speak the hitherto unspeakable during nine stunning days in June 1979. Neither they, nor the system which falsely claimed to govern in their name, would be the same again.

The Impact

Political scientist Bogdan Szajkowski has described those nine days in June as a "psychological earthquake, an opportunity for mass political catharsis."[75] But the pope's pilgrimage was also a massive moral, even spiritual, earthquake in which millions of Poles decided that it was time to live "as if": "as if" they were free men and women.

The temptation to romanticize these unprecedented events is strong, and precisely so as not to diminish the impact of John Paul's pilgrimage, it should be firmly resisted. Yet one cannot help be struck by the fact that virtually every Pole with whom one discusses this history today—and irrespective of that person's religious or political convictions—identifies the 1979 pilgrimage as the fulcrum of the Revolution of 1989, and the point at which Poland irreversibly turned toward a noncommunist future.

To historian and dissident Adam Michnik, who three years before had challenged his colleagues on the left to get over their traditional anticlericalism, the pope's pilgrimage was a "lesson in dignity," a "national plebiscite," "Poland's second baptism." Despite the mass character of the events, John Paul not only "spoke to all of us," but "to each of us individually." And his message, according to Michnik, was a call to break through the self-centeredness and atomization characteristic of life within the culture of the lie. Michnik believed that the pope had revived the Polish tradition of sacrifice: a tradition which, the historian readily argued, had its deepest roots in Poland's Christian tradition.[76]

Janusz Onyszkiewicz, a "Catholic with certain doubts" who became Solidarity's spokesman in 1981, described the pilgrimage as the point at which "we" and "they" were decisively clarified in the struggle between "the society" and "the power." Prior to June 1979, it had been very clear who "they" were: the regime. But it was not clear who "we" were: how many of "us" there were, and how much "we" could trust each other. "Then the pope came and the 'we' was clear: 'we' are the society, and the country is ours. 'They' are just an artificial crust." Onyszkiewicz remembered the intensity of feeling that permeated the events of the pilgrimage, the feeling that, absent the omnipresent threat from the east, "the pope could have swept the whole business away" by lifting a finger. That was not to be, in 1979. But the fact that people felt their moral and social power during those nine days was a major moral and psychological victory, a historical turning point from which there could be no retreat. The pope had exorcised the fear that kept the "we" of society from coalescing.[77]

Cardinal Franciszek Macharski, who succeeded John Paul as

archbishop of Kraków six months before the pilgrimage, reached for a historical analogy: John Paul in June 1979 was acting, like Pope Leo the Great, as the *defensor civitatis*, the defender of the city who met and challenged the barbarians who had been threatening, not just the city, but civilization itself. But the pope could do this, Macharski suggested, precisely because he put politics into its proper place: which was not first place. The pope could be *defensor civitatis* and *defensor hominis*, the defender of man and of a true humanism, because he was by conviction and vocation the servant of the *redemptor hominis*, the redeemer of man. Nor should this be understood as mere tactics, the pope eschewing a frontal assault on communism simply because "the power" had all the means of coercion at its disposal. Rather, John Paul brought to the struggle, and particularly to the June 1979 pilgrimage, the viewpoint of a philosopher and theologian convinced that communism's deepest flaw was in the arena of truth, and that its economic, political, and social failures were expressions of its fundamental errors about the nature of the human person. And so it was a matter of morally required strategy, not just of pragmatic tactics, to locate the confrontation with communism at that most basic level of its failure.[78]

None of these participants in and observers of the June 1979 pilgrimage would deny that there was another, simpler, even simplistic level to the mass reaction that the pope inspired: the level of the anonymous Polish miner who, when asked, why be religious in a communist state, answered, "To praise the Mother of God and to spite those bastards."[79] But when John Paul told his fellow Poles in June 1979 that "the future of Poland will depend on how many people are mature enough to be nonconformist," the key word was "mature."[80] And there was, really, no essential contradiction between the miner's wanting to "spite those bastards" and the pope's call to maturity: the evidence being the peaceful, nonviolent, and dignified way in which millions of Poles (who doubtless wanted to "spite those bastards") conducted themselves during the pilgrimage. In other circumstances, under other leadership, and inspired by other themes, the mass demonstrations of disaffection that took place in Poland in June 1979 could have led in short order to cataclysmic rioting and bloodshed. Instead, they led to the solidarity from which came Solidarity.

That solidarity grew out of an unspoken but widespread social compact that seemed to form in Poland in June 1979: as Father Józef Tischner describes it, people said, to themselves and to each other, "Let's stop lying." Thus "we" and "they" were further clarified: "we" would try to "live in the truth" (as Václav Havel would later describe the experience); "they" would continue to live within the lie. Given the opportunity, Father Tischner explained, people "instinctively understood" the importance of a movement of moral renewal as the basis for any serious attempt to confront "the power."[81]

Father Maciej Zięba, O.P., who was a twenty-five-year-old student and worker at the time of the pope's pilgrimage, also remembered it in these terms—as a moment of truth that broke through "the artificial world around us," the world of the lie. The Church had previously given Zięba "the first experience in my life" of freedom. But when John Paul, playing on the fact that "land" and "earth" are the same word in Polish, prayed in Victory Square, "Come, Holy Spirit, renew the face of the earth . . . of *this* land!", people knew that "*something* had to change." No one knew how it was going to turn out. "We might have to live and die under communism. But what I wanted to do was to live without being a liar. The 1979 visit gave us the hope that this was possible."[82]

This virtually universal conviction that the pope's 1979 pilgrimage was the beginning of the end of Polish communism precisely because it was a great moment of national moral regeneration helps explain why the economistic explanation of the Revolution of 1989 is so unsatisfactory. Of course those thirteen millions Poles who prayed and sang with John Paul II in June 1979 were dissatisfied with the way "those bastards" had botched the Polish economy. But they had been dissatisfied for a long time. And so, as Timothy Garton Ash put it, "the economic crisis was . . . a necessary, but by no means a sufficient, cause of the revolution. The decisive causes are to be found in the realm of consciousness rather than of being"—put another way, in the realm of conscience rather than of subsistence.[83]

Solidarity banners and poems gave voice to this revolution of the spirit within a year. One homegrown banner in the remote village of Ustrzyki Dolne put the people's sentiments into a stinging peasant image:

we don't care about life
the pig also lives
we want a life of dignity[84]

Or, as the poet of the Rzeszów commune would sing in 1981,

The times are past
when they closed our mouths
with sausage.[85]

It cannot be said that western commentators picked up on the moral revolution which took place in Poland between June 2 and June 10, 1979. The veteran Vatican watchers at the Italian daily, *Corriere Della Sera*, were not atypical in their analysis of the pilgrimage: John Paul's visit was "a sign of détente and openness from a pope who comes from the East and wants to build a strong, lasting bridge to it."[86] John Paul was, of course, committed to bridge-building. But no lasting bridges between East and West could be built on the basis of the Yalta imperial system. Nor could East and West be reconnected without the span provided by central Europe. Something, as Father Zięba later put it, had to change.

Enter, on the foundations of social solidarity, Solidarity.

The Workers Reject the Workers' State

The history of Solidarity, and especially of its early period, have been ably told elsewhere and there is no need to repeat that chronology here.[87] Our focus is on the Church and the union: the linkage symbolically captured by those famous photographs taken at Gdańsk's Lenin Shipyards, the epicenter of the Solidarity earthquake, during the crucial strike in August 1980—the photographs of the locked shipyard gates, and of the workers barricaded behind the ikon of the Black Madonna and the portrait of John Paul II; the photographs of the priests hearing outdoor confessions just inside the gates.

It began, as it had in 1956, 1970, and 1976, with governmentally imposed price increases. Then, while the 17,000 workers at the shipyards were protesting the price increases, the management fired Anna Walentynowicz, a crane operator and veteran independent labor activist. The workers then struck and Lech Wałęsa, a suspended electrician who climbed back into the yards over the 12-foot-tall perimeter fence, took over the leadership of the strike committee. Bishop Lech Kaczmarek of Gdańsk, mediating quietly between the local authorities and the striking workers who had barricaded themselves into the shipyards, suggested that things might be kept calm if the Church could offer pastoral services to the workers. The authorities agreed, and on August 17, Father Henryk Jankowski, Wałęsa's pastor at St. Bridget's church in Gdańsk, said the first open-air Mass in the shipyards and blessed a great wooden cross that the shipyard carpenters had built as a memorial to the workers killed in 1970.

Negotiations continued at the yards, and the workers' position was strengthened on the night of August 22, when *Więź* editor Tadeusz Mazowiecki and historian Bronisław Geremek arrived in Gdańsk bringing a message of support from intellectual dissidents in Warsaw. Wałęsa promptly recruited Mazowiecki and Geremek as advisers, and thus was born (in part through the midwifery of the Clubs of the Catholic Intelligentsia) the worker-intellectual coalition that made Solidarity such a potent adversary for the communist regime.

On August 26, with the situation still unresolved in Gdańsk and the threat of Soviet intervention hanging heavily in the summer air, Cardinal Wyszyński preached a powerful sermon at the Jasna Góra monastery in Częstochowa, calling for "calm, balance, prudence, wisdom, and responsibility for the whole Polish Nation." The cardinal's sermon was promptly bowdlerized by the state-run radio and press agency and turned into a critique of the striking workers who, with no other immediate source of information, were badly disappointed. Word of the potential rift quickly got back to the headquarters of the bishops' conference in Warsaw, and that same night the Main Council of the conference issued an emergency communiqué stressing that civic peace was impossible without freedom, including the freedom to form independent trade unions—the point on which the Gdańsk strikers had decided to make their stand. All doubts about the Church's position were then erased as the bishops' communiqué quoted the relevant passage from the documents of the Second Vatican Council: "Among the fundamental rights of the individual must be numbered the right to form themselves into associations which truly represent them and are able to cooperate in organizing economic life properly, and the right to play their part in the activities of such associations without risk of reprisal."[88]

Solidarity, which was born during those two stirring August weeks in the Lenin Shipyards, was a test of whether any revolution in the modern world could be both self-regulating and nonviolent. The history of modern revolutionary practice, and the theory of revolution first adumbrated during the French Terror, suggested that both were impossible dreams. Initial intentions notwithstanding, revolutions inevitably took on a life of their own, and that life inevitably led to (when it did not begin in) violence.

Solidarity challenged that history. It challenged it in part on the basis of Cardinal Wyszyński's own approach, honed over thirty hard years of struggle: firmness of principle; a long-term strategic vision; flexible tactics. And the aging cardinal recognized the affinities between himself and these new activists, unequivocally telling Warsaw Solidarity chief Zbigniew Bujak on October 19, just before a crisis broke out over the union's legal registration, "I am with you." By October, the cardinal knew that the lessons he had taught, of principle combined with self-regulation and self-limitation in the service of a true Polish patriotism, had been learned.

But perhaps the most striking aspect of Solidarity's challenge to the sanguinary history of modern revolutionary action was its nonviolence.

Even in 1979, according to historian Norman Davies, "the Romantic tradition still [reigned] supreme in the Polish mind."[89] And in the history of Polish Romanticism, violent, if ultimately quixotic, attempts to throw off the burden of foreign occupation were a staple and celebrated feature of the national experience. Every literate Pole had read the great trilogy of novels by Nobel laureate Henryk Sienkiewicz, a national epic in which such knights of derring-do as Pan Yan Skshetuski, Pan Michal Volodyovski, and the Polish Falstaff, Pan Onufry Zagloba, charged back and forth over Poland, Lithuania, and Ukraine (the lands of the old Polish-Lithuanian Commonwealth) in violent pursuit of glory and in violent defense of fatherland and faith.[90] Every Polish schoolchild had learned the poetry and read the plays of Adam Mickiewicz, with their Romantic recollection of past martial triumphs, their depiction of Poland as the "Christ of

Nations," crucified for Europe's sins, and their celebrations of the unquenchable Polish spirit.

Not least among the contributions of Pope John Paul II to the Revolution of 1989—and to the nonviolence of the Solidarity revolution that set the pattern for everything else—was the pope's ability to both harness and discipline this Romantic tradition. From his inaugural sermon on October 22, 1978, when he cited Sienkiewicz by name, through the nine days of June 1979, John Paul returned time and again to this literary tradition for allusions, references, and images. But he married Polish Romanticism to nonviolence. When John Paul reached into his deep store of traditional Polish images, when he drew on Mickiewicz's Romantic national messianism and spoke of Poland's special role in Europe, and when he called for moral resistance to the communist culture of the lie and to the system that culture had created, the pope also insisted that a morally acceptable resistance had to be nonviolent: as a matter of principle, not merely as a matter of pragmatic tactics. The truth about man with which John Paul wished to confront communism included the truth that violence turns another human being into an object: which was precisely what communism also did. Father Józef Tischner suggests that what John Paul taught the Poles was "a new way of being a partisan."[91] Or, and to borrow from Camus: John Paul rechanneled the tradition of Polish Romanticism such that the Poles, refusing to be victims any longer, also refused to be executioners.[92]

The result of this challenge to the modern revolutionary tradition was a profound inversion of the vanguard claims of Marxism-Leninism. As Timothy Garton Ash put it,

> In eighteen days Poland's workers had blown a huge hole through the Leninist myth that the working class cannot see beyond immediate economic wants, and is therefore doomed to founder in mere economistic *tredyunionizm* until its sights are raised by a communist party. [During the Solidarity August of 1980] the roles [were] reversed: the party clung to economic issues, while the workers raised their own sights to the higher plane of human rights and political participation. It was the beginning of a workers' revolution against a "Workers' State."[93]

And that inversion could not have taken place, in Poland, without the Catholic Church and specifically without the steady catechesis of human rights preached by the Church since the 1960s.

Thus on August 31, 1980, Lech Wałęsa, whose denim jacket regularly displayed a miniature of the Black Madonna, signed the Gdańsk agreement authorizing "independent, self-governing trade unions" with a huge souvenir pen (from the 1979 pilgrimage, of course) topped by a giant photo of John Paul II. And thus the Solidarity chairman at Poznań, asked in 1981 what had been the most important change in the workers' lives since the days of August 1980, said, "That—and [pointed] to a large cross on the [factory] wall."[94]

Beyond Romanticism

Like the pope's 1979 pilgrimage, the rise of Solidarity was such a splendid instance of the good guys battling against long odds and finally beating the bad guys that the temptation to romanticize the whole business can be almost irresistible. Yet it would, paradoxically, demean the accomplishments of the founders of the first independent trade union in the communist world—which was, as everyone understood at the time, far more than a trade union—if that temptation was indulged. The story, warts and all, is sweet enough not to require additional sugar coating.

The union leadership and followership, including the crucial worker-intellectual coalition, was cross-hatched with tensions. (Jacek Kuroń once quipped that Wałęsa should have gotten another Nobel Peace Prize for keeping the movement's factions away from each other's throats.[95]) The leaders made tactical errors in the struggle with the government that went on continuously from the signing of the Gdańsk agreement to the imposition of martial law on December 13, 1981. Part of the problem was the very uniqueness of Solidarity: the trade union that couldn't be (officially) but had to be (because of the bizarre and unnatural situation) a political opposition. Hard words were exchanged between men and women whom millions idealized as heroes. Personal ambitions and ideological convictions sometimes got in the way of the common cause. All of this came out into the open even more clearly after the communist crack-up, when the Solidarity coalition came apart in the spring of 1990 over differences that various factions and personalities had with the government of Prime Minister Tadeusz Mazowiecki. As Timothy Garton

Ash put it at the time, "recent history offers few spectacles sadder than this one of friends and comrades who had gone through so much together, with such dignity, honor, wit, and yes, solidarity, now belaboring each other [rhetorically] with rusty clubs and blows beneath the belt."[96] That, alas, is what frequently happens when normal politics breaks out from under the rubble of the totalitarian state.

And yet for all that we now see its flaws, Solidarity was a great success: a great moral success, and a great political success. Solidarity decisively broke the expectation, depressingly widespread in western elite circles as well as in the Kremlin, that the future was, somehow, on the side of Marxism-Leninism. Solidarity demonstrated, empirically, that there were in fact two revolutionary traditions in the modern world, and that the depredations which had grown out of the French Revolutionary tradition could be met by a morally driven commitment to the democratic revolutionary tradition of Jefferson and Madison. Solidarity did what armies could never have done, absent a nuclear holocaust: it killed the Warsaw Pact. Few western students of this history have so great a claim on our attention as Timothy Garton Ash. And his summary of the meaning of Solidarity is both tempered and just: "Solidarity . . . was a pioneering Polish form of social self-organization, with the general objective of achieving, by means of peaceful, popular pressure combined with elite negotiation, the end of communism. In this it succeeded. . . ."[97] Moreover, Solidarity's success in Poland had effects far beyond Poland borders:

> Elements of the new politics developed by Solidarity in Poland—
> the forms of peaceful protest and civic resistance, the negotiations
> symbolized by the [1989] Round Table—spread directly to its
> neighbors. Poland was first. If the division of Europe which we call
> in shorthand "Yalta" began in Poland in 1945, then there is an
> important sense in which the end of "Yalta" also began in Poland.
> No country did more for the cause of liberty in Europe in the
> 1980s, and no country paid a higher price.[98]

Nor should the celebrant of the Church's contribution to Solidarity's accomplishments pass over the tensions that existed between the Polish Church and the leadership of the new "trade union plus." The Church was accustomed to being the sole institutional opposition to Poland's communist regime: if the pattern of confrontation between Church and state was wearisome at times, it was also familiar. Solidarity added a new face card to the deck. Church leaders, including Cardinal Wyszyński and his successor, Cardinal Józef Glemp, committed to reforms but determined to avoid the specter of Soviet invasion and occupation, were concerned about the union's ability to be self-regulating. Threats of Soviet intervention were relayed to the Church leadership (by, among others, American intelligence services) throughout 1980–1981. And on each of these occasions, the Polish bishops' conference, in addition to asking the regime to act responsibly, also warned Solidarity not to push too far.[99]

But despite these tensions the Church never broke the pledge that Cardinal Wyszyński made to Zbigniew Bujak in October 1980: "I am with you." Nor did John Paul, from Rome, cease to draw the world's attention to the Polish situation: which was his unique way of bringing the glare of publicity onto Leonid Brezhnev, in the hope that that might prevent a repetition of the events of 1968 in Czechoslovakia, when Soviet tanks crushed the Prague Spring. The Church had helped give birth to Solidarity, and, for all the arguments that, not unnaturally, take place between parents and children, it would not abandon its child, which had grown to 10 million strong within a year of John Paul's 1979 pilgrimage.

That commitment would be tested to the full in 1981.

The Year of Troubles

In the aftermath of the communist crack-up, the entire process that led to the collapse of the Warsaw Pact and then of the Soviet Union itself seems to have had a historical inexorability about it. That is the way things often look in retrospect. But that is not the way they looked in 1981.

To Leonid Brezhnev, Yuri Andropov, and the other aging masters of the Kremlin, Solidarity, backed by the Roman Catholic Church, was a frontal assault on what had become the two unchallengeable shibboleths of the Yalta imperial system: the supremacy of the party within each Warsaw Pact nation, and the allegiance of each nation's rulers to Moscow. Moreover, all of this agitation was going on in Poland, the keystone of the entire external empire erected by Stalin in the aftermath of World War II. Americans may have ceased to believe in the domino theory after Vietnam. But the theory was alive and well in Moscow: and, according to Leonid Brezhnev's reading of the game board, if the Polish domino fell, it just might take everything else with it.[100]

The connection between Brezhnev's imperial anxieties and the attempt by a Turk, Mehmet Ali Agca, to assassinate Pope John Paul II on May 13, 1981 remains a matter of intense speculation. Agca's links to Bulgarian intelligence do seem to have been proven. And the notion that the Bulgarians would attempt such an action on their own is simply not credible, given the nature of the relationships between Warsaw Pact secret services and Moscow Center. A Soviet connection to the assassination also satisfies the obvious and venerable query, cui bono? Who would benefit? If John Paul was indeed the key to the rise of Solidarity, and if Solidarity challenged the post-Yalta order in Poland, and if Poland was *the* domino in the Yalta imperial system, then Agca's assassination attempt in St. Peter's Square does look like an attempt to decapitate the leadership of the social and political resistance within Poland. Nor, on this analysis, need we indulge in unprovable hypotheses about the pope writing Brezhnev, threatening to return to the Polish barricades in the event of a Soviet intervention, and Brezhnev muttering, in the manner of Henry II, "who will free me from this turbulent priest?" With or without such a letter, which some claim he wrote in December 1980, John Paul had already done an enormous amount of damage in the Soviet leadership's eyes: and more damage seemed likely.

What we can know with certainty is that the shooting of the pope cast a pall over a Poland already beset by wildcat strikes and Solidarity-authorized strikes, and by the struggle over the formation of Rural Solidarity. Then, two weeks after Agca shot the pope, Cardinal Wyszyński died of cancer in Warsaw on May 28, 1981. His successor, Archbishop (later Cardinal) Józef Glemp, was principal concelebrant at the Mass with which Solidarity's first congress began on September 5. But Glemp lacked the unsurpassed moral authority of Wyszyński and John Paul was incapacitated (although he did work throughout his hospitalization and subsequent recuperation on the encyclical *Laborem Exercens*, a strong defense of workers' rights which he issued on September

15 shortly after the conclusion of the first round of the Solidarity congress). Meanwhile, the situation throughout the country continued to deteriorate, and on October 18, General Wojciech Jaruzelski replaced Stanisław Kania as leader of the Polish communist party and de facto head of state.

The denouement was not long in coming. Jaruzelski met with Primate Glemp and Lech Wałęsa on November 4, but it seems that by then the decision had been taken to deal with the situation by other means. At 11:57 P.M. on the night of December 12, 1981, 3.4 million private telephones went dead simultaneously across Poland. Tanks rolled through the streets of Warsaw; road blocks were set up throughout the country. Solidarity's leaders, meeting in emergency session in Gdańsk, were arrested in their hotels. (Wałęsa, who had refused to hide despite the threat of arrest, was seized at his apartment.) The Polish army and the SB had "invaded their own country."[101] Then, at 6 A.M., General Jaruzelski went on radio and television to announce that a "state of war" had been introduced and that authority would be henceforth exercised by a Military Council of National Salvation. "By first light, Poland resembled a huge concentration camp with armed personnel carriers and police patrols on the streets of all major towns."[102]

It was a technicality in Poland's communist legal code (which had no provision for "martial law" as such) that led Jaruzelski to define what he had done as a "state of war." But, technicalities aside, it was a wholly apt image. The Polish state had declared war on the Polish people. "The power" had declared war on "the society." Whatever else he may or may not have accomplished in the dark hours of the night of December 12–13, 1981, General Wojciech Jaruzelski had made inescapably explicit what had long seemed obvious to all but the blind, the ideologically besotted, or the corrupt: the "grotesque disharmony" between the regime that ruled Poland and Poland's national traditions.[103]

The Hard Road to Freedom: 1982–1989

The imposition of martial law had its ironically amusing moments. Father Stanisław Małkowski, a Solidarity priest in Warsaw, was arrested that first night and taken to jail. The SB told him that he would have to sign a loyalty oath to the regime. Małkowski said that he could not possibly do such a thing without consulting with his religious superior, Archbishop Glemp. The SB said that that was impossible. Małkowski replied that, in that case, he'd have to consult with the Holy Spirit, and how long might he have for the discussion? "Ten minutes," replied the SB. "And," remembered Father Małkowski, "the Holy Spirit told me that I couldn't sign." Father Małkowski was released and sent off to a rural parish.[104]

According to former Solidarity spokesman Janusz Onyszkiewicz, Jaruzelski's "state of war," and its attempt to restore a "normal" situation in Poland, was based on four misconceptions, three of which illustrated the degree to which Poland's communists had failed to comprehend the moral revolution that had begun in June 1979 and given birth to Solidarity the following year.

The first misconception was that Solidarity had been hijacked by a gang of extremists whose elimination would lead to a situation in which "people came back to their senses."

The second was that, post-Solidarity, it would be possible to reatomize Polish society while concurrently improving the economic situation which the party leaders believed to be the root of popular discontent. The goal, on the Hungarian model, was the "Kádárization" of Poland.

The third misconception was that the Church, which the regime knew would not endorse violent resistance, would, in the end, come around and make arrangements with the government over the corpse, so to speak, of Solidarity.

And the final misconception was that the West, driven by the concerns of its bankers over a Polish debt default, would accommodate itself to the new Polish order after the ritual condemnations of martial law.[105]

In retrospect, the Jaruzelski regime's quest for a return to post-Yalta "normalcy" seems ludicrous: it was impossible to turn the clock back to the days before June 1979 and August 1980. But it was not impossible to make life miserable. And so the martial law period in Poland (which formally ended in July 1983) and the years that followed were a time of decomposition. The Polish party and regime withered away "like the slow retreat of a plague," the economy collapsed even further, and a grim bitterness of spirit infected much of society.[106]

It was also a time of some confusion and uncertainty for the

Polish Church, the only institution in the country to be strengthened by both the rise of Solidarity and the "state of war."[107]
Cardinal Glemp was, in many respects, in an impossible position,
as would have been any successor of Cardinal Wyszyński's other
than Karol Wojtyła. Glemp bore Wyszyński's title, and he seems
to have enjoyed an almost filial relationship with Wyszyński,
whose secretary he had once been; but there was no way in which
he could carry, even by episcopal ordination and papal appointment, the moral authority that came to Wyszyński by reason of
his unique biography. Glemp was physically unprepossessing,
while Wyszyński was imposing. A doctor of both civil and canon
law, he lacked the late cardinal's feel for the popular religious
image and allusion. Moreover, and despite the fact that he had
been an active supporter of workers while bishop of Warmia-
Olsztyn, Glemp seemed to prefer to deal with the regime through
top-level negotiations between Church and state in which he
would act as a patron or protector of Solidarity—which was not
the role the interned, or later freed, Solidarity leaders had in mind
for themselves or for the cardinal. Cardinal Glemp was also
clumsy at dealing with the press, a particular liability given
Warsaw's emergence as an international media center; the result
was that his words were often misunderstood even when he was
taking positions in support of the suppressed union. Finally,
Glemp, as Wyszyński's designated heir, shared the old primate's
concern for Church unity, but now faced a situation in which the
increasingly volatile younger Polish clergy were demanding that
the Church leadership take a more vocal and public stance
against the Jaruzelski regime. In similar circumstances in the past,
Wyszyński could appeal (subtly) to the authority of his person;
he, after all, had pronounced the "*Non possumus*" and had suffered three years of internment as a result. Glemp could only
invoke the authority of his office, and thus contribute to his repu-
tation as an "authoritarian."

Cardinal Glemp was a devoted churchman and a Polish
patriot. But however one weighs the cardinal's strengths and
weaknesses, Glemp could not and did not exercise the kind of
authority as primate that Wyszyński enjoyed. In the first instance,
and after Wyszyński's death, everyone understood that the real
primate of Poland was in Rome and was not going to be silent
about matters in his homeland. Secondly, the Polish episcopate

strengthened its collegial and collaborative processes during the 1980s, such that it was ever more "the episcopate," not the primate, in whose name the Church's policy was made and the Church's public statements issued. Thirdly, the demography of dissent had dramatically changed in the country: there were 10 million "dissidents" in Poland by August 1981—the members of Solidarity. These were men and women who, in Alain Besançon's handsome formulation, had "regained the private ownership of their tongues."[108] Their relationship to the Church and its primate was bound to be different than that which prevailed when Cardinal Wyszyński was, indisputably, the *interrex*.

The Resistance Church

The resistance Church that emerged in Poland in response to the "state of war" was ikonically represented by the "Solidarity altar" in Nowa Huta's church of St. Maximilian Mary Kolbe, consecrated by Pope John Paul II during his second pilgrimage to Poland in 1983. On the front of the altar cloth was the inscription, "Mother Of Solidarity, Pray For Us," with "Solidarity" in the union's characteristic jumbly red lettering. Behind the altar was a 7-foot-tall triptych: its centerpiece was the Black Madonna; the left panel was a photograph of the pope holding his head in anguish and prayer; and the right panel was a portrait of Father Jerzy Popiełuszko. (Ten years after martial law, young couples still brought their newly baptized infants to the Solidarity altar to dedicate them to the Holy Mother of Jasna Góra.)

During the early 1980s, it was Father Popiełuszko who came to embody, in a singular way, the resistance Church and its defiance of the Jaruzelski regime's attempt to "normalize" the situation in Poland. Popiełuszko's parish church, St. Stanisław Kostka, was just off Warsaw's "Square of the Defense of the Paris Commune" (now renamed "Woodrow Wilson Square," as it had been before 1945). The neighborhood, Żoliborz, was traditionally bohemian and left wing in its politics: one of the few places in Poland where one might still find an intellectually respectable Marxist. Just after the imposition of martial law, in January 1982, the thirty-five-year-old Father Popiełuszko (whom Cardinal Wyszyński had appointed as chaplain to striking workers at the Warsaw steel mills in August

1980) instituted a monthly "Mass for the Fatherland" at St. Stanisław Kostka. The Mass, and Popiełuszko's quiet eloquence, began to attract enormous crowds from all over Warsaw, indeed from all over the country: "the church would be filled to capacity with some three thousand people, while as many as ten or twelve thousand more stood outside, often in cold or snowy weather."[109]

In those sermons Father Popiełuszko spelled out the implications of John Paul II's challenge to the Poles, to "vanquish evil with good." According to his friend Father Antonin Lewek, Popiełuszko "courageously spoke about Christian ideals of social justice, of freedom, truth, love, and the need to defend basic human rights and the dignity of man as God's child."[110] He preached nonviolence. But he also insisted on resistance: the resistance that would come when people lived "as if." By the very fact of the "Mass for the Fatherland," Father Popiełuszko was asking his people: "Which side will you take? The side of good or the side of evil? Truth or falsehood? Love or hatred?"[111] It was neither sophisticated theology nor sophisticated politics. But it was moral dynamite. And it was unprecedented. As *New York Times* correspondent Michael Kaufman put it later,

> Nowhere else from East Berlin to Vladivostok could anyone stand before ten or fifteen thousand people and use a microphone to condemn the errors of state and party. Nowhere, in that vast stretch encompassing some four hundred million people was anyone else openly telling a crowd that defiance of authority was an obligation of the heart, of religion, manhood, and nationhood.[112]

All of which posed a sufficient threat to the regime that the SB decided to murder Father Jerzy Popiełuszko.

He was driving back to Warsaw from pastoral duties in Bydgoszcz on October 19, 1984, when his car was stopped by three officers of the state security. They beat him to death, and then dumped his battered and trussed body into the Vistula River near Włocławek. On October 20, the state radio announced that Popiełuszko had disappeared and was presumed to have been kidnapped by unknown parties. By the next day, thousands of people from all over the country were flocking to the church in Żoliborz, where Masses were being said every hour. Lech Wałęsa arrived at 11 A.M. on October 21 and, voice shaking, pleaded with the crowd to remain nonviolent: "Dear countrymen: There is a great danger hanging over our Fatherland. I appeal to you, please, do not let anyone provoke you to bloodshed! I beg you to maintain peace and to pray constantly for Father Jerzy."[113] For ten days, the crowds packed the church and the churchyard by the tens of thousands.

And then, on October 30, came the evil news that Father Popiełuszko's body had been dredged from the river. The Stanisław Kostka church was packed, with thirty priests concelebrating at the altar, when the news swept the building. Father Lewek urged the people to remember Jesus' weeping over the death of Lazarus, to cry but not to strike out in anger. And then

> Something very moving happened. The crying crowd managed to show that they forgive. Three times they repeated after the priests, "And forgive us our trespasses as we forgive those who trespass against us. And forgive us our trespasses as we forgive. . . ." It was a Christian answer to the un-Christian deed of the murderers.[114]

Father Popiełuszko was to have been buried in Warsaw's Powazki Cemetery. But the steelworkers whom Popiełuszko had served organized a petition, signed by some 10,000 people, urging Primate Glemp (who had clashed privately with Father Popiełuszko on several occasions) to permit the burial of the priest at St. Stanisław Kostka. A workers' delegation, accompanied by Father Jerzy's mother, met with Glemp on November 1, and it was agreed that an exception would be made. And thus it was that on November 3, 1984, at a funeral Mass celebrated by Cardinal Glemp with hundreds of thousands of Warsawians in the streets, Father Jerzy Popiełuszko, the martyr priest of Solidarity, was laid to rest in his churchyard.[115]

The grave immediately became a shrine, and one of the great pilgrimage sites in a land of pilgrimage. As Janusz Onyszkiewicz put it years later, the Stanisław Kostka churchyard was "a piece of free Poland: around Father Popiełuszko's grave was Solidarity's sanctuary."[116] The new sanctuary continued, symbolically, the ministry of Father Jerzy Popiełuszko, whose sermons had linked the Polish resistance of the 1980s to the Polish defeat of the Teutonic Knights in the fifteenth century, to the 1920 victory over the Red Army, and to the 1944 Warsaw Uprising, reminding his people time and again that "one cannot murder hopes."[117]

The Popiełuszko church and gravesite were also the most

famous example of one of the striking phenomena of the resistant Polish Church in the 1980s: what might be called "moral extraterritoriality." Much as embassies enjoy "extraterritorial" status in host countries and are considered the sovereign territory of the country represented, so did a number of Solidarity churches throughout Poland become virtual embassies from "the society" to itself: places where "the society" could be itself, and strengthen itself, without the incursion of "the power."

Lech Wałęsa's parish, St. Bridget's in Gdańsk, was one of these: the pastor, Father Jankowski, decorated the church with modern art works memorializing prisoners of conscience. So were the Ark and Kolbe churches in Nowa Huta. At the latter, Father Kazimierz Jancarz, the spiritual father of the Lenin Steelworks who was given to describing himself as "just a proletarian" (and who in fact looked like a linebacker for the Chicago Bears), led a comprehensive program of resistance: moral, cultural, social, economic, and political. Father Jancarz stressed that 1989 was an evolution, not a revolution: "because there were no corpses, and that's very important." But the evolution he fostered through the resistance ministry at the Kolbe church in the 1980s had (nonviolently) revolutionary consequences.

Every Thursday there would be Mass at 6 P.M., followed by an educational program. This might involve a debate on the current situation (Wałęsa and many of those who were to become the Solidarity parliamentary faction in 1989 came and spoke), or a lecture on some aspect of Polish history: "We tried," said Father Jancarz, "to give people back their memory." The parish also organized an unofficial Christian university for the Nowa Huta workers, which ran for four years in the mid-1980s. For four to six hours every other Saturday, the workers studied economics, "real history," sociology, psychology, and the technical aspects of organizing and public relations with teachers from the Polish Academy of Sciences, the Jagiellonian University, and the Kraków Polytechnic. Fifty workers were enrolled for each semester, and four semesters got them a degree. The "university" eventually graduated some 400 people, including Father Jancarz himself: "I took the program and learned a lot from it."

Then there were the "evenings of independent Polish culture," in which the church basement was given over to graphics exhibits, theater, political cabarets, jazz, or symphonic music.

Nothing was announced beforehand; publicity was by word of mouth. And between 700 and 1,000 people always attended. (As for the artists, "the only censor was a sense of ethics," according to Father Jancarz.)

The Kolbe church also became the country's first independent television station, run by people sacked at the state-run TV. Over the years, videocams were used to make cassettes for private distribution, but the "station" eventually got broadcasting facilities and did the first film on the life of Jerzy Popiełuszko.

All of this was done in the conviction that "communism had destroyed the normal structures of human life and community, and we had to try to put them back together again." This meant, of course, catechism for the children, a student chaplaincy, and the regular sacramental life of the parish. But it also meant going out to the people where they lived, in their flats and their workplaces. And it meant creating an oasis of independent culture through the "moral extraterritoriality" enjoyed by the Kolbe church.[118]

The Endgame

Adam Michnik insisted, to all who would listen, that Poland between the July 1983 lifting of martial law and the Revolution of 1989 was not "socialism with a human face . . . [but] communism with a few teeth knocked out."[119] In those grim years, the kinds of programs pioneered by the Kolbe church kept the spirit of Solidarity alive. But they also embodied (and deepened) the broader cultural aspects of the final revolution, and thus helped armor people against the embitterment that threatened to overwhelm the land. As Timothy Garton Ash would put it at the time, "an entire world of learning and culture exists independent of the state that claims to control it—a real world of consciousness floating high and free, like Mohammed's coffin, above the false world of being."[120] According to Father Mieczysław Maliński, the Church fought the regime's attempt to enforce a "culture of closed mouths"—which is, of course, no culture at all, because no conversation means no culture.[121]

And the Church's creation of the space for an "independent culture" meshed nicely with the new resistance strategy of the

Solidarity leadership who, during their time in jail, had decided that the reconstruction of civil society was the essential precondition to any serious political and economic change. As Warsaw Solidarity leader Zbigniew Bujak put it, "Once, resistance had meant taking up a gun. Now, people instinctively took up typewriters."[122]

In other words, just as Gandhi had fought the British monopoly on salt in the Raj, so Solidarity and the Church in the mid-1980s challenged "the government's monopoly over information, history, and cultural life."[123] Information was key: as Father Maliński put it a few years later, people came to their church to find out "what the hell was going on in the rest of Poland."[124] So, too, was continuing a high-level discussion of the moral bases of resistance—thus *Tygodnik Powszechny* remained a crucial instrument of the resistance. And there was extensive underground publishing: among other works from the West, Michael Novak's *The Spirit of Democratic Capitalism* was translated into *samizdat* and was "very influential," especially among the Catholic intellectuals in the resistance.[125]

These educational and cultural efforts to maintain and extend the nonviolent Solidarity revolution were given two large boosts by the second and third pilgrimages of John Paul II to his homeland. In May 1983, just before the formal lifting of martial law, the pope came to Poland for eight days and preached against demoralization. "Mother of Jasna Góra," he prayed, "help us to persevere in hope." If John Paul's first pilgrimage in June 1979 broke the fever of the fear that was the basis of social control in the totalitarian state, then the second pilgrimage in 1983 broke the fever of hopelessness that had set in with the "state of war."[126] The pope's third pilgrimage, in June 1987, was an attempt to lay a firm theological and philosophical foundation for the resurrection of Solidarity, through a series of sermons on the true Christian meaning of "solidarity": themes that the pope addressed in detail, and not by geographic accident, in Gdańsk and Gdynia.[127] And shortly after his 1987 visit, the pope published the social encyclical *Sollicitudo Rei Socialis,* which highlighted the "right of economic initiative" and criticized its suppression "in the name of an alleged 'equality,' " which "provokes a sense of frustration or desperation and predisposes people to opt out of national life. . . ."[128] Immediately after the encyclical's publication, the Polish episcopate issued a communiqué declaring that "in the light of Catholic social teaching, it is essential to extend considerably the role of the private sector in the national economy."[129]

But John Paul did more than preach powerful sermons and issue detailed social encyclicals. In a crucial symbolic gesture whose planning had involved much controversy with the Jaruzelski regime, the pope met during his 1983 pilgrimage with Lech Wałęsa. It was billed as a "strictly private meeting," but as Father Józef Tischner put it at the time, bluntly and accurately, "there are no private meetings with the pope."[130] Moreover, and perhaps even more significantly for the long run, the pope, during his 1983 meetings with Jaruzelski, refused to accept a kind of "corporatist solution" in which the Church would enjoy religious and cultural independence while cooperating with the state (through "Catholic unions" or an officially sanctioned Catholic "opposition") to reorganize economic and social life. Some in the Polish Church favored such an accommodation: both to break the impasse that martial law had created and to reestablish the Church as the regime's principal interlocutor. But the pope would not have it. Solidarity had its own integrity and the right to its own independent life, and the Church would support that.[131] There would be no deals behind Solidarity's back.

The government's pressure on the resistance Church continued: in 1988 and 1989, five priests died violently "under suspicious circumstances."[132] But by 1988 the regime's days were rapidly drawing to a close. In April and May, workers at Nowa Huta, and then at the Gdańsk shipyards, struck: and their strike demands, while in the first instance about pay, also included the restoration of the still illegal Solidarity. Demonstrations followed in Warsaw, Kraków, Lublin, and Łódź, with young workers and students chanting "There's no freedom without Solidarity." By late fall the regime was indicating a willingness to negotiate over a different set of social and political arrangements.

But negotiate with whom? Here, once again, the Jaruzelski government tried to play the "Catholic card," suggesting to the Church leadership that it was the obvious choice to represent "society" in any such negotiations. That the Church yet again refused to be put into this position "broke the logjam," according to Janusz Onyszkiewicz, and forced the regime to begin a dialogue with Solidarity after seven long years. (Onyszkiewicz also believes that the pope's commitment to Solidarity was a decisive factor in the Church's decision.)[133]

Thus the regime agreed to the famous Round Table negotiations that began on February 6, 1989, and in which virtually all parties to the social civil war that had been contested since 1947 took a role. Finally, and as a result of those negotiations, partially free elections were held on June 4, 1989, with Solidarity-backed candidates winning all 161 openly contested seats in the Sejm, the lower house of the Polish parliament, and 99 out of 100 seats in the newly created Senate. By August 24, after further political maneuverings, Wałęsa's old adviser from the 1980 Days of August, the intensely Catholic Tadeusz Mazowiecki, had been sworn in as post war Poland's first noncommunist prime minister, with Jacek Kuroń as labor minister and Bronisław Geremek as leader of the Solidarity parliamentary faction.

Father Jerzy Popiełuszko had been right: hopes could not be murdered.

The Challenge of the Free Society

Given the economic and political dislocations that have, inevitably, followed hard on the heels of the fall of Polish communism, there is an understandable tendency in some quarters to look back on the period from 1947 to 1989 with a bit of nostalgia: as a simpler time, in which decisions were easier because the identities of both good guys and bad guys were so patently clear. There is, it must be said, a bit of selective memory going on here: not everyone in Poland saw the situation with crystalline moral clarity; not everyone was a resister; and many people made the grubby daily compromises that were part and parcel of life within the communist culture of the lie. The conflict between "the society" and "the power" went on within individual consciences, as well as between, say, the resistance and the SB. Even in the 1980s, Poland was not one gigantic Robin Hood's band, with General Jaruzelski as the sheriff of Nottingham Forest.

But there is also an important truth hiding inside that wistful longing for a simpler past. Things *are* much more complicated in postcommunist Poland. The issues are no longer as clear as they were in the days when there was one goal—the demise of communism—on which every resistance faction could agree. Now the issues are less susceptible to broad coalition building: full-bore marketization or a more measured approach? Parliamentary democracy or a strong presidency? Poland-in-Europe or a revival of nationalism and Polish exceptionalism? Punishment for former communists or a generous drawing of the curtain across a period of the nation's past? Communism taught two generations of Poles that there was only one correct interpretation of reality and only one correct answer to every social, economic, and political question: and for all that many Poles regarded that answer as so much nonsense, the mental habit of thinking in terms of "one correct answer" has proven hard to shake in the early days of the Third Polish Republic.[134]

Moreover, the moral situation is no longer defined in grand terms as between "us" and "them." But that Manichaean habit of mind endures, and it has created difficulties for Poland's new democracy. "Incorrect" answers to the issues are still thought, in some quarters, to be the result of personal mendacity, corruption, ambition, or cantankerousness, rather than as honest differences of opinion on contingent matters. Or, as Timothy Garton Ash has put it, it is sometimes easier to "live in the truth" than to work with the half truths and compromises that are the normal medium of political exchange in a democratic regime.[135]

Things are also more complicated for the Polish Church. The forty-two-year state of emergency, so to speak, is over. A resistance Church has had to learn how to take up the tasks of democratic culture formation in a political situation in which Catholic social teaching can provide guidelines but no legislative answers, and in a social environment in which there is little tradition of "democratic etiquette."[136] A Church that maintained its strength during forty-two years of repression by celebrating (and demanding) unity-through-uniformity is now exploring the boundaries of unity-within-legitimate-diversity: within the Church, and in terms of the Church's address to social and political issues.

This latter task has been made even more difficult by the peculiar history of Polish communism. The constitutional "separation of Church and state" in communist Poland was a facade behind which the state tried to control the Church: and thus there is a certain disinclination among today's Church leadership to accept at face value the claim that "separation" on the American model (much less the American model as interpreted by, say, the American Civil Liberties Union) is somehow a necessary legal expression of one's commitment to the first human right of religious freedom. Permissive abortion laws were introduced by the Gomułka regime in the mid-1950s as a direct attack on the Church's sexual ethic and its moral construal of family life: and thus it should not have been surprising that the Church pushed quickly for a repeal of those laws, which symbolically incarnated the immorality of communist "legality" insofar as Church leaders were concerned.

On the other hand, on these questions and on such issues as religious education in publicly supported schools, it cannot be said that the Church leadership has learned the arts of persuasion. It, too, had become accustomed to dealing in faits accomplis. As Bishop Tadeusz Gocłowski, Bishop Józef Życiński, and *Tygodnik Powszechny* editor Jerzy Turowicz (three men with different political views) all concede, the Church is struggling to define the relationship between its vocation as teacher and its role in culture formation, on the one hand, and its commitment not to engage in partisan politics, on the other.[137] Journalist Kazimierz Wóycicki believes that the Church needs to develop a "new language to speak to society."[138] Cardinal Macharski, returning to his Leonine image, argues that the Church is no longer the *defensor civitatis*, the defender of the "city"; how, then, shall it be the *defensor hominis*, the defender of man, in service to the *redemptor hominis*, the redeemer of man, in a democracy? The Church's goal, in other words, has to be a situation in which the Church no longer enjoys a virtual monopoly on goodness. How shall it pursue that goal without losing its own unique integrity?

But it should not be thought that the confusions about the relationship between moral norms and democratic politics are solely the Church's affair. There is in fact a lot to be sorted out on this front across Polish society as a whole. And, again, the communist hangover is a major problem. Totalitarianism imposed its own bizarre morality on society, by massive coercion if necessary. One reaction to that coercion has been to swing the pendulum entirely in the other direction. Thus one now hears Poles talking about the necessity of creating "a state with a neutral *Weltanschauung*": as if democracy could only be built on a foundation of moral neutrality.[139] But this is impossible. How would one do it? What sustains the tolerance that in turn makes democratic pluralism possible, if not a virtuous citizenry?

The question, not unlike that in the United States, is one of boundaries: it is a question of agreement on the nature and extent of the moral perimeter of a good and democratic society. Drawn too stringently, the perimeter becomes a noose and the politics of consent erode into the politics of one faction's coercion. Drawn too loosely, the perimeter simply disappears and coercion rears its head in another form: raw majoritarianism, in which every-thing—including, it would have to be presumed, basic human rights—is up for a vote. The United States has not resolved these questions in over two hundred years of constitutional democracy. It would be fatuous to expect that they should have been resolved in Poland in two or three years.

What journalist Kazimierz Wóycicki called the "tremendous challenge of living in freedom," especially after the "artificial life" of communism, is now the defining issue in all post-totalitarian societies. As Dostoevsky's Grand Inquisitor reminds us, tyranny makes for an easier life in many respects. Freedom is not only exhilarating; freedom is frightening. And of all the possible ways of organizing a free society, democracy is, as Churchill famously said, simply the best of a set of unsatisfactory options.

Some of those who once celebrated the Polish Church's contri-bution to the anticommunist resistance now seem to want to return the Church to the sanctuary, allowing occasional ecclesias-tical forays into the public square as the need to preach tolerance intensifies from time to time. But that solution is impossible, given the history of the Church's role in Polish national life. And even if it were, somehow, possible, it would be undesirable. The final revolution—the revolution of the spirit in which people came to understand that politics was not, and could not, be first—made the Revolution of 1989 possible. By reminding democracy that it, too, stands under the judgment of moral norms that transcend the will of legislatures and presidents, the final revolution can make an indispensable contribution to the ongoing political and economic revolution that will, God willing, still be underway in Poland a century from now.

SIX

Czechoslovakia:
A Church Reborn in Resistance

Václav Havel, playwright and quondam antipolitician chosen president of Czechoslovakia in 1989, has been celebrated throughout the world as the author, director, protagonist, and impresario of the Velvet Revolution in his country. And with good reason, for his leadership, which reflected widespread respect for his personal integrity, was indispensable. Havel showed great political skill in November and December 1989. But he also defined the moral nature of the revolution in exquisitely apt terms, as he had once defined with insight and literary elegance the moral corruption that was the essence of the communist system overthrown by the revolutionaries of the Magic Lantern Theater.[1] Still, Václav Havel would probably acknowledge that, like Churchill, his was the voice that gave the roar produced by a lion greater than himself. A significant part of that roar came from an institution once thought to have been tamed by the communists into an aging and domesticated house cat without will, tooth, or claws: the Roman Catholic Church in Czechoslovakia.

Two years after the revolution, in the fall of 1991, Father Oto Mádr, an elfin man of seventy-four dressed in sweater and faded brown suit, was sitting in the office of the Prague-based theological journal he edits: lost, momentarily, in memory. Father Mádr was trying to recall the precise words he had written for the primate of Czechoslovakia, Cardinal František Tomášek, at the outset of the upheaval that toppled Czechoslovakia's neo-Stalinist regime in six heady weeks—words that would be read to a cheering throng by another dissident priest, Father Václav Malý, the thirty-nine-year-old master of ceremonies at several of the great public events of the Velvet Revolution. After a brief moment

Father Mádr's memory cleared and Cardinal Tomášek's call to public resistance rang out again, however softly for its being repeated in the cramped offices of *Teologické Texty* rather than from a balcony overlooking 250,000 protesters in Prague's Wenceslas Square:

Citizens of Bohemia, Moravia, and Slovakia:

I returned from Rome some hours ago. . . . I must not remain silent at the very moment when you have joined together in a mighty protest against the great injustice visited upon us over four decades. It is impossible to have confidence in a state leadership that is unwilling to speak the truth, and that denies basic human rights and freedoms. . . . These people cannot be trusted. . . . We are surrounded by countries that, in the past or presently, have destroyed the [prison] bars of the totalitarian system. . . . We must not wait any longer. The time has come to act. We need a democratic government. . . . *We are with you, friends, in the struggle for freedom.*

For forty years we have been oppressed by totalitarianism. With gratitude and respect, I am addressing with special urgency the victims of cruel violence. You are the object of Christ's words: "Blessed are those who hunger and thirst for righteousness, for they shall be satisfied.". . . I pray that you take the way of nonviolence. Let us fight for the good by good means. Our oppressors are showing us how short-lived the victories of hatred, evil, and revenge are. . . .

And I also want to address you, my Catholic brothers and sisters, joined by your priests. In this hour of destiny for our country, not a single one of you may stand apart. Raise your voice again: this time, in unity with all other citizens, Czechs and Slovaks, members of other nationalities, believers and unbelievers. Religious liberty cannot be separated from other human rights. Freedom is indivisible.

Let me end with the words that once rang through our history: "With God's help, our destiny is in our hands."[2]

Father Mádr's text, its endorsement by the octogenarian Cardinal Tomášek, and its triumphant proclamation by Father Malý, was the symbolic culmination of forty-one years of intense struggle, much of it underground and all of it dangerous. Mádr, Tomášek, and Malý among the Czech clergy; the underground bishop Ján Chryzostom Korec in Slovakia; lay leaders like Václav and Kamila Benda, Pavel Bratinka, Silvester Krčméry, and

František Mikloško—these were people who, according to Czechoslovakia's Stalinist and neo-Stalinist leaders, were not supposed to happen. Or if they happened, they were to be immediately and ruthlessly suppressed. But there they were, among the leaders of Havel's Civic Forum and its Slovak counterpart, Public Against Violence. Their personal resistance gave birth, over time, to a reborn Church. And that Church in turn helped midwife the rebirth of democracy in Czechoslovakia.

From Gigantism to "Normalization"

Communism, the West was often reminded during the days of détente, was "not monolithic." Which was, in a sense, true: some communist regimes, and their distortions of human life and community, were even more repulsive than others. Czechoslovakia's communist leaders could take credit, if that be the word, for two of the more grotesque political expressions of Stalinist ideology during the forty years of the Yalta imperial system: the gigantism of Klement Gottwald and his successors in the first decades after World War II, and the neo-Stalinist "normalization" program of Gustáv Husák that followed the imposition of the Brezhnev Doctrine and the collapse of the Prague Spring of 1968.

Czechoslovakia lies in "central," not "eastern," Europe (Prague is some hundred miles *west* of Vienna), and as one contemporary guidebook puts it, life in the Czech lands and Slovakia has been "formed and deformed by the cataclysmic pressures of a millennium of continental madness."[3] "Deformation" nicely captures the impact of the regime of Klement Gottwald, the head of the Czechoslovak communist party who seized power in 1948 and immediately began to implement a draconian system of social control modeled on the practices first perfected by Gottwald's Kremlin master, Josef Stalin.

Gottwald, a notorious lecher and drunkard, made some efforts to link his enterprise to Czech (if not Slovak) history: in one memorably absurd locution, Gottwald, asked why his militantly atheistic regime was financially supporting the renovation of Prague's Bethlehem Chapel (the headquarters of Jan Hus during the pre-Reformation controversies that roiled Bohemia in the early fifteenth century) answered that "Five hundred years ago, the people of Prague were already fighting for communism."[4] But a Stalinist cult of personality, and Stalinist gigantism of a particularly vulgar sort, were the true hallmarks of the regime that Gottwald created, and which survived his widely unlamented death in 1953.

There was, for example, The Statue.

Gottwald himself having failed to mummify satisfactorily when, on his demise, attempts were made to transform him into a Czechoslovak Lenin on display in his own mausoleum, Czechoslovakia's communist leaders settled for erecting a colossal statue of Stalin, about a hundred feet tall, on a hillside in the Letná gardens overlooking Prague's splendid baroque Old Town. Completed in 1955 and dedicated amidst an orgy of rhetoric, the statue (which depicted Stalin leading a worker, a female heroine, a soldier, and a botanist into the classless future) was a perfect expression of communist taste and communist contempt for Prague's magnificent architectural heritage. Alas for the designers, the statue's dedication was followed, within a year, by Nikita Khrushchev's famous speech denouncing Stalin's distortions of orthodox communist ideology and his cult of personality: after which, the Prague Stalin was immediately covered with scaffolding. Six years of argument followed, and in October 1962, the inspiration of the Gottwald regime was dynamited, leaving behind a massive concrete plinth (inside which a rock club was formed, after the 1989 revolution).

Vulgar gigantism typified Czechoslovak communism before the Prague Spring in ways other than the architectural. Mass gymnastic displays (in 1960, over three-quarters of a million athletes gyrated together) were a regular feature of public life: fittingly enough, they were dubbed the *Spartakiáda*. The buildings along Prague's Wenceslas Square, site of massive rallies which workers were obliged to attend on May Day and other feasts on the communist liturgical calendar, were festooned with great signs ("We shall overfulfill the Plan by 143%!"). And the square's lampposts still carry the ubiquitous loudspeakers through which what must have seemed an endless stream of blather poured forth from the guardians of ideological orthodoxy.

Nor did Khrushchev's strictures against Stalin's "cult of personality" prevent two generations of Czechoslovak schoolchildren from being dragooned through the wonders of the Klement

Gottwald Museum (now a savings bank) and the Museum of the National Security Corps and the Army of the Interior Ministry. The latter, a tribute to the border patrol and to the loathed secret police, the "StB" (*Stati Bezpecnost*), contained what was perhaps the single most telling symbol of Czechoslovak communism: the stuffed remains of "Brek," a guard dog "who pounced on sixty fleeing miscreants, sustained two shot-gun wounds"—and was, presumably, a model to be emulated by the children whose education would be enriched by contemplation of his canine services to Real Existing Socialism.[5]

The Stalinism of Klement Gottwald and his immediate successors was brutish and cruel: the dictatorship of thugs. But there was something even more sinister about the sophisticated neo-Stalinism of Gustáv Husák in the years from 1969 to 1989. For it was during the Husák period that the "culture of the lie" so brilliantly dissected by Václav Havel metastasized and came close to killing civic culture and civil society in Czechoslovakia.

Alexander Dubček's 1968 Prague Spring, and the Soviet bloc invasion that crushed it that summer, had demonstrated two things: that a generation of Stalinist ideological indoctrination had not "taken" in Czechoslovakia, and that the alternative to firm Czechoslovak communist control of the country was Soviet occupation. Control was thus reasserted in the person of the Gustáv Husák, himself a former victim of a Stalin-era purge, who was chosen first secretary of the Czechoslovakian communist party in April 1969 on a platform of "normalization." The statistics of the immediate score settling were bad enough: 150,000 fled the country; 500,000 were expelled from the party; perhaps another million lost their jobs or were demoted. But the devil's bargain that Husák eventually enforced on the people of Czechoslovakia—embodied in Václav Havel's parable of the greengrocer (see Chapter 2)—was worse.

The people of the Czech lands, in particular, have more than a little of the "good soldier Švejk"—satirist Jaroslav Hašek's fictional antihero and rebel against absurd authority—in them. Thus the initial reaction to the destruction of the hopes generated by the Prague Spring was an outburst of public Švejkism. Prague citizens politely gave directions to Soviet tank crews: without telling them that they had just reversed the street signs. The leader of the invading Warsaw Pact forces, marshal of the Red Army Andrei

Grechko, was nicknamed "El Grechko" after "his tanks strafed a particularly interesting design onto the National Museum" at the top of Wenceslas Square. Dissident students forced the cancellation of a meeting with new party secretary Husák by chanting continually, "Long live the Party! Long live Husák!"[6] There were even moments of more direct nose thumbing: a happy mob of Prague celebrants sacked the Aeroflot office in Wenceslas Square when the Czechoslovak national ice hockey team beat the hated Soviets in 1969. And at a far graver level there was the self-martyrdom of Jan Palach, the student who immolated himself in front of Prague's National Museum in January 1969, and whose funeral procession was composed of 800,000 mourning citizens.

But defiance—overt or Švejkist—is only possible while morale remains high. And that is precisely what Husák's "normalization" killed: public morale. Rebellion may have continued privately, behind closed doors. But, over time, Kafkaesque symbols like the sign in the greengrocer's window replaced Švejkism. And Czechoslovakia under "normalization" was reduced to what one mournful observer called "a Biafra of the spirit."

Husák's "normalization" had its physically cruel antecedents in the repressions of the Gottwald years. Under "normalization," the StB became an ever more ubiquitous presence in Czechoslovak life; and the reach of its agents was expanded by an order of magnitude through the workings of a nationwide network of informants and accomplices (a phenomenon that, in itself, contributed to the moral pollution of the country). Dissidents were routinely beaten during interrogations. Menial manual labor was the lot of those who were politically active against the regime; Pavel Bratinka, now the leader of a neoconservative political party and Prague think tank, used to translate articles from *Commentary* and the *Salisbury Review* for underground circulation while working as a stoker.[7] Children were punished (by denial of educational, travel, and employment opportunities) for the ideological deviance of their parents, and spouses were abused by StB interrogators and house-searchers for the political activities of their (often imprisoned) husbands or wives.

But Real Existing Socialism under the Husák regime differed from pre-1968 Gottwaldism in that it reached back to the old Roman tyrannical principle of "bread and circuses" as its chief means of social control over the torpid mass of the population. Husák's "deal" was, in effect, that Czechoslovakia would be fed and entertained (within limits) for so long as ideological ortho- doxy was publicly sustained.[8] The regime knew that such protes- tations of ideological fervor as rang through Wenceslas Square on May Day were false. So did most of those chanting the approved slogans and applauding the stultifying rhetoric of the party hacks. But that was the deal: they pretend to pay us, we pretend to work; they pretend to preach, we pretend to believe; they pretend to be our representatives, we pretend to elect them. "Normalization" under Husák was not the absurd world of Šwejk, a world which could be lampooned and thus escaped. "Normalization" after the collapse of the Prague Spring was the more cruelly absurd world of Kafka, from which there was no exit, and in which a pervasive and soul-rotting cynicism became the dominant attitude of both rulers and ruled. It was, to go back once again to Havel, the cul- ture of the lie. And both masters and serfs were liars, to one degree or another.[9]

Husákian "normalization" was not entirely successful, of course. Dissent continued: most prominently in Charter 77, the landmark human rights manifesto issued by a wide-ranging group of independent cultural leaders, former communists, and church people in 1977. (Husák's regime displayed its true and awful col- ors at the funeral of Jan Patočka, one of the three leaders of the Chartists, who died of a cerebral hemorrhage after an intensive StB interrogation on his Charter activities. At his funeral, a gov- ernment helicopter hovered a few yards above Patočka's open grave while attempts were made to read a memorial statement.[10]) After the Polish upheavals of 1979 and 1980, and then after the martial law period in Poland, Czechoslovak dissidents and activists met clandestinely in the heavily wooded areas along the Polish-Czechoslovak border with Solidarity leaders, in a kind of ongoing seminar into the problems and prospects of resistance.

But unlike Poland, Czechoslovakia lacked a unified center of ongoing, institutional, nationwide, anticommunist opposition (such as the Polish Church). And, until the mid-1980s, the Czechoslovak resistance tended to be more fragmented than in Poland, lacking, as it did, a focal point such as Solidarity. Husákian "normalization," which had been more successful in atomizing Czechoslovak society (especially in the Czech lands of Bohemia and Moravia) than had the Polish communists, made organizing all the more difficult.

Yet thanks to the dogged efforts of the Chartists the thinking and organizing went on, in this, one of the most successfully repressed of the Warsaw Pact countries. And that thinking and organizing, amplified by the activism (and prayers) of an underground Church that, by the mid-1980s, came bursting into a new and defiant public life, produced the Velvet Revolution of 1989 in six breathtaking weeks. Gottwald and Husák, the old Stalinism and the new, failed. And if it was Václav Havel who embodied the mind and heart of the opposition which produced that failure, it was the Roman Catholic Church, which Gottwald and Husák thought they had brought to heel, that nourished and gave expression to the religious dimensions of the Revolution's soul.

A Taste of Ashes

In talking with older veterans of the relentless communist persecution of the Catholic Church in Czechoslovakia, one often hears the summary phrase, "Everything was destroyed." It is, of course, an exaggeration, if an understandable and pardonable one: for "everything" was not destroyed. The life and ministry of the Church continued, if under terribly restrictive conditions. Believers transmitted their faith to their children. Priests were ordained, some clandestinely. The sacraments were celebrated, if but occasionally in some areas. A modicum of religious instruction took place. The Church and the Faith survived Czechoslovak communism. But there was indeed a tremendous amount of institutional destruction. And the phrase, "everything was destroyed," aptly captures the intention, if not the final accomplishment, of Klement Gottwald, Gustáv Husák, and their cronies.

That was not what the Church's leaders expected at the end of the Second World War—the war that became inevitable at Munich, bitterly remembered in Czechoslovakia as the world-historical decision that was taken "about us, without us." After the war, according to Father Oto Mádr, and with the reconstitution of a Czechoslovak democracy that had, it was hoped, learned from the mistakes (including the anticlericalism) of the interwar republic, the Church was full of optimism about the future. And that optimism translated itself into action, for the period immediately after the war saw the flowering of a number of new Catholic movements, involving youth ministry, family life, and religious publishing.[11]

Then came Gottwald and the communists, and the Church became, in Václav Benda's phrase, "the first exemplary object of systematic repression."[12] At the time of the 1948 coup that stopped Czechoslovak democracy for forty-one hard years, Catholics represented some two-thirds of the population of the country, and were the overwhelming majority in Slovakia. Gottwald's strategy toward this potential source of resistance was two-pronged: to break the Church's institutional network wherever possible, and to control (through a combination of legal restrictions and cooptation) whatever was left. (The communists were also eager to sever the Church's lifeline to Rome, and the apostolic nuncio was, accordingly, expelled.)

The breakage was considerable. The new movements were quickly dismantled and their leaders shipped off to prisons and labor camps. Archbishop Josef Beran of Prague (a leader in the anti-Nazi resistance who had survived three years in the concentration camps, including Dachau) and all the other bishops in the country were interned or imprisoned, as were leading clerical and lay activists: the notorious uranium mines in Bohemia, a contemporary analogue to the Sardinian pits to which Christians were consigned in the days of the catacombs, were a frequent destination for the prisoners. Eleven of thirteen seminaries were closed. Religious orders were banned in 1950: the monks, brothers, and nuns were evicted from their monasteries and convents in the course of two nights. Novices were conscripted or sent home; some 11,000 of those under vows were dispatched for "reeducation" to prisons and labor camps where most of them spent an average of five years in circumstances of malnutrition, overwork, and disease that led to an appalling death rate. (The heads of these communities were, in many cases, not released until the Prague Spring.)[13] The Church's schools were closed and its extensive land holdings confiscated. Church publications were shut down. In the Carpatho-Ruthenian districts of eastern Slovakia, the Greek Catholic Church was wholly suppressed after forcible attempts to merge these Byzantine-rite Catholics into the Orthodox Church failed; the Rusyns' one bishop, Pavol Gojdic, died in Leopoldov prison in 1960.[14]

What could not be destroyed was subjected to the most severe controls: as Bishop František Lobkowicz, a student under Czechoslovak Stalinism and a young priest during the "normalization," put it, "They wanted us to be afraid, always."[15] The StB worked tirelessly to penetrate Church organizations, and there is little doubt that some priests ordained during the forty-one years of persecution were active agents of the internal security service. Then there was Article 178 of the criminal code, according to which "the clergy can carry out their ministry only with the prior approval of the state," but which also regulated the activities of anyone involved in "pastoral activity" and which promised state sanctions against anyone attempting to "obstruct" the state's oversight of the Church.[16] Under Article 178, clergy were "licensed" as employees of the state; the revocation of a license meant that a priest could no longer function publicly and had to seek some other form of employment, lest he be arrested for parasitism. The present archbishop of Prague, for example, Miloslav Vlk, spent fifteen years as a window washer when his license was revoked. The ideal cleric, to the Czechoslovak communist leadership, was one who limited himself to a cultic role, performed only occasionally.

Communist attempts to control the dwindling Czechoslovak presbyterate (there were 7,000 priests in the country in 1948, and about 3,000 in 1985) included close attention to the two remaining seminaries in the country, in Litoměřice and Bratislava. Students for the priesthood could attend seminary only with state permission (and pressure was brought to bear on secondary school teachers who might be inclined to approve such an application for a local student—"What has happened to your political work?" they would be asked by the StB). Moreover, those admitted to seminary knew that their teachers were usually collaborators of one sort or another, and that their fellow students were not always what they appeared to be.[17] Foreign theological journals and books were banned as, after 1974, were radios.[18]

Perhaps the most notorious of the Czechoslovak communists' schemes to control the clergy by means of cooptation was the priests' organization, "Pacem in Terris," which functioned as a propaganda mouthpiece on matters of foreign and domestic policy throughout the Husák "normalization." Some of these "pax terriers," as dissident laypeople styled them, were dedicated supporters of the communist regime. Others joined "Pacem in Terris" out of weakness: the StB network quickly identified priests who liked to travel, or who wanted a plum assignment, or who were short of money; and if many resisted these blandishments, others succumbed. A third group of "Pacem in Terris" members involved those who knew that the "pax terriers" were an embarrassment to the Church (at best), but who thought that a formal affiliation with the organization was necessary if they were going to be able to function pastorally—if they wanted to repair their church, or get religious books, or conduct catechism classes with less hassle than usual.[19]

Whatever the motivation, though, the fact of "Pacem in Terris" not only provided the regime with an instrument for its propaganda purposes; it depressed the spirits of those activist laity who were making an effort to preserve an independent religious life, according to Václav Vaško, the premier historian of the persecuted Czechoslovak Church. "Pacem in Terris" also led to a kind of schizophrenia within the clergy, a private "war within each priest." But that schizophrenia in turn created what Vaško describes as "the lie that 'Pacem in Terris' [and other such forms of collaboration were] the only way to save the Church for the future." The net result, for both activist laity and those clergy susceptible to this falsehood, was, according to Vaško, "demoralization": which was, again, the overarching goal of Husákian "normalization."[20]

The suborning of priests and the manipulation of seminarians were parts of the regime's efforts to control the Church's formal leadership. But the communists' determination to bring the Church to heel showed itself more broadly in the use of the state-run educational system as a carrot—or stick—by which to reward or threaten religiously serious parents. Parents' employment and travel opportunities were dependent on their declining to request religious education for their children; and parents who did so request knew that they were thereby constraining their children's educational and professional opportunities as well as their own. Constant StB pressure to maintain ideological conformity was visited on teachers, and slogans like "There will never be prosperity until the last priest is struck down by the last remaining stone from the last remaining church" were features of secondary school life in intensely Catholic Slovakia—where teachers were also paid a bonus for dissuading their students from attending religious education classes.[21] Employment discrimination was also the fate of those who chose to be married in a religious ceremony—with the result that, while rates of baptism remained relatively high throughout the forty-one years of communism in Czechoslovakia, only 3 percent of Catholics getting married in Czechoslovakia publicly celebrated a church wedding, by the late 1980s.[22]

In the face of this relentless repression—the overt repression of the Gottwald period and in the aftermath of the Prague Spring, and the more subtle (and insidious) repression of the Husák "normalization"—the human solidarity that makes civil society possible began to break down. Kamila Benda, wife of philosopher and Charter 77 activist Václav Benda, recalled that, during the eight years she and her husband were denied a telephone, not one neighbor in their apartment building ever offered Mrs. Benda the use of a phone; the neighbors had, doubtless, observed the fifteen searches that the StB had conducted in the Bendas' flat, and had surely noted that every visitor to the apartment was subsequently interrogated by the internal security forces. Sympathy—in the form of a friendly word, or a few clothes for the Benda children, or a little money—was always expressed privately, never publicly: "It was always one-on-one," said Mrs. Benda. "There were never three."[23]

But if there was acquiescence and cowardice, even within the Church community, there were also many great acts of courage. Father Oto Mádr was condemned to death in 1951 as a "spy," and for the next year awoke every morning with the expectation that he would be shot, that day. His sentence was then reduced to life imprisonment, of which he eventually served fifteen years. It was, he recalled, a "very happy period of my life, with many conversions. . . . [Being in prison was] very fine, it gave the Church a new apostolate." The apostolate of the prisons and work camps was, to be sure, distinctive. Father Mádr would celebrate Mass clandestinely, ten drops of sacramental wine having been coaxed out of dried grapes. Communion was then distributed throughout the camp by the barber, who, during his round of weekly haircuts and shaves, carried small pieces of Eucharistic bread with him in the only ciborium available: a piece of cigarette paper. Father Mádr also remains proud of the prison "Catholic weekly" in which he wrote news, a biblical meditation, perhaps a fragment of a sermon: on a folded bit of paper, about two inches square, which "had to be small so that we could eat it" if necessary (which meant: if detected).[24]

The Slovak lay activist Silvester Krčméry, imprisoned thirteen years for "treason" (i.e., the evangelization of young people and workers, and the translation of papal social encyclicals into Slovak), also looked back on his days in prisons and labor camps—seven years of which were in the isolation cells reserved for particularly recalcitrant offenders—with a measure of quiet satisfaction. As Dr. Krčméry put it, "It was not very gay, but it was bearable because of God, and because of our spiritual life. In isolation, meditation was like spiritual weightlessness—you lost contact with the room and the prison."[25]

Acts of quiet heroism—and resistance—went on by the countless thousands throughout the forty-one years. Bishop Lobkowicz, remembering his days as a young priest, recalled that it was "easier to get lost in the big apartment skyscrapers"—and thus conduct a Bible class, or a discussion of the pope's most recent statement on the family.[26] Father Malý, whose license had been revoked and who faced over 250 StB interrogations because of his Charter 77 activities, used his time as a manual laborer, stoking boilers in Prague's Meteor Hotel, to develop new techniques of evangelization, presenting the Gospel to his rough-hewn co-workers not as a set of catechism answers, but as an invitation to follow Christ into a fuller way of life.[27] Kamila Benda was allowed to visit her husband quarterly during his four years in prison: for an hour each time, with a guard present to enforce the rule against the discussion of anything but family affairs. And on every visit, she brought her husband communion, concealed in the palm of her hand and given to her by a close friend, a Dominican priest, himself functioning underground.[28] None of these brave men and women, today, thinks of him or herself as a "martyr-confessor." Yet that, according to the ancient tradition of the Church, is precisely what they were.

Still, and for all the quiet heroism and the occasional acts of public defiance, Husák's "normalization" meant that the Church, and particularly the leadership structures of the Church, had a thick hand constantly around its windpipe. And that fact led to

one of the most controversial initiatives in the *Ostpolitik* of Pope
Paul VI, the attempt to reach a modus non moriendi with the
communist government of Czechoslovakia.

Efforts by the Holy See to break through the ice field of confrontation with Czechoslovak communism began even before
Husák's days in power. In 1965, at the personal request of Paul VI,
Archbishop Beran, who symbolized the Church's refusal to have
any truck with the regime, accepted the red hat of a cardinal and
exile in Rome. It was thought, presumably, that the archbishop
was an obstacle to any reasonable accommodation with the
regime. Negotiations between the state and the Holy See followed,
beginning in 1966. And in 1973 four residential bishops were
appointed after the candidates had been vetted by Archbishop
Agostino Casaroli and his colleague, Msgr. Giovanni Cheli. Two
of them, however, Josef Vrána and Josef Feranec, had been leading
members of "Pacem in Terris" and were consequently snubbed by
the Catholic laity.[29]

The *Ostpolitik* of the Holy See in Czechoslovakia was driven
by a deep concern about the eventual eradication of the Church's
hierarchy (and thus, over time, of its sacramental life); and so the
focus remained on the appointment of bishops after the initial
agreement of 1973. In its attempts to create a decent atmosphere
for negotiation, the Holy See even went so far as to curtail the
activities of one of the true heroes of Catholic resistance in
Czechoslovakia, Bishop Ján Chryzostom Korec. Korec, a Jesuit,
had been secretly ordained to the episcopate in 1951 at age
twenty-seven (at the time of his appointment, Korec was
wrestling oil barrels in a Bratislava warehouse). He managed to
function clandestinely as a bishop until 1960 when, discovered,
he was dispatched to prison with a twelve-year sentence. Released
during the Prague Spring, he was sent back to jail to finish his
original term in 1974, but international pressure forced his
release. Korec then worked in Bratislava as a factory laborer, elevator repairman, and night watchman, all the while continuing
his underground episcopal ministry. But on August 24, 1976, a
Vatican envoy, Father John Bukovsky, came to Czechoslovakia
and told Korec that Pope Paul VI had asked that he cease his
underground activities as a bishop, and particularly that he stop
ordaining priests clandestinely. This request, according to Father
Bukovsky, was the result of a governmental demarche in which

the Czechoslovak communists had informed the Holy See that repression of the Church would ease when the activities of the underground Church stopped. Korec protested to Bukovsky that the Holy See's position was mistaken and that the Vatican's hopes were sure to be frustrated, given the mendacity typical of the regime. But Bukovsky said that the pope's mind was made up, and Korec agreed to obey. Alas, the result was precisely as Bishop Korec had predicted: there was no letup in repression.[30]

Indeed, no new bishops were permitted in Czechoslovakia between 1973 and the Velvet Revolution; by that point, ten of the country's thirteen dioceses were without a residential bishop, a situation without parallel in communist countries (with the obvious exception of Albania, where no clergy were permitted at all). Moreover, under the influence of the *Ostpolitik* and out of his sense of loyalty and obedience to the Holy See and the Holy Father, the primate of Bohemia, Cardinal František Tomášek, took what many activist Catholics perceived as a weak and ineffectual stance toward the regime, going so far in 1977 as to criticize Catholic participation in Charter 77.

Thus the situation by the late 1970s was grim in the extreme. An underground Church was alive and vigorous, if under constant pressure, especially in Slovakia. But the "legal" Church was both penetrated and manipulated. An aging clergy made access to public sacramental life difficult. The machinations of "Pacem in Terris," and of bishops perceived as excessively acquiescent to the state, strained relations between the formal ecclesiastical leadership and lay activists. Serious religious education had been denied to two generations of Czechs and Slovaks, and Catholic intellectual life was almost wholly clandestine. Catholics determined to practice their faith continued to suffer educational, employment, and civil disabilities, and were continually harassed by the StB. Charter 77 had energized a new human rights movement amidst the torpor of Husákian "normalization," but those priests and laity who signed the Charter got no help, and in fact criticism, from their formal religious leaders. Even the lifeline to Rome seemed strained to the breaking point: Vatican *Ostpolitik* was widely viewed with dismay by the most dedicated priests and laity, who believed that the Church, had it remained on this course, "would have sunk into a catastrophe."[31]

The taste of ashes was in many mouths.

Rebirth in Resistance

On April 11, 1985, 1,100 priests, a third of the presbyterate of Czechoslovakia, concelebrated Mass at the Moravian shrine of Velehrad: "We felt how strong we were," remembered Bishop František Lobkowicz, then a thirty-six-year-old pastor.[32] At the Mass, Cardinal Tomášek, then eighty-six years old, read a letter from Pope John Paul II, urging the priests "in the spirit of St. Methodius to continue intrepidly on the path of evangelization and testimony, even if the present situation makes it arduous, difficult, and even bitter."[33] Three months later, on July 5, 1985, the phoenix of the Czechoslovakian Church decisively rose from the ashes of "normalization," as some 150,000 to 200,000 Catholic pilgrims came to Velehrad to mark the 1,100th anniversary of the death of St. Methodius. The communists had long tried to promote and transform the event, which turned into the country's largest independent gathering since the collapse of the Prague Spring, as an official "peace festival." But when communist leaders welcomed the visitors to Velehrad in these terms, the Catholics roared back, "This is a pilgrimage! We want the pope! We want Mass!"[34]

There had been, clearly, a dramatic change in the state of affairs from the Vatican-ordered cessation of Bishop Korec's underground activities in 1976 to this explosion of Catholic energy at Velehrad in 1985. A Church that had seemed almost supine, in public terms, was now defending itself on the basis of the universally acknowledged right of religious freedom. Moreover, the Church had begun to assert itself publicly as a vocal institutional supporter of human rights for all, and had thus become a major obstacle to "normalization" as construed by the Husák regime. What had happened?

The resurrection of the Czechoslovakian Church and its transformation into a public defender of the rights of all began in earnest on October 16, 1978, with the election of Pope John Paul II. That, at least, is the view one hears from all the major participants in the reconstruction of public Czechoslovak Catholicism. It was not, of course, the case that the Church had died, prior to 1978. But its public face was, so to speak, heavily veiled. John Paul II helped lift the veil, and in so doing bridged the gap between the legal and illegal Church, between the official Church and its underground, in ways that would help shape the Velvet Revolution and topple the Husák regime eleven years later.

What was it about the election of John Paul II that would cause the Slovak historian František Mikloško to describe it thirteen years later as "historic" and "of tremendous importance" to the revolution?[35] In the first instance, activist Czechs and Slovaks now believed that they had a pope who "understood their situation": a pope who was a fellow Slav, who had lived under communism and struggled against it, and who embodied the successful resistance of the Polish Church, to which many Catholic Czechoslovaks looked for a model of effective Catholicism under totalitarian conditions.[36] As Father Václav Malý put it, "We saw the pope differently than some seemed to do in the West. From the outset, we saw someone in Rome who was an example of deep faith, who understood the communists, who wasn't naive, and who defended us. The pope played an enormously important role [in shaping the revolution]."[37]

Bishop František Lobkowicz remembered in particular the electrifying impact of the pope's inaugural homily, with its call, "Open the doors to Christ . . . . Be not afraid!" "The communists wanted us to be afraid," said Lobkowicz. "After that, we weren't afraid anymore."[38] Historian Václav Vaško remembered that occasion, and the new pope's persistent emphasis on human rights in the early days of his papal ministry, as a signal to the Church leadership in Czechoslovakia that it could no longer remain silent: that it had to speak, not in terms of demanding benefices from the state, but in defense of rights that it enjoyed because of the very humanity of its members. The new pope, Vaško recalled, had brought the catechesis of the Church and the approach of Charter 77 into sync with each other.[39] Those deeply involved with the underground or illegal Church were also keenly aware of the help that the clandestine Church had been given by Karol Wojtyła when he was archbishop of Kraków.

This public papal emphasis on inalienable human rights as the prior rights of persons, not as goods to be requisitioned politically from the state, struck many Czech and Slovak Catholic activists as a distinctively new mode of Vatican *Ostpolitik*.[40] Charter 77 activist and philosopher Václav Benda also found in the new pope's teaching a bridge between Catholic theological humanism and the concept of a "parallel polis" on which he had been working with other Chartists.[41]

Communism, especially under Husák's "normalization," had cut most of the sinews and tendons of civil society in Czechoslovakia. Thus the first step in resistance to the communist culture of the lie had to be cultural, not political: effective resistance would begin with the reconstitution of civil society. And that process of civic rejuvenation would be born from the decisions of individuals to live "in the truth," to live "as if" they were free people. As Benda put it in May 1978, "If the chief form of the present political evil is a restrictive heaviness that all citizens carry on their shoulders and at the same time bear *within* them, then the only possibility is to shake that evil off, escape its power, and to seek truth [through] . . . a genuine quest in which everything 'good and evil' in the development of politics will be re-examined, thought through, and reinterpreted. . . . The election of Pope John Paul II demonstrates that such a view . . . is not just a personal folly of mine, and that it can become realistic on a worldwide scale . . . ."[42]

The second conclave of 1978, the new pope's strong public emphasis on human rights, the example of his historic visit to Poland in June 1979, and, one may surmise, conversations between the two Slavic churchmen, also had a profound impact on Cardinal František Tomášek, the archbishop of Prague. During the pontificate of Paul VI, Tomášek had been something less than a visible sign of contradiction against the government, and for many reasons. He was an obedient son of the Church, and as the *Ostpolitik* of Paul VI seemed to require a stance other than confrontation, Tomášek was, accordingly, rather quiet on public matters. His criticism of Catholic participation in Charter 77 may well have been shaped in part by this *Ostpolitik*-driven concern for a certain public calm in the relations between Church and state; according to Father Václav Malý, Cardinal Tomášek was also worried that Church involvement with the Charter would require an untoward politicization of a religious institution.[43] Then there was the problem of the "pax terriers," and the aging cardinal's evident lack of certainty about the ultimate loyalties of many of his clerical troops. Nor would Tomášek have found support from those of his fellow bishops able to function publicly (especially Vrána and Feranec) for a more vigorous resistance against the pressures of the government.

Tomášek's situation changed, dramatically, with the election of John Paul II: and so did Cardinal Tomášek. Tomášek could, with Wojtyła in Rome, be assured of public papal support for a forthright defense of the Church's rights and the basic human rights of believers. The 1982 instruction from the Vatican's Congregation for the Clergy, banning priests' involvement with partisan politics, led to a decline in the numbers and influence of "Pacem in Terris" (as John Paul II surely knew it would).[44] Assured of his flanks being covered, so to speak, Cardinal Tomášek also began to surround himself in the early 1980s with a group of priest advisors committed to a more activist role for the Church; the group included Father Mádr, Father Josef Zvěřina, and Father Tomáš Halík. (It may be taken as yet another sign of Tomášek's personal revolution—and personal integrity—that Father Zvěřina, whom Father Malý would later describe as having been, with Father Mádr, one of the two "pillars" of the resistance Church in the 1970s, had publicly chastised Cardinal Tomášek for his criticism of Catholic participation in Charter 77.[45])

This triad of advisers, whose counsel would later be amplified by the cardinal's conversations with the banned Father Malý, helped Tomášek to see the Charter, not as a partisan instrument, but as a civic initiative: moreover, an initiative aimed, not at the seizure of political power, but at forming the intellectual and moral basis of a broad coalition of defenders of human dignity and human rights, including the first right of religious freedom. Thus Tomášek came to the view that the participation of ex-communists and nonbelievers in the Charter was not a trap for the Church, but was in fact one of the movement's strengths. Father Malý recalled that it was also important for the cardinal that human rights be understood, among the believers, as "growing from the roots of the Gospel and the Gospel imperative to care for the persecuted": a case that was, again, far easier to make given the preaching of John Paul II on his pastoral visits around the world.[46]

The net result, as Pavel Bratinka put it several years later, was "this singular spectacle of the cardinal getting older *and tougher* at the same time."[47] Václav Benda, under great pressure from the

StB in the late 1970s and early 1980s, felt the difference personally, in the support he received from the Church while he was
imprisoned for his Charter activities. And from 1983, when
Cardinal Tomášek gave his blessing to another Catholic activist,
Marie Ruth Kréková, as the spokesman for the Charter (earlier
spokesmen having been picked off by the StB, one by one, and
jailed), the octogenarian primate was "fully engaged" with the
Catholic resistance, according to Benda. Nor did Benda deem it
wholly coincidental that it was during this period, the mid-1980s,
that the Catholic and Christian component became the largest
part of the human rights movement: which was the de facto political opposition, precisely because it was the moral-cultural opposition to "normalization."[48]

Thus under the inspiration of the Polish pope, and with the support of the aging and toughening primate, Czech and Slovak
Catholics began to play a more prominent role in forging what
former U.S. ambassador to Czechoslovakia William H. Luers
described as a new type of resistance "community—subtle, anti-
party, anti-ideology, ethical and ultimately very powerful."[49] It
was a community whose power derived, in part, from the alternative it modeled in the face of the communist state. The state fostered atomization and distrust; the resistance was built on personal
friendships and personal trust. The regime lied; the resistance community tried to "live in truth." The regime debased politics; the
resistance practiced "antipolitics." The regime owned the state; the
resistance tried to rebuild civil society. The regime enforced ideological orthodoxy; the resistance was a coalition across many
points of view. The result was what Václav Havel called a rebirth
of "love, tolerance, nonviolence, the human spirit, and forgiveness"—the "bacteriologic weapons" that eventually, in November
and December 1989, cowed the army, the StB, and the police.[50]
That the Catholic Church in Czechoslovakia was able to help set
that "framework" for the resistance, as Václav Benda put it, was
due in no small part to the personal revolution of the man who, in
his late eighties, would be saluted familiarly as "Frantši Tomášek"
by cheering nonviolent resisters in front of the archbishop's palace
near Prague Castle.[51] And that the cardinal's revolution was influenced by John Paul's preaching of the final revolution, we need
not doubt.

Three events in the mid-and-late 1980s embodied and gave public expression to the Church's emergence as a major force in the resistance to communism in Czechoslovakia.

The first of these was the previously mentioned 1985 pilgrimage to the Cistercian monastery at Velehrad in Moravia, to mark the 1,100th anniversary of the death of St. Methodius—with his brother St. Cyril, one of the two "apostles to the Slavs" whom John Paul II had named co-patrons of Europe (with St. Benedict) and whose ministry the pope had celebrated in the June 1985 encyclical, *Slavorum Apostoli*. To many of those who took part in this great public manifestation of a renascent and resistant Czechoslovak Catholicism, "Velehrad" was the equivalent of the pope's pilgrimage to Poland in June 1979. As in Poland, the sheer numbers of pilgrimage participants broke through the fears generated by social atomization, confirmed that "we" (society) were larger than "they" (the state), and demonstrated that "we" could assert ourselves in the confidence that "we" were not alone. In that sense, the mere fact of the Velehrad pilgrimage was empirical proof to those present (and to those who later heard of it by word of mouth, or through Vatican Radio and Radio Free Europe) that Husákian "normalization" was a human—and thus political— failure. Former dissident Pavel Bratinka also believes that Velehrad was one of the defining moments at which the Husák regime's self-assurance began to crack: never before had people dared to shout down their masters, and with chants of "We want Mass, we want the pope," no less. From this point on, in Bratinka's analysis, the regime's self-confidence waned while the self-assurance of the resistance community grew.[52]

Father Václav Malý is another leader of the resistance who, in retrospect, sees Velehrad as a key turning point. The pilgrimage linked popular piety to the civic opposition; it encouraged believers to think that they could act together in witness to the Gospel; it taught those present that the manipulative efforts of the regime (which, it will be remembered, tried to present the Methodius commemoration as a "peace festival") could be successfully resisted. Finally, according to Malý, Velehrad was an important event in the history of the pre-revolution because it brought together Czechs and Slovaks in one place, and in a common religious act that had great public resonance.[53]

(The Velehrad pilgrimage was also the occasion for the revival of a bit of Šwejkist humor. There was, as usual, an argument after the event about the precise numbers who had attended. Cardinal Tomášek's office said 150,000; the government said 50,000. Church people said, "We're both right: We're counting ours, and they're counting theirs."[54])

The second crucial public expression of this new Catholic activism that, in time, helped shape the Velvet Revolution was the petition for religious freedom organized by a Moravian peasant, Augustin Navrátil, in 1988–1989. The reform communism of Alexander Dubček, twenty years before, had been reform "from above." The 1988–1989 Navrátil petition, wrote Timothy Garton Ash, was the quintessence of reform "from below."[55] Pavel Bratinka put it this way: "The communists ridiculed Cardinal Tomášek as a 'general without an army.' Navrátil decided to create an army."[56]

The 1988–1989 petition was actually the third appeal for religious freedom that Augustin Navrátil had organized since he was first moved to activism by his aggravation over the regime's removal of one of the traditional crosses found in the fields of Moravia. The first was in 1976, and was composed of seventeen points. It garnered 700 signatures locally in Moravia before Navrátil was jailed in a psychiatric hospital. On his second try, in 1984–1985, Navrátil expanded the petition to twenty points, and circulated it among the various government ministries, asking whether it was legal to solicit signatures to the appeal. The StB was the only bureaucracy willing to declare itself "competent" in the matter; Navrátil was arrested, interrogated, and sent to the psychiatric section of a prison hospital, where he was diagnosed as suffering from "paranoia quaerulans." (Garton Ash suggests, aptly enough, that what possessed Augustin Navrátil was really a "divine stubbornness."[57]) The judge in his case arguing that he was a danger to society, Navrátil was incarcerated for almost a year. Proving the judge's point, although not in the way the judge intended, Navrátil, on his release, started to organize his third petition, which began circulating in December 1987 and continued to attract signatures for the next two years.

The 1988–1989 Navrátil petition, whose thirty-one points spelled out the implications for Czechoslovakia of the fundamental democratic principle of the separation of Church and state, was a watershed event in the "pre-revolution"—the events and the moral reawakening that finally gave birth, in November and December 1989, to the Velvet Revolution.[58] The petition sought redress for the multiple grievances of Czech and Slovak Catholics; but in doing so it articulated, and gave its signatories the opportunity to affirm, publicly, such basic human rights as the rights of free speech, assembly, and habeas corpus. The petition championed the freedom of the press. And it demanded respect for contracts in a law-governed society. Thus the third Navrátil petition became a kind of public referendum, not simply on the condition of the Church, but on basic human rights for all. What began as a moral-cultural, indeed religious, initiative came to have great public (and political) consequences.

The petition, which had garnered some 600,000 signatures by late 1989, was also a kind of recall election measuring the people's attitude toward Husákian "normalization" and the communist state: and Protestants and nonbelievers joined Catholics in registering an overwhelming rejection of the regime's lies and repressions. That rejection doubtless explains the regime's reaction: Augustin Navrátil was returned, yet again, to a psychiatric prison. But the very fact that so many Czechs and Slovaks would publicly identify themselves with a petition that was, at bottom, a fundamental assault on the moral legitimacy of the communist regime indicated that the change in the correlation of forces some Catholics first sensed at Velehrad—regime demoralization paralleled by an increasing confidence within the resistance community—was building. Cardinal Tomášek was, evidently, determined that the momentum would intensify even further: the man who had once rejected Catholic participation in Charter 77 now told his people that it was their duty to sign the Navrátil petition: because "cowardice and fear are not becoming to a true Christian."[59]

The third Navrátil petition was thus another important benchmark on the hard road to the Velvet Revolution. Its content was important in itself; and the petition graphically illustrated, in concrete circumstances, Pope John Paul II's frequent claim that religious freedom was the first of human rights and the sure guarantee of any scheme of human rights in a society fit for human beings. According to Kamila Benda, the petition also had five important public consequences for the "pre-revolution." Navrátil's "divine stubbornness" in mounting three petitions over a dozen years—with the third becoming a great national campaign—showed that the regime could be beaten, if the resistance was tenacious enough. Secondly, the petition was a Catholic initiative in which thousands of non-Catholics joined: and thus the bonds between the Church and the broader resistance community were reinforced in ways that transcended the historic Catholic/Protestant and religious/secular antipathies that the regime might have manipulated. Third, Cardinal Tomášek's support further strengthened the primate's position as a public symbol of resistance. Fourth, the petition forced many people to put themselves on the line, publicly, which not only strengthened the moral foundations of the resistance community but also compounded the regime's difficulties (not even the StB could arrest 600,000 dissidents). And, finally, like Velehrad, the petition was a joint effort of Czechs and Slovaks, thus frustrating the regime's continuing efforts to exacerbate tensions between the two groups.[60]

The third defining event in the renaissance of resistant Catholicism in Czechoslovakia during the pre-revolutionary period took place on March 25, 1988. In an attack on peaceful Catholic demonstrators that came to be known as "the Good Friday of Bratislava," the Husák regime demonstrated beyond any reasonable doubt that it had no intention of pursuing even a modest policy of glasnost along the lines pioneered by Mikhail Gorbachev in the USSR.

Earlier in the year, the Slovak activist and historian František Mikloško had called for a peaceful public rally in Bratislava's Hviezdoslavovo Square, in front of the Slovak National Theater, to petition the government for religious freedom and new bishops. The regime's response to Mikloško's call to action was a brutal expression of the neo-Stalinist paranoia that still gripped the Czechoslovak communist party. František Mikloško himself was held in preventive custody for the forty-eight hours before the rally. In Prague, Václav Benda, who had lent his support to the Slovak initiative, was interrogated for six hours and then kept in his flat on March 25, in order to prevent his attendance in Bratislava. Bishop Korec, Dr. Silvester Krčméry, and other well-known Slovak activists were physically detained or otherwise prevented from leaving their homes. A police blockade was set up on the roads for 100 kilometers around Bratislava.[61]

And still thousands of Slovaks came—the exact numbers are in dispute, but it may have been as high as 15,000—with candles, in the rain, to pray and sing in the square. They were met with a ferocious police attack featuring water cannons, tear gas, and dogs. The police and StB were even beyond worrying about public relations: BBC and Australian TV crews were beaten, which resulted in a wave of international protests against the Husák regime.[62]

The "Good Friday of Bratislava" confirmed Václav Benda's judgment about the utter irreformability of the Husák regime. As Bishop Korec would put it, "Not even the most narrow-minded of policemen could have thought that girls with rosaries and candles in their hands posed a threat to Bratislava or central Europe."[63] But it may also have shown, in a way that could not have been perceived at the time, just how desperate the regime really was. The Kremlin was doing who-knew-what. The resistance community was broadening its scope within Czechoslovakia. The once acquiescent Church was fully engaged with the resistance, and on the basis of the kind of moral-cultural activism to which the regime had no response save water cannons and attack dogs. Things must have looked very bad indeed, to the communist leaders ensconced in Prague Castle.

Which was, in retrospect, an accurate judgment: for their writ had but twenty months to run.

St. Agnes's Gentle Revolution

The Czechs call it the *masakr*. And because of it, the time and place at which the Velvet Revolution began can be established with considerable precision. The *masakr* took place on Friday night, November 17, 1989, on Národní, a boulevard running from the Vltava River to Wenceslas Square in Prague's Old Town. Fifty thousand students, many of whom had been active in the resistance community, marched up Národní toward the Square under the auspices of the League of Young Socialists and with the permission of the authorities. Their aim was to commemorate the fiftieth anniversary of the death of a Czech student, Jan Opletal, who had been murdered by the Nazis; but the connections between repressions past and present were not to be denied, and the students, although remaining entirely nonviolent, began to chant antiregime slogans. Suddenly, about halfway toward their destination, the students were confronted by the "white helmets" and truncheons of the riot police and the "red berets" of an antiterrorist squad. Refusing to disperse, the students tried to talk with the troops surrounding them; some handed out flowers to the red berets; others lit candles on the ground and with arms raised, chanted "We have bare hands." After what must have seemed like hours of mounting tension, the white helmets and red berets attacked, without warning. Men, women, and teenagers were beaten senseless. Hundreds were hospitalized but, mercifully, no one was killed.

And by the next day, the candles lit along Národní had ignited the nonviolent fire of the Velvet Revolution. Kamila Benda, two of whose sons had been leaders of the November 17 demonstration, remembered that evening as the point at which people decided that enough was finally enough; the regime could not be allowed to attack unarmed students with impunity.[64] On Sunday evening, November 19, at a meeting convened by Václav Havel, *Občanske Forum* (Civic Forum) was created as an umbrella organization linking the many parts of the Czech resistance community; shortly thereafter, *Verejnosť Proti Násiliu* (Public Against Violence) was formed for similar purposes in Bratislava. (In the classic Havel manner, Civic Forum's signature button, in the red, white, and blue of the Czechoslovak flag, featured a stylized smiling face.) Six weeks later, after a series of mass demonstrations, strikes, and negotiations between the regime and the resistance, the heirs of Klement Gottwald folded their hand and the crowds who had chanted "Havel to the Castle" got their wish, as the leader of Civic Forum was duly installed as president of Czechoslovakia.[65]

Catholic participation in both Civic Forum and Public Against Violence was intense, and much of it has already been noted. Indeed, the Church since 1985 had become such a pillar of the resistance community that Father Václav Malý, in reading the proclamation that Father Oto Mádr had drafted for Cardinal Tomášek, could refer to the eighty-nine-year-old primate as the "third great symbol" of the resistance, along with Havel and Alexander Dubček, the suddenly rehabilitated leader of the Prague Spring. And the crowds cheered their "Frantši Tomášek."

But the cardinal's role in the Velvet Revolution was rather more than symbolic. According to Václav Benda, who was one of the key Catholic intellectuals in Civic Forum and thus privy to the debates that went on in the Magic Lantern Theater, the communist government of Miloš Jakeš, in the early days of the revolution, approached Tomášek with the proposal that he act as a mediator between the opposition and the government. But even were the regime sincere about real reform (which Tomášek had good reason to doubt), putting the primate in the position of "mediator" between two parties would have both split the resistance community and suggested a kind of legitimacy to the regime's political position. The primate, further demonstrating just how he was becoming "older and tougher" (and cagier), understood this and refused the mediator's role, thus putting the Church firmly and irrevocably on the side of the people and sustaining the broad resistance coalition.[66] Cardinal Tomášek's decision drove one more (very large) nail into the coffin of Czechoslovak neo-Stalinism.

The chronology of the Velvet Revolution has been detailed elsewhere, but one more distinctively Catholic moment in the immediate overture to the Velvet Revolution ought to be noted.[67] For centuries, a Catholic legend had it that miraculous things would happen when Blessed Agnes of Bohemia, the thirteenth century sister of King Václav I who abandoned her riches to live among the poor, was canonized. That long-awaited event took place in Rome on November 12, 1989, five days before the *masakr* that sparked the Velvet Revolution. And the very fact of the celebration in St. Peter's Square had its repercussions in Czechoslovakia in the weeks that followed: as Bishop František Lobkowicz put it, people in the underground Church who had not seen each other in forty years met at the canonization, experienced the degree to which the Church had survived both Gottwald's Stalinism and Husák's "normalization," and were reunited just in time to reforge the links that would prove helpful in the revolutionary maelstrom ahead.[68]

But whatever the unplanned tactical advantages conferred by the canonization, the coincidence between the proclamation of Agnes's sanctity and the Velvet Revolution was too striking for anyone to ignore—even the secular intellectuals in Civic Forum. As one of Havel's aides said during the *Te Deum* sung in St. Vitus's Cathedral to celebrate the playwright's installation as president on December 29, "St. Agnes had her hand under our gentle revolution."[69] Who, after those astonishing six weeks, could disagree?

The Lazarus Church

On October 22, 1991, the bishops of the Czech and Slovak Federal Republic concelebrated Mass at the same St. Vitus's

Cathedral, high atop Hradčany, Prague's castle promontory, to mark the thirteenth anniversary of the installation of Pope John Paul II. The principal celebrant and homilist was the newly created cardinal, Ján Chryzostom Korec, S.J., the former repairman and night watchman. The first words of greeting at the Mass were spoken by Prague archbishop Miloslav Vlk, the erstwhile window washer. At the far end of the line of concelebrants was the youngest of the bishops, František Lobkowicz, who had been warned during his compulsory army service, shortly after his priestly ordination, "It is forbidden to speak about your ideas."[70] Among the congregants that evening were Václav and Kamila Benda, who had once celebrated silent and clandestine communion services in prison, and Václav Vaško, the historian who spent eight years painstakingly chronicling communism's attempted destruction of Catholicism in Czechoslovakia. (By a splendid coincidence—or act of Providence, perhaps—Vaško's Catholic publishing house, *Zvon*, now occupies the former headquarters of "Pacem in Terris"; Vaško's own office had been the fiefdom of the chief "pax terrier."[71]) To see these men and women, once so hard pressed, now alive and whole, publicly religious, and shaping the political future of their country, was to witness what many of them regard as little less than a miracle.[72]

It is almost impossible for a believer who has never experienced the kind of persecution visited upon the Catholics of the Czech lands and Slovakia, and who has never lived the exhilaration of their liberation, to comprehend their outlook on the world and the Church in the aftermath of the revolution. One can only imagine that it must be something like the experience of Lazarus when he found himself surprisingly alive in the heat, glare, and beauty of the Judean sun.

The daylight of freedom can, of course, be disorienting and troublesome.[73] Particularly among the older clergy, memories of life before Gottwaldism remain very much alive: and the temptation to think that the forty-one-year nightmare is over, and that it is now time to return to the status quo ante, must be very strong indeed. But the country, or perhaps better, the society inherited by Cardinal Korec and Archbishop Vlk and Bishop Lobkowicz and Father Malý and the Bendas and Pavel Bratinka and František Mikloško and Silvester Krčméry is not what it was in 1948. Things did not stay the same during the nightmare. Society became more atomized, more fragmented, more materialistic. And yet the same people who had once learned radical mistrust through the corrosive activities of the StB have also lived through the experience of the Revolution of 1989, and the final revolution of the spirit that preceded it.

Thus Catholicism in the Czech lands and Slovakia in the 1990s and beyond will test the possibilities of reevangelization in what is, particularly in Bohemia and Moravia, a post-Christian society. The emphasis in that phrase is usually put on *post*. But in this case it might just as well be on *Christian*, and in the Czech lands as well as in Slovakia. The clerical and lay leaders of Czechoslovak Catholicism today have a rich cultural heritage on which to draw. And they are responsible for a Church whose moral authority, in the wake of the Velvet Revolution, is high indeed.

While the problems of post-totalitarianism present themselves distinctively in the Czech lands and in Slovakia, both nations, and the Church within them, are beset by a complex of social and psychological problems that might be called the "communist hangover." The low-grade hedonism of Husákian "normalization" has given way, among some young people, to upscale hedonism of the familiar western sort.[74] The fear engendered by the StB has taken its toll; mistrust of others' intentions, a lack of the instinct for cooperation, passivity, the breakdown of a sense of personal responsibility, and other expressions of the social disintegration produced by communism remain part of the population's psychic baggage. Tolerance is not a particularly well-developed virtue, and the communist-encouraged habit of regarding those with whom one disagrees as enemies has proven hard to break.[75] The state was a burden, but the state also absolved individuals from the responsibility of defining a role and position in society; and many seem to find it hard to take the initiative in this respect even today, whether the issue is economic life or social life more broadly. Václav Benda worries that many Czechs and Slovaks misunderstood the nature of their own revolution, and are thus disappointed and frustrated that it didn't result in an immediate upsurge in consumer satisfactions.[76] Jan Kotas, a twenty-year-old Prague seminarian, put the problem of residual statism in these terms: "I think that, after the revolution, we expected paradise here. Now we have learned that [even a democratic] state cannot give us paradise. And that is good."[77] True enough; but it is also disorienting.

For Father Václav Malý, the communist hangover is primarily

a pastoral problem, one that gives focus to his preaching and to his efforts to organize his parish and its lay leadership. (Malý had been offered a government position after the revolution, but said that he wanted to be what he was: a priest and pastor.) Hatred, class warfare, mistrust, and the omnipresence of enemies (internal as well as foreign) were the themes constantly hammered home by communist propaganda: and for all that the propaganda was understood as just that, propaganda, it had its effects on attitudes and behaviors, as did the internal security apparatus and its networks of collaboration. In that atmosphere, said Malý, forgiveness and trust were signs of weakness. Thus the Church today has to preach these as basic moral values, worthy of free people, and crucial to living in a humane, and democratic, society. Trust as strength, forgiveness as a sign of character, self-sacrifice as something other than neurosis: the reevangelization of the post-totalitarian society has to begin at this level. People have to learn how to live in freedom. Men and women who had long thought of themselves merely as political objects have to learn to think of themselves as citizens aware of their individual dignity and their responsibility for public affairs: personal conversion is, in this sense, one of the essential bases of a genuine democracy. For believers, as Father Malý put it, the task is to move from "defending ourselves" to "offering ourselves" in service to the common good.[78] (Some Czechoslovak Catholics believe that this reevangelization of virtue and the virtues will be more readily acceptable to the agnostic intellectual and professional classes than to the workers; interestingly enough, and in something of a contrast to Poland, it was from the intelligentsia, including the artistic intelligentsia, that much of the Church's new membership came in the period just after the Velvet Revolution.)

As in Poland, lay and clerical activists during the pre-revolution and the revolution now sometimes find themselves in disagreement on issues and Church priorities. Some prominent Catholic activists, for example, are concerned that Church authorities focused too much on institutional rebuilding in the immediate aftermath of the communist crack-up. Pavel Bratinka, for example, believes that the Church was hurt in the eyes of the public by its urgency about the restoration of confiscated Church property, and by not making it clear that many of these properties would be used for the kind of charitable activity which people looked to the

Church to provide. Bratinka, as a classic economic liberal, would readily admit that property is important, and particularly for the freedom of the Church: Czechs and Slovaks had just had forty-one years of experience in what happens to a Church without property. On the other hand, a hierarchy and clergy perceived, fairly or not, as primarily concerned with institutional stabilization surely run the risk of making their task of reevangelization even more difficult. It was precisely by acting as *defensor hominis*, even if that brought further pressures on it as an institution, that the Church built up a great deal of moral credit during the 1980s. The wise investment of that moral capital requires a Church that is, and is seen to be, primarily evangelical, sacramental, and charitable in its activities. Father Malý's challenge, that Catholics in Czechoslovakia shift from defending themselves to offering themselves, has institutional as well as personal implications.

Then there is the question of national unity. Slovak nationalism had traditionally been identified with Slovak Catholicism. And that Catholicism has been seen as one of the cultural distinctions between the Slovaks and their (Hussite and agnostic) cousins in the Czech lands. Yet in the years immediately following the Velvet Revolution, Slovak nationalism—and indeed calls for Slovak separatism—also became the instrument by which ex-communists (whose detachment from their former convictions was not entirely clear) sought to reestablish a position of power in the region.[79] The Slovak church leadership, many older Slovaks, and not a few contemporary Catholic political leaders in Slovakia remember the anticlericalism and Czech cultural hegemonism of the interwar Masaryk and Beneš governments. The Czechs remember that the Slovak regime of Msgr. Jozef Tiso from 1939 to 1945 was allied to Nazi Germany. Then there are the more recent memories of Czech-Slovak cooperation and mutual aid under the Gottwald and Husák regimes.

All of these memories, compounded by a heady mix of ethnic and political pressures, have created a tremendous challenge to the Church's formal leadership in both Slovakia and the Czech lands, and to those former Catholic dissidents like František Mikloško, Ján Čarnogurský, Pavel Bratinka, and Václav Benda who now share the responsibility of governing a democratic Czechoslovakia. The pressures cut in several directions. If a genuinely widespread and popular movement for Slovak independence emerges, the Church leadership of Slovakia (already concerned about its ability to speak effectively to its people in a country beset by all the temptations of consumerism) would find it extremely difficult to make the case for maintaining the federation. If, on the other hand, and in the Czech lands, the Slovak Church is perceived as helping to split the country for a second time since its independence, much of the moral authority built up by Cardinal Tomášek and the resistance Church may be lost. The Holy See seems to have made clear, if quietly and indirectly, its preference that Czechoslovakia not be broken up: for that might trigger an escalating and volatile pattern of ethnic/national revanchism throughout central and eastern Europe, of the sort that exacerbated Yugoslavia's bloody conflict in recent years. But the Holy See is unlikely to bring public pressure to bear against intensely Catholic Slovakia.

Thus the Lazarus Church of Czechoslovakia finds itself under new forms of pressure in the wake of its triumphant reassertion of human dignity and human rights during the 1980s. The final revolution clearly does not mean the end of politics; in post-totalitarian societies, it means the beginning of politics. The romance of the Velvet Revolution has gone. Perhaps it is good that it has. For that means, as President Havel put it in his 1991 New Year's Day address, that "time and history [have] come back into our lives. The gloomy skies of boredom and stultifying inaction have cleared, and we can only marvel at the vast range of possibilities a truly free political climate can offer, and at how it continues to astonish us, in both the good and bad senses of the word."

Yet one part of that astonishment has been the discovery that "the heritage of the past few decades has proven worse than . . . could possibly have [been] anticipated in the joyous atmosphere of those first few months of freedom."[80] And thus the question in postrevolutionary Czechoslovakia is the degree to which the experience of the final revolution, the revolution of the spirit, might temper the passions that were frozen beneath the field ice of Czechoslovakian communism, and whose release back into public life has been one of the inevitable prices of freedom.

SEVEN

No Monopolies on Virtue: Christian Conviction and the Democratic Prospect

The final revolution is not the end of history. It is the restoration of history to human dimensions.

As Hannah Arendt pointed out a generation ago, one of the ugliest aspects of the totalitarian project (especially in its Marxist-Leninist form) was its conscious effort to accelerate the human drama: to hold down the "fast forward" control on history so as to hasten the coming of the day of (mundane) redemption. And if there was a bit of breakage along the way, well, humankind had long ago learned that famous lesson about the relationship of eggs to omelets. Besides, those who had discerned the truth of history had every right, indeed had a responsibility, to quicken the arrival of the promised future.[1]

The final revolution—the revolution of conscience and the revitalization of the human spirit that, by radically relativizing the pretensions of the political, makes possible a politics that can support human flourishing—restores the natural rhythms of history and society. That is what happened in central and eastern Europe as the final revolution unfolded in the 1980s: as a measure of normality was restored to the pace of history, civil society was slowly and painfully recreated. And that form of normality, living "as if," or "living in the truth," in turn made possible a political revolution in 1989 that did not simply replicate the brutalities of the system it sought to replace.

Normality means just that, normality, and not perfection. Those who find themselves disenchanted with the Revolution of 1989 because of the politics that have followed the communist crack-up need to think again about the meaning of "normal" pol-

191

itics. (Americans in particular might remember the sorry condition of their republic in the years immediately following the Treaty of Paris in 1783.) The Revolution of 1989 was made by men and women, not by angels: and the results have been, predictably enough, very human indeed.

Moreover, the final revolution is a constant reminder that the consummation of human fulfillment is in the time-beyond-time, in the Kingdom come in its full glory. Short of that Kingdom, the business of history and politics is striving. And striving means the possibility of sin and failure. Indeed, human striving means that sin and failure are inevitable. The horizon of possibility provided by the transcendent Kingdom-to-come helps keep human striving (and its attendant sins and failures) in perspective. It also keeps alive the hope without which politics degenerates into the cynical contest for power in its basest form: the capacity to coerce consent (or at least acquiescence) to one's will.

The Revolution of 1989 was, to be sure, a very different kind of revolution—indeed, it broke the pattern of *revolution* as we have understood the term since 1789. The Revolution of 1989 was a revolution of restoration: not a restoration of the ancien régime, but a recovery of normal politics after the fevered megapolitics of communism. And the "1989 difference" derived in no small part from the final revolution that preceded the political revolution, which in turn destroyed the Yalta imperial system and thereby finished Marxism-Leninism as an ideological force in world history.

Ironically or providentially, and despite its draconian efforts to snuff out religious sensibilities, communism helped prepare its own demise by providing occasions that were an existential window into the Kingdom against which all earthly kingdoms are measured and found wanting: the Kingdom whose promise gives meaning to human striving in history. Cardinal Stefan Wyszyński planning the Great Novena during his internment; Father Kazimierz Jancarz organizing his "evenings of independent Polish culture"; Father Oto Mádr writing his underground "Catholic weekly" in prison on a two-inch-square scrap of paper; Kamila Benda taking communion surreptitiously to her interned husband; Father Václav Malý working out a new style of catechesis in the boiler room of the Meteor Hotel; millions of beleaguered parents teaching their faith to their children—these were moments in which the Kingdom beyond history touched the world of human striving in ways whose impact we cannot empirically measure. But that these graced moments shaped the Revolution of 1989 is witnessed to by virtually all those concerned, even those who do not share the Christian convictions of these modern martyr-confessors.

In the catacomb Christianity of central and eastern Europe, as well as in the more public activities of the Church, men and women grew strong enough to resist communist oppression without themselves becoming embittered or violent. The spiritual energy of the resistance Church helped restore history to a human scale, and thus helped to channel the energies of the broader dissident community into forms of resistance that were commensurate with the resisters' commitments to democracy and a law-governed, "normal" society.[2]

The final revolution made possible the distinctive moral quality of the political Revolution of 1989.

The Communist Hangover

How one reads both the Revolution of 1989 and the postrevolutionary struggle to establish democracy and the free economy in the countries of the late Warsaw Pact is determined in large measure by how one reads communism. If communism was simply a clumsy, inefficient form of authoritarianism, incapable of competing economically with the worlds of capitalist democracy, then the Revolution of 1989 was in truth a matter of "delayed modernization," and communism's replacement by more efficient economic and political institutions should have been a fairly simple business. But that is not what communism was.

Communism was, first and foremost, a heresy: it was a defective and deforming vision of the human person, human community, human history, and human destiny. Communist economic foolishness and the communist terror were both expressions of communism's fundamental anthropological toxicity. And yet communism exercised a powerful grip on the imaginations of millions of people. Why? Because communism was a radically mundane form of the hope for human regeneration through the inbreaking of a Kingdom of truth and righteousness that had shaped western consciousness and culture since the days of the

Jewish prophets. Therein lay communism's power to attract, and its power to coerce. And the doctrinal delusion of communism led, time and again, to a debased personal and social morality. People lied, overtly and covertly. Language was degraded and the meanings of terms inverted. Trust between people eroded. Corruption, large and small, was epidemic. Social atomization and fragmentation destroyed the tissues of human solidarity. Cynicism and passivity abounded.

To miss the moral degradation wrought by communism is to have missed communism—and to misconstrue the tasks that lay ahead for the new democracies. Moreover, when one adds to these moral elements of communism's destructiveness the economic, social, and ecological wreckage caused by Lenin's heirs, the real wonder is not that postcommunist societies are in various forms of crisis; the real wonder is that there has been impressive progress in the transitions to democracy and the market.[3]

Because of the very nature of the disease from which central and eastern Europe is recovering, the gravest immediate threat to the democratic prospect in the region may not lie in the economic shock therapy of rapid marketization, or even in those eruptions of repressed national and ethnic grievances that have so focused western attention in recent years, but in the moral hangover that was inevitable after the great debauch of communism. Absent a continuing moral regeneration—absent a deeper appropriation of the truths of the final revolution—the moral detritus of the communist past may yet come to haunt the long-suffering peoples of *Mitteleuropa* (and points east).

The "inner migration" on which many people embarked during the communist years had its strengthening aspects. But it could not, by itself, resurrect a democratic etiquette or ground a sense of personal moral obligation to the common good.[4] This suggests that rebuilding the torn or atrophied tissues of civil society ought to have a high priority in the new democracies.

The reconstitution of "civil society" was the political key to the Revolution of 1989's effective resistance to communism, according to those who led the way to a postcommunist future. But civil society is not merely a tool for resisting tyranny: it is the essential foundation on which democracy—self-government of, by, and for the people, in a law-governed society that cherishes and protects basic human rights—rests.

As they work out the practical political consequences of the victory of freedom, the new democracies will be threatened by both a false populism and a false formalism. The false populism will not be very good at handling the problem of losers: and one of the building blocks of democracy is the protection of losers' rights, after the election. The false formalism will focus so exclusively on structures that it will neglect the moral and cultural foundations of a political system in which both constitutional and statutory law must be held accountable to norms that transcend the polity—if the polity is not going to become a tyranny. Thus the new democracies, and their friends, will have to take action to ensure that what was re-created at great cost—the civil society which is the best safeguard against false populism and false formalism—is strengthened for the future.

And in the central and eastern European context, where Catholicism played such an important role in the rescue of civil society from the moral and social bog of communism, this immediately raises the question of the Church's roles in the post-totalitarian order. How shall the Church help "rebuild a world of freedom," as Pope John Paul II has described the postcommunist task?[5]

The Church Being Itself

Whether the focus is on ecclesiastical life or public life, the first task of the Church is to be the Church: to be the community of faith, sacramental worship, and charity that proclaims Christ as the light of the nations, the *lumen gentium* in whom is found the definitive revelation of the true meaning of human life and aspiration.[6] Because the Church is first and always a witness to the saving acts of God in Christ, the Church is "in the nature of [a] sacrament—a sign and instrument, that is, of communion with God and of unity among all men."[7] It is, in short, because the Church is the Church, and not simply another interest group in society, that it can offer a genuinely distinctive service to public life.

The unhappy experience of the churches of western Europe in recent decades holds a lesson for the Church in the new democracies of the old Yalta imperial system. As the eminent Lutheran theologian Wolfhart Pannenberg has put it, the churches' failures at culture formation in the established democracies of western Europe are in part of the churches' own making:

> [The] churches themselves have in many ways bought into a secular mindset. In preaching, teaching, congregational life, and sometimes in liturgy, they have pursued a course of accommodation to secularism. In this way they hope to get a more sympathetic hearing for the Christian message. It is now apparent, however, that the strategy of accommodation is self-defeating.[8]

It is self-defeating because the strategy of accommodation reflects a lack of Christian confidence in what is most distinctive about the Christian message. A softer, even more humane, secularism with incense and bells is not likely to attract many converts (or reconverts). The churches that were most confident of their unique vocational responsibilities were the churches best able to resist the communist assault. The churches most confidently preaching Jesus Christ, crucified and risen, as the transcendent answer to the deepest longings of the human heart are the churches most likely to revive Christianity where it has died in central and eastern Europe, and to strengthen it for the future where it is now strong.[9]

And it is precisely a confident Christianity that will make a useful contribution to the process of democratic consolidation in the new democracies. Western elites tend to think of the relationship between vibrant Jewish and Christian religious and moral conviction, and democratic vitality, as a zero-sum game, somewhat on the model of the Ayatollah Khomeini and Iran: the greater the religious and moral conviction, the weaker the democracy. But this caricature of a much more complex (and thus interesting) relationship is caused in part because western elites tend to think of democracy in excessively formulaic terms, as a mere matter of agreement on procedures (increasingly, about litigation!) rather than as a substantive experiment in self-governance. But democracy is self-evidently more than procedures. Democratic politics is impossible, over the long haul, without democratic civility. And democratic civility is impossible without a virtuous people, confident of their own ability to choose wisely, and committed to protecting individual liberty amidst genuine pluralism while concurrently promoting the common good.

Put another way, democratic politics is only possible when politics is understood to be penultimate. Thus democracy is sustained and strengthened by religious and moral convictions that honor the political world while relativizing its claims to omnicompetence. It is not, after all, a zero-sum game.

Moreover, it is precisely an intensely and self-consciously Christian Church that is an effective sign of the transcendent destiny of human life and an effective teacher and pastor in the world of public affairs. Again, Wolfhart Pannenberg:

> What the Church does most distinctively serves the world most powerfully. It is precisely as a liturgical worshiping community that the Church is most effectively a sign of the ultimate destiny of every human being and of humanity as a whole. That ultimate destiny of all human beings is to be one with God and, through that unity, one with one another. Human beings can associate in many ways in order to achieve a measure of community, even of communion. A gang of criminals is undoubtedly a community of sorts. But the kingdom of God is not community-in-general. It is communion with God through Christ in the power of the Spirit. That communion is the destiny of humankind, and the Church, especially in her liturgical life, is the present image of that destiny. Thus the life of the Church is itself an integral part of the message of the Church, namely, the proposal to the world of its future in the kingdom of God.[10]

Thus the first task of the Church in the new democracies that emerged from the Revolution of 1989 is not to offer sage counsel on the relative merits of presidential or parliamentary systems, or to gauge the pace of privatization and marketization. It is to be the Church, the bearer and embodiment of the message of the Kingdom that, by challenging the pretensions of the political, opens the social space on which a politics of consent can replace the politics of coercion. The communists understood that, and persecuted the Church accordingly. Democrats ought to be as perceptive as communists about the Church's first political task.

James Billington is another scholar who has grasped the relationship between a vibrant Christian faith and the process of democratic consolidation in post-totalitarian societies. Billington describes the history of the twentieth century as a great "global drama" in several acts. Act I was the trauma of "total war," in the two world conflagrations that destroyed the old European order. Act II was the "totalitarian peace" of the Cold War. Act III was the Revolution of 1989 and the New Russian Revolution of

1991: "the victory of freedom and the emergence of a liberal political and economic order" as the model of choice for post-totalitarian and post-authoritarian societies. But freedom's victory will not be complete (and thus capable of ensuring a reasonably stable future) without a successful passage through Act IV.

And Act IV is the drama of cultural personality, "the renewed search for unique identities in the midst of creeping technological uniformities." Act IV is "a search for spiritual depth in an increasingly two-dimensional universe: a search for a source of responsibility amidst the fluidity of freedom."[11] Act IV is the continuation of the final revolution amidst the many political and economic tasks of democratic consolidation. Americans in particular should be able to understand that the results of that search-for-responsibility will bear heavily on the democratic prospect in the new democracies: for "religious roots and moral convictions independent of government were prerequisite to the establishment and future health of representative government in America—as George Washington clearly noted in his farewell address."[12]

Thus what is so often assumed to be a dangerous cultural contradiction of late twentieth-century life—"a global process that seems to be both moving forward to democratization and back to religion"—may in fact be one process, with one *telos* or (worldly) destiny: for "democracy arose historically out of religion" and religion may well be "necessary to underpin [democracy] ethically."[13] The "contradiction" is not so contradictory after all: when, that is, one understands that democracy's roots in the culture of the West lie in soil enriched for centuries by Jewish and Christian understandings of the nature and destiny of human beings.

There are no guarantees that the Catholic Church will seize the opportunities for democratic culture formation that have been presented to it by the communist crack-up, and by its own immense prestige in central and eastern Europe as one of the premier agents of the collapse of the Yalta imperial system. When Polish country pastors (and the occasional bishop) instruct their congregants in precisely which political party to support in free elections, the Church is not only making itself look foolish: it is jeopardizing its capacity to play its most important political role in consolidating Polish democracy, which is precisely a *pre*-political role. When Catholic identity is so densely interwoven with ethnic identity that the Church loses its sacramental capacity to be a "sign . . . of unity among all men," something has also been lost in terms of the consolidation of democracy.

Enter, once again, Pope John Paul II.

Truth and Freedom

The challenge for post-totalitarian Catholicism in central and eastern Europe is a bit of a paradox: to be true to its own self-understanding as a sacrament of the Kingdom (against the world for the world, as it were), and to give concrete expression to its expressed convictions about democracy, the Church that has long enjoyed a virtual monopoly on goodness in many settings must now work for the day when that monopoly is broken. The resistance Church, the refuge of truth and decency in a sea of communist mendacity, must give way to the culture-forming Church, the teacher and pastor of democratic societies.

John Paul II, architect of the Revolution of 1989 by reason of his preaching of the final revolution, has had a number of things to say about all of this, and many of them have centered on the relationship between truth and freedom in a democratic polity. The pope has clearly and unambiguously committed the Church to a strategy of persuasion, not coercion: as he put it in his 1990 encyclical on Christian mission, "The Church proposes; she imposes nothing."[14] But John Paul is also convinced that democracy cannot be built on foundations of moral indifference. Perhaps most provocatively (and to some ears, threateningly), the pope laid out this challenge to the democratic future in *Centesimus Annus*, his 1991 encyclical which was in part a meditation of the moral meaning of "1989":

> Nowadays there is a tendency to claim that agnosticism and skeptical relativism are the philosophy and the basic attitude which correspond to democratic forms of political life. Those who are convinced that they know the truth and firmly adhere to it are considered unreliable from a democratic point of view, since they do not accept that truth is determined by the majority, or that it is subject to variation according to different political trends. It must be observed in this regard that if there is no ultimate truth to guide and direct political activity, then ideas and convictions can easily

be manipulated for reasons of power. As history demonstrates, a democracy without values easily turns into open or thinly disguised totalitarianism.[15]

What was the pope trying to say in this controversial passage? As ever in parsing John Paul II, one has to begin with his Christological anthropology: with the pope's classic Christian convictions about man, and about man redeemed by Christ. There, the pope believes, is where one starts to discern the truth about politics. "Politics" properly understood is never a matter of mere systems. Politics is an expression of one's anthropology, of one's conception of the human person.

And the pope's conception, inspired by Genesis 1.27 and drawing from the wisdom of both the Christian West and the Christian East, is a dramatic one: "We are all living ikons of Him who is our origin and our final destiny."[16] Man is for man the road to God. And human beings, living by faith through grace, are thereby opened up to a wider vision of the human condition, a vision in which our freedom to seek the truth leads us to the truth that makes us free. "Those who, enlightened by faith, discover in themselves and in their brothers and sisters the features of this ikon are able to have a more penetrating and universal vision of the human person and the world about us."[17] But that vision, like the talents in the Gospel parable of the three stewards, is not to be hidden away as a kind of private treasure: rather, it is meant to illuminate the road of history and the tasks of politics. For, aware of their "ikonic" condition, Christians "must unite their efforts to those of all people of good will in order to offer to humanity the contribution of the light which comes to them by faith."[18] And that light is of special consequence for those emerging from the dark night of totalitarian occupation: the "true humanism" of Christian faith is a socially formative and politically powerful reminder that "every kind of immanentism, by proposing a reductionist image of man, deprives him of that transcendent dimension which alone can remove from him the prospect of final annihilation."[19]

The Church's "truth about man" is thus the foundation of its conception of politics, including (better, especially) democratic politics. Like Lincoln, John Paul asks how it is that governments "so conceived and so dedicated can long endure." His answer is that they cannot endure—or they cannot endure in service to the justice, freedom, civil peace, public order, and prosperity that is their responsibility—if they ignore the truth about man, or if they reduce the instruments of governance to an ensemble of legalistic procedures. The answer to the false humanism of communism cannot be a radical skepticism about the nature and destiny of the human person, for that will only lead, in time, to new forms of oppression. The answer that provided the effective antidote to communism can also provide the sure foundation of democracies committed to liberty and justice for all: and the answer is a true humanism that takes full account of man's transcendent origin and destiny.[20]

The pope's convictions on this matter of truth, freedom, and democracy explain dimensions of the new interaction of the Church and politics in central and eastern Europe that have been widely criticized in the West (and in parts of the old Warsaw Pact) since the communist crack-up. Take, for example, the matter of Poland's abortion laws. As we have seen, the Gomułka regime's permissive abortion laws in the mid-1950s were a direct attack on the Church's sexual ethic and on its moral teaching about family life. So, on historical grounds alone, one ought to have expected the Church to press vigorously for a repeal of legislation that was understood by all the parties concerned to be an essential component of the communist attack on Catholicism. But it would be a mistake to think of the Church's activism in Poland on behalf of laws more protective of unborn human life as matters of historical score settling alone.

John Paul and the Polish bishops are convinced that there can be no democracy and no true freedom without rigorous public protection of basic human rights. And among those basic rights they include the right to life of the unborn. Thus their call for legal protection for the unborn should not be construed, even in the intensely Catholic Polish context, as a matter of the Church "imposing its morality" on society as a whole. Rather, for John Paul and the Polish episcopate, the right-to-life issue is (in its public dimensions) the premier civil rights issue of the day. On the basis of bitter historical experience (in which the Nazi extermination of those deemed to suffer under the burden of *lebensunwertes Leben*, "life not worth living," figures prominently), John Paul believes that radically constricting the boundaries of the community for which society assumes a common responsibility is the opening wedge to social evil on a massive scale. So, from the pope's point of view, the Polish abortion controversy has never been simply a matter of whipping the troops into line, so to speak: it has everything to do with the future of Polish democracy.[21]

To suggest that this commitment to civil rights in a law-governed democracy is the best prism through which to view the abortion controversy in postcommunist Poland is not to suggest that the Polish episcopate has learned how to be an effective and compelling moral educator in its new political circumstances. It has not, as several members of the Polish hierarchy have conceded. But the reduction of the abortion question in Poland to a question of whether the alleged "black totalitarianism" of the Church will succeed "red totalitarianism" is an unfortunate misconception of this very basic, and very painful, debate.[22]

The Church as moral educator and teacher of the truth about man has had a whole host of grave moral issues to confront in the years immediately following the communist crack-up. One of the most difficult has been the question of the accountability of former communist leaders: which is not, again, an issue of score-settling, but rather a profound question of how one cleanses the moral atmosphere of societies long polluted by the communist culture of the lie. The issue has been made even more vexing because many of those who once benefited by their acquiescence to the communist system have now made a very good deal for themselves under the new democratic and capitalist order, precisely because their former connections gave them an advantaged position in the new order. The Church has counseled forgiveness: Catholics who held fast against communist tyranny should now forgive those who were not so strong. On the other hand, the long tradition of the Church has held that forgiveness absent repentance, confession, a "firm purpose of amendment," and a suitable penance is a hollow gesture. On the other, other hand, a government is not a confessor. How does one stand up for the truth—in this case, about history and culpability—while at the same time getting on with the immense task of repairing the extraordinary damage done by two generations of communist idiocy? The morally contentious situation of the new democracies of central and eastern Europe is further evidence for the truth of John Courtney Murray's claim that democracies are always experiments: democracy is, by its very nature, an unfinished business, for no one can ever be certain that there will be sufficient virtue "in the people" to sustain this historically strange business of self-government through republican political institutions with constitutionally and legally restricted powers. In that sense, and in many others, there is no cause for Americans and other western Christians to look askance at the raucous and occasionally divisive nature of political life in the new democracies born during the Revolution of 1989. We, too, have no guarantees that democracy will last.

The Peace and Freedom Connection

There is another matter on which western Christians need to examine their consciences in the wake of the Revolution of 1989: and that is the question of whether the free Church of the West gave adequate support to its persecuted brethren behind the iron curtain.

The answer one gets to that question, from a great many knowledgeable churchmen and churchwomen, across the political spectrum in the countries of the old Yalta imperial system, is, frankly, "No."[23] Some say it sadly; others are still angry at what they regard as their betrayal. And there are many in central and eastern Europe, formerly known as "dissidents," who are touchingly grateful to those western Christians who did speak up on their behalf. But why, they wonder, were those Christians so often regarded as "dissidents" in their own western communities? And why were the institutional churches, including western bishops' conferences, so quiet in the face of such relentless persecution of their brethren?

Why, in short, did so very much more attention get paid to nuclear weapons than to the suffering and persecuted Church, in the years after the Second Vatican Council and particularly in the 1980s?

The Revolution of 1989 falsified the central claim of the renascent "peace movement" that began in the late 1970s and reached a public apogee in the United States with the "nuclear freeze" agitations of the early 1980s: the claim that nuclear weapons were themselves at the root of the conflict between the democracies and the communist world. On this analysis, the first order of business was to remove (or drastically scale down) the weapons: which would lead, inevitably, to a reduction in ten-

sions. Those who argued that this got the problem precisely backward—because the weapons were an expression of a fundamental
ideological (indeed, moral) conflict whose resolution was the precondition to any satisfactory efforts at arms control and disarmament—were regularly (and often bitterly) informed that they did
not care enough about the fate of the earth.[24]

The verdict of history is now in, and it ought to be quite clear:
the threat of nuclear warfare dramatically diminished as communist regimes began to change. The Revolution of 1989 and the
New Russian Revolution—carried out by people, "dissidents,"
who were rarely supported by western peace activists—ought to
have put an end to the "weapons versus regimes" argument: the
root issue was the regimes, and the problems posed by the
weapons (which were, to be sure, grave indeed) were resolved
once the issue of regimes was resolved. Which means, to put the
matter simply but accurately, when communism lost and the
democracies won.

That so many prominent western Christians failed to comprehend this linkage between communism and the threat of nuclear
war—or, even worse, failed to understand how their concern for
peace was being manipulated by communists in ways that made
life even harder for their already beset coreligionists—is a very
great sadness. But the failure of the Church of the West has to be
confronted, if western Christians are to take adequate stock of
their own record during this great drama. Nor should it be said
that this was merely a matter of certain fringe characters out in
the fever swamps (like the Dutch Pax Christi activist who
informed a 1990 conference on the theology of suffering that
communism was a splendid economic and political system which
failed in central and eastern Europe because the people in that
region were not "sufficiently mature" to be communists.[25]) The
myopia also affected distinguished scholars like the Flemish
Dominican, Edward Schillebeeckx, who was the keynote speaker
at an international colloquium on peace held in Prague in
September 1984. The conference was, of course, organized by
"Pacem in Terris," and the usual pax terrier politics prevailed.
Father Václav Malý's gentle if forthright criticism of Father
Schillebeeckx, later smuggled out to the West and published in
the documentary journal, *RCDA—Religion in Communist Dom-
inated Areas*, deftly cut to the nub of the issue:

Dear Professor Schillebeeckx:

. . . [Y]ou have been unwittingly used; many Christians are very disturbed by your participation in the Prague colloquium. I firmly believe that you were motivated by the best of intentions which, of course, in this conjunction served an evil purpose. Peace and respect for the inviolability of human rights are inseparable. Peace propaganda must be suspect if it is conducted by a government that suppresses every spontaneous expression of its citizens' convictions, if they differ from the officially dictated directives. . . .

I am a Catholic priest unable to serve my Church publicly because I am involved, among other things, in the Charter 77 citizens' program in which many Christians are trying to [make] their contribution to the achievement of peaceful coexistence. The only response on the part of our state authorities to such peaceful endeavors are police surveillance, discrimination in employment, and imprisonment.

Dear Professor Schillebeeckx, please accept my words as fraternal warning so that in the future you avoid similar pitfalls. It would cause enormous harm to our whole Church if your meritorious theological work were degraded by such ill-advised, albeit well-intended steps. I should like to assure you that at any future occasion we shall be happy to welcome you here for mutual exchange of the experiences of our faith.

> With fraternal respect, in Christ,
> Fr. Václav Malý
> Catholic priest deprived
> of state license[26]

"Peace and respect for the inviolability of human rights are inseparable": that is what a considerable segment of the leadership and the opinion elite in western Christian churches forgot, in the last fifteen years of the Cold War. Having forgotten that, the Church became susceptible to the allure of "relevance" as defined by elite opinion in the secular culture. It was a failure of imagination, of nerve, and of Christian responsibility on which the western Church ought to reflect very carefully indeed.

Surprises from the Lord of History

In the wake of the euphoria that followed Karol Wojtyła's triumphant 1979 return to Poland as the first Slavic Bishop of Rome, the distinguished Polish philosopher Leszek Kołakowski (then in exile for his anticommunist writings) posed a hard question to the Catholic Church in his native land: Did the Church oppose the totalitarian system in all its dimensions, or was the Church primarily exercised about the system's atheism?[27] Suppose, for example, that the Polish regime were to drop programmatic atheism from its agenda. Would the Church continue in opposition, or would it withdraw from the struggle so long as its own interests were recognized by the government?

Kołakowski's query had doubtless occurred to others in the secular opposition to the Yalta imperial system throughout central and eastern Europe. If the alleged affinities between Catholicism and certain odious forms of politics had been exaggerated from time to time by the Church's enemies, it was nonetheless true that Catholicism had, over the centuries, found it possible to coexist with a wide array of regimes, some of them altogether unsavory by contemporary standards. Moreover, there was, in the European context, a long history of tension between the Church and particular schools of democratic thought. Continental liberalism, unlike its more eclectic American counterpart, was deeply and abidingly anticlerical (and indeed anti-Catholic). Nor had this historic tension been ameliorated during the post–World War II period in central and eastern Europe by the experience of vibrant Christian Democratic parties, as had been the case in western Europe. So Kołakowski's tough question cannot be dismissed as mere effrontery. There were indeed questions to be explored and issues to be resolved.

On the other hand, there were questions to be put to Kołakowski's question.

In the first instance, atheism and the communist project could not be so easily disentangled as Kołakowski's question seemed to imply (and as Kołakowski himself, in later years, admitted). The vain attempts of sundry "Christian Marxists" of the late 1960s and 1970s to the contrary notwithstanding, what was clear in 1917 seemed clear again in the early 1990s: atheism was not a disposable part of communist ideology. In fact, it was an essential component of Marxism-Leninism as a comprehensive worldview, a *Weltanschauung*. Absent principled, programmatic atheism—not skeptical agnosticism, but full-bore atheism—totalitarianism would not be totalitarianism. Totalitarian claims would be, well, less than total. God would have His innings. Absent atheism, totalitarianism's emblematic slogan (first enunciated by Mussolini) simply collapsed: "Everything within the state, nothing outside the state, nothing against the state." The linkage between atheism and Marxism-Leninism was not attributable merely to the personal crotchets of Karl Marx and Vladimir Ulyanov. It was built in, necessary, indispensable to the communist project of "objectifying" society.

Secondly, totalitarianism and the Church were two revolutionary traditions locked into inescapable conflict because of their radically different construals of the moral order. As Pope John Paul II put it two years after the Revolution of 1989, "The state or party that claims to be able to lead history toward perfect goodness and that sets itself above all values cannot tolerate the affirmation of an objective criterion of good and evil beyond the will of those in power, since such a criterion could be used to judge their actions."[28] Thus the totalitarian assault on the Church—to eliminate the Church if possible, to co-opt and subjugate it as an instrument of the state's ideological purposes if necessary—was unavoidable. It was required by the logic of the totalitarian project itself.

The Church could, as the Polish experience demonstrated, work in defense of the national interest with a communist regime that recognized (as a momentary tactical concession of its own) the reality of the Church as a cultural, social, and political force. Thus Cardinal Stefan Wyszyński twice intervened in national affairs (in 1956 and 1970) to calm public unrest at the request of Poland's communist government. Both the primate and the Polish government of the day recognized that the alternative to Church-sanctioned public order in those circumstances was quite probably direct Soviet intervention: which would mean massive Polish bloodshed. But such pragmatic judgments and arrangements in Poland were always set in the context of an assumed, irreversible incompatibility. It was, after all, the same Cardinal Wyszyński who, at the cost of three years imprisonment, had led the Polish bishops in 1953 in their heroic *Non possumus!*"

In short, the answer to Leszek Kołakowski's question was an unavoidable one, given the realities: as a matter of first principles, the Church opposed the totalitarian project in all its dimensions. It could not be otherwise, given the nature of the Church and the claims of Marxism-Leninism. The Church had its own inescapable pastoral obligations, to be sure: as Pope Pius XI put it in 1929, "If it were a question of saving a few souls, of preventing greater evil, we would have the courage to deal even with the devil in person."[29] But any such dealing with the principalities and powers would be done with eyes open: as John Paul II would describe the diplomacy of the Church, "the Holy See remains open to relations with every country and system, whereby it basically seeks the good, which is simply the welfare of humanity." But that diplomacy took on a distinctive coloration when the negotiating partners were communists—at least in the *Ostpolitik* of John Paul II. "We are convinced that such a dialogue cannot be easy," said John Paul, "since it starts from diametrically opposed worldviews." But one tried.[30]

Out of that trying came much of the religious energy that helped shape the uniqueness of the Revolution of 1989. And out of that distinctive revolution of restoration came, not convergence, but victory: victory for democracy over communism, victory for freedom over tyranny, victory for a true humanism over a false conception of human nature and human destiny. All in all it was, as the Catholic bishops of Europe put it in December 1991, a series of "extraordinary events in which the love and mercy which God the Father has for all His children [could] almost be touched."[31]

We cannot know what the future of freedom will bring in central and eastern Europe. The consolidation of democracy in the countries of the late and unlamented Yalta imperial system will be difficult and arduous. There will be setbacks along the way. But the Revolution of 1989 was also a reminder that the Lord of history—the Lord of the final revolution, if you will—is still capable of surprises. Christians believe in faith that the future is, finally, assured: that God will restore all things in Christ, in the Kingdom in which swords will be beaten into plowshares and every tear wiped away. But between now and then—between Easter and the return of the Lord in glory—there is history, and there is the life of the Church, which must ever hold itself open to the possibility of the new, the surprising, and the unexpected.

Because of their faith in the promised future, contemporary Christians can say, with St. Paul, "I forget what lies behind and strain forward to what lies ahead" (Philippians 3.13–14).

Thus the Christian can never be a fatalist. And that is why Christian faith finally proved more resilient than communism. Communism was, in its cold heart of hearts, fatalistic. Christians, on the other hand, "can be certain that the future will offer to us . . . the manifestation of a new aspect of the fullness of Christ."[32]

And so the final revolution will continue. The Revolution of 1989, an expression of this revolution of the spirit, was a reminder that there are still surprises left in history, and that the good guys do indeed sometimes win. As we approach the twenty-first century, the curious mix of good and evil that characterizes all things human—and especially all things political—will remain. But we may also be sure that the Lord of history has not yet exhausted His supply of wonders on the road to the New Jerusalem.

Notes

Introduction: The Final Revolution

1. James H. Billington, *Fire in the Minds of Men: Origins of the Revolutionary Faith* (New York: Basic Books, 1980), p. 3.

2. Ibid., p. 265.

3. Cited in ibid., p. 6.

4. Cited in ibid., p. 5.

5. Ibid., p. 9.

6. The classic work is Norman Cohn, *The Pursuit of the Millennium*, revised and expanded edition (New York: Oxford University Press, 1970). Cohn explores the linkage between the medieval millenarians and modern totalitarianism in the "Conclusion" to his study, which has appeared, thus far, in three editions. The "Conclusions" in the 1957 and 1961 editions of Cohn's work (published by, respectively, Essential Books and Harper Torchbooks) make the point in a more extended fashion than Cohn's more concise "Conclusion" to the most recent edition. References here are thus to Cohn, 1957; Cohn, 1961; and Cohn, 1970.

7. Cohn, 1970, p. 284.

8. See Sigmund Mowinckel, *He That Cometh: The Messiah Concept in the Old Testament and Later Judaism* (Oxford: Basil Blackwell, 1959).

9. See Eusebius, *Ecclesiastical History* III.5, par. 196. See also Joseph Klausner, *From Jesus to Paul* (New York: Macmillan, 1944), pp. 598–99.

10. Cohn, 1970, p. 29.

11. Ibid., pp. 13, 98, 123, 259–60.

12. Ibid., p. 29.

13. Ibid.

14. Ibid.

15. Ibid.

16. See ibid., p. 75.

17. Ibid., p. 120.

18. Ibid., p. 215.

19. Ibid., pp. 264, 275.
20. Cohn, 1961, p. 319.
21. Ibid., p. 309.
22. Cohn, 1970, pp. 108–9.
23. Ibid., p. 109. Cohn continues: "And it is no less true—if even more paradoxical—that the phrase 'the Third Reich,' first coined in 1923 by the publicist Moeller van den Bruck and later adopted as a name for that 'new order' which was supposed to last a thousand years, would have had but little emotional significance if the fantasy of a third and most glorious dispensation had not, over the centuries, entered into the common stock of European social mythology" (ibid.).
24. On Bonneville, see Billington, *Fire in the Minds of Men*, pp. 33–43. On Buonarotti, see ibid., pp. 87–99.
25. See Cohn, 1970, pp. 261–80.
26. See Billington, *Fire in the Minds of Men*, p. 94.
27. Ibid., p. 8.
28. Ibid., p. 9.
29. Norman Cohn sees here in the sixteenth century another partial prefigurement of the twentieth:

> Only in the story of the radical Taborites and of the New Jerusalem at Münster can one perceive hints of the process which seems to be normal in modern totalitarian states—how the collective impetus flags, until it is only by means of incessant propaganda and terror that the true believers can induce the increasingly weary masses to continue along the path prescribed by the paranoiac myth. [But] even these two movements were crushed before they reached the next stage, when leadership passes from the true believers to out-and-out cynics who use the same methods and the same myth for the simple purpose of securing, reinforcing and extending their own monopoly of political power. (Cohn, 1957, p. 314)

In sum: the Middle Ages, for all their inventiveness (and especially in the worlds of the lurid), could not produce a foreshadowing of Leonid Brezhnev.

30. Billington, *Fire in the Minds of Men*, p. 14.

Chapter 1. Not by Politics Alone:
Unwrapping the Revolution of 1989

1. *Foreign Affairs Chronology, 1978–1989* (New York: Council on Foreign Relations, 1990), p. 34.
2. See Zbigniew Brzezinski, *The Grand Failure: The Birth and Death of Communism in the Twentieth Century* (New York: Scribner's, 1989),

and Jeane J. Kirkpatrick, *The Withering Away of the Totalitarian States
. . . and Other Surprises* (Washington, DC: American Enterprise
Institute, 1990).

3. Ralf Dahrendorf, *Reflections on the Revolution in Europe* (New
York: Times Books/Random House, 1990).

4. Garton Ash's journalism, which has, not inaptly, been compared
to Orwell's, has been gathered into two collections: *The Uses of
Adversity: Essays on the Fate of Central Europe* (New York: Vintage
Books, 1990), and *We the People: The Revolution of '89 Witnessed in
Warsaw, Budapest, Berlin & Prague* (Cambridge, U.K.: Granta Books,
1990) (available in the United States under the title *The Magic Lantern*).
Earlier in the decade, Garton Ash wrote an award-winning study enti-
tled *The Polish Revolution: Solidarity* (Sevenoaks, U.K.: Hodder and
Stoughton, 1985). All three volumes are indispensable sources of data
and insight.

5. James H. Billington, "The Crisis of Communism and the Future of
Freedom," *Ethics and International Affairs* V (1991), p. 87.

6. John Clark and Aaron Wildavsky, *The Moral Collapse of Communism: Poland as a Cautionary Tale* (San Francisco: ICS Press, 1990).

7. Sidney Blumenthal, *Pledging Allegiance—The Last Campaign of
the Cold War* (New York: HarperCollins, 1990). The citation is from
William C. Bodie's review, "How Gorbachev Saved Reagan, Bush, and
the World," in *The National Interest* 23 (Spring 1991), p. 101.

8. Dahrendorf, *Reflections*, pp. 16–17. Jeane Kirkpatrick offered a
sophisticated variant on the "Gorbachev did it" account when she
argued that Gorbachev's decision to keep the Soviet troops in their bar-
racks during the Revolution of 1989 broke the back of the communist
regimes of the old Warsaw Pact by revealing their illegitimacy: that is,
by making clear that their power rested solely on a foundation of coercive force. See Kirkpatrick, *The Withering Away*, pp. 3, 81.

9. Michael Howard, "The Springtime of Nations," *Foreign Affairs*
69:1, pp. 19–20, 23.

10. William H. McNeill, "Winds of Change," *Foreign Affairs* 69:4
(Fall 1990), p. 152.

11. Robert G. Kaiser, "Gorbachev: Triumph and Failure," *Foreign
Affairs* 70:2 (Spring 1991), p. 160.

12. Martin Malia, "A New Russian Revolution?" *New York Review
of Books*, July 18, 1991, p. 29.

13. "The Anatomy of a Reticence," in Václav Havel, *Open Letters:
Selected Writings, 1965–1990* (New York: Knopf, 1991), pp. 291–322.
"Anatomy" was first released in April 1985.

14. Havel put the problem in these terms:

For thirty-seven years every possible and impossible open space in Czechoslovakia has been decorated with slogans such as "Building up our homeland strengthens peace," "The Soviet Union, guarantor of world peace," "For the even greater flowering of the peaceful labor of our people!" and so on and so forth. For thirty-seven years our newspapers and the other media have been saturated with the same weary clichés about peace. For thirty-seven years our citizens have been required to carry the same old peace placards in the mandatory parades. For thirty-seven years a few individuals clever enough to establish themselves as our professional "peace fighters," being particularly adept at repeating the official pronouncements, have engaged in extensive peace-congress tourism at state expense. For thirty-seven years, in other words, "the struggle for peace" has been part and parcel of the ideological facade within which we live. Yet every citizen knows from a thousand daily, intensely personal experiences that this official facade conceals an utterly different reality that is growing ever more disheartening: the wasteland of life in a totalitarian state, with its all-powerful center and all-powerless inhabitants. ("Anatomy of a Reticence," pp. 293–94)

15. Ibid., p. 298.
16. Havel again:

Some time ago, two appealing young Italian women arrived in Prague with a declaration of women calling for all things good: respect for human rights, disarmament, demilitarization of children's education, respect for all human beings. They were collecting signatures from both parts of our divided Europe. I found them touching: they could easily have been cruising the Mediterranean on yachts with wealthy husbands (they could surely have found some)—yet here they were, rattling around Europe, trying to make the world better. I felt all the sorrier for them because virtually none of the better-known Prague women dissidents wanted to sign (the petitioners understandably did not even try to approach nondissidents). The reason was not that Prague women dissidents could not agree with the content of the declaration. Without conferring in any way about it, they all, individually, agreed on a different reason: it seemed to them ridiculous that they should sign something *as women*. Men, who had nothing to sign, treated this feminine action with gallant attentiveness and a quiet smile, while among the ladies the prevalent mood was one of vigorous distaste for the whole matter, a distaste all the more vigorous for the fact that they were not absolved from deciding whether to sign or not; they experienced no need to be gallant. . . . (ibid., pp. 306–7)

17. Ibid., p. 311.
18. Ibid., pp. 313–15.
19. The SDI case is suggestive of yet another cluster of ironies at the intersection of religion and international politics in the 1980s. In terms of American domestic politics, the Reagan administration's initial proclamation of a "Strategic Defense Initiative" (which involved the repackag-

ing of several existing research programs whose funding was significantly increased) was less the result of a carefully considered and dramatic shift in strategic doctrine than it was an attempt to blunt the antinuclear weapons pressure from the freeze movement in general, and in particular what officials feared would be the political fallout from the antideterrence posture of the National Conference of Catholic Bishops in their 1983 pastoral letter, "The Challenge of Peace." (Celebrants of the bishops' letter will object that the letter gave a "strictly conditioned moral acceptance" to deterrence. But the letter was widely perceived, in the relevant media and political communities, as an attack on both Reagan administration nuclear weapons policy and on the deterrence system itself. The bishops' conference did nothing to challenge this widespread reading of their work. And thus the impression stuck.) On this analysis, the bishops could be regarded as something like the fathers of SDI.

But consider the many ironies in the fire here. The first is that the bishops (committed as they were to the orthodoxies of the arms control fraternity on this subject) wanted nothing to do with SDI, and in fact expressed grave reservations about the strategic defense program in their 1985 follow-up report to "The Challenge of Peace." The second irony is that the system the bishops rejected—SDI—may have helped produce the result the bishops claimed to want in 1983: peace in Europe with significant nuclear disarmament. (The bishops, it should also be remembered, were also highly skeptical about the emplacement of Pershing II missiles in western Europe during the INF modernization program—another Reagan administration decision that arguably had a positive impact in creating the political conditions for the possibility of the Revolution of 1989.)

On the relationship between SDI and Soviet arms control proposals, see also Max M. Kampelman, *Entering New Worlds: The Memoirs of a Private Man in Public Life* (New York: HarperCollins, 1991).

20. See Václav Havel, *Letters to Olga, June 1979–September 1982* (New York: Henry Holt, 1989), and Adam Michnik, *Letters from Prison and Other Essays* (Berkeley: University of California Press, 1985).

21. For an eloquent example of how the case for freedom could be pressed in and out of season, see Max M. Kampelman, *Three Years at the East-West Divide* (New York: Freedom House, 1983). On the intersection of security issues and human rights issues in U.S./Soviet relations throughout the Helsinki process, see Carol O'Hallaron, "Risky Business: Linking Human Rights and Defence Issues at the Vienna CSCE," *Cambridge Review of International Affairs* 4:1 (Spring 1990), pp. 27–39.

22. Francis Fukuyama, "The End of History?" *The National Interest* 16 (Summer 1989), pp. 3–18. See also Francis Fukuyama, *The End of History and the Last Man* (New York: Free Press, 1992).

23. Fukuyama, "The End of History?" p. 18.

24. One of the reasons the word got around in central and eastern Europe was the fact of those remarkable broadcast services that provided an information link to the West (and to the truth): Radio Free Europe, Radio Liberty, Vatican Radio, the BBC, and Deutsche Welle. Too little appreciated in the West, these services are still cited by activists from the 1980s as having made a considerable difference, particularly when the going got rough.

25. See Garton Ash, *We the People*, pp. 26–29:

> On the overcast Sunday morning I went to the polls in Żoliborz with my indomitable underground publisher, Andrzej Rosner, his wife Ania, and their seven-year-old daughter Zuzia. . . . Andrzej and Ania were handed their complicated ballot papers: separate white ones for each seat in the *sejm*; the "National List" of thirty-five prominent Party-coalition candidates, who merely had to get fifty per cent of the vote to take uncontested seats; and a long pink paper listing all the candidates for the Senate. Ignoring the curtained booths, Andrzej and Ania sat down at a table and began the glorious work of deletion; for in yet another blunder, the Party-coalition side had insisted that voting should be by crossing out the undesired candidates. Zzzick, zzzick, went the pens, as my friends crossed out name after official name, taking their time about it, savoring the moment. . . .
>
> It looked much the same all over Warsaw. By mid-morning there were long queues. "You see, it's after Mass," was the explanation given me for the length of the queues in almost every case: that and the sheer complexity of the voting procedures. Some voters came directly from their children's First Communion, trailing little girls in long white dresses. The first communion and the first election. And not only for the children. "Yes, sir," confided one not-so-young couple, holding hands and simpering, "it's our first time!" . . .
>
> In the corridor [of another voting place in Praga, a working class suburb of Warsaw] I was approached by an old man, in some perplexity. "Excuse me," he said, "Bylinksi—is he ours (*nasz*)?" Yes, I said, he's ours. Zzzick, zzzick, went the pen, as he crossed out all the National List, muttering to himself, "I've had enough of them, all these years. . . ."

Chapter 2. Calling Good and Evil by Name: The Communist Lie Confronted

1. Václav Havel, "New Year's Address," in *Open Letters*, p. 390.

2. Ibid., pp. 391–92.

3. Pope John Paul II had a similar view of the distinctive nature of communist tyranny. As he put it in the 1991 encyclical *Centesimus*

Annus, in his chapter "The Year 1989," politics under the totalitarian system "becomes a 'secular religion' which operates under the illusion of creating paradise in this world. But no political society . . . can ever be confused with the Kingdom of God. The Gospel parable of the weeds among the wheat (cf. *Matthew* 13.24–30; 36–40) teaches that it is for God alone to separate the subjects of the Kingdom from the subjects of the Evil One, and that this judgment will take place at the end of time. By presuming to anticipate judgment here and now, man puts himself in the place of God and sets himself against the patience of God" (25). Man also, as the pope knew full well, did horrible things in this world because of this particular form of presumption.

4. As did Henry Kissinger in 1970. See Elmo R. Zumwalt, Jr., *On Watch* (New York: Quadrangle, 1976), p. 319.

5. Václav Havel, "The Power of the Powerless," in Havel et al., *The Power of the Powerless: Citizens Against the State in Central-Eastern Europe* (Armonk: M.E. Sharpe, 1990), pp. 27–28.

Havel's essay was written in 1978 and had a great impact among the leaders of what would become the Revolution of 1989. Zbigniew Bujak, a leader in Solidarity, said this about the essay to Havel's translator, Paul Wilson:

> This essay reached us at the Ursus factory in 1979 at a point when we felt we were at the end of the road. Inspired by KOR [the Polish Workers' Defense Committee], we had been speaking out on the shop floor, talking to people, participating in public meetings, trying to speak the truth about the factory, the country, and politics. There came a moment when people thought we were crazy. Why were we doing this? Why were we taking such risks? Not seeing any immediate and tangible results, we began to doubt the purposefulness of what we were doing. Shouldn't we be coming up with other methods, other ways?
>
> Then came the essay by Havel. Reading it gave us the theoretical under-pinnings for our activity. It maintained our spirits; we did not give up, and a year later—in August 1980—it became clear that the party apparatus and the factory management were afraid of us. We mattered. And the rank and file saw us as leaders of the movement. When I look at the victo-ries of Solidarity and Charter 77, I see in them an astonishing fulfillment of the prophecies and knowledge contained in Havel's essay. (cited in Havel, *Open Letters*, pp. 125–26)

6. Ibid., p. 28.
7. Ibid.
8. Ibid., p. 30.
9. Ibid., p. 31.
10. Ibid., p. 25.
11. Ibid.
12. Ibid., pp. 25, 29.

13. The image of "moral schizophrenia" was suggested to me by the bishop of Tarnów in Poland, the philosopher Józef Życiński.

14. Havel, "The Power of the Powerless," p. 31.

15. I am indebted for this description of the moral dilemma of relationships under communism to Janusz Onyszkiewicz, former spokesman of Solidarity and, at the time of our conversation (June 1991), vice minister of national defense of the Republic of Poland.

16. See Andrzej Micewski, *Cardinal Wyszyński: A Biography* (San Diego: Harcourt Brace Jovanovich, 1984), pp. 195–96.

17. Ibid., p. 264.

18. Ibid., p. 426–27.

19. Ibid., p. 244. Bishops' servants seemed to be a favorite target of the Polish SB, the secret police. Bishop Życiński of Tarnów, who was installed as ordinary of his diocese after the revolution, told me that the SB had attempted to recruit his predecessor's drivers. Życiński also showed me, with a trace of pride, the door in the tile stove in the drawing room of his residence "where the bug was."

20. Havel, "The Power of the Powerless," p. 72.

21. Ibid., pp. 72–73.

22. In a conversation we had on June 15, 1991, at the editorial offices of the Catholic journal *Tygodnik Powszechny* in Kraków.

23. Cited in Norman Davies, *God's Playground: A History of Poland*, Vol. 1 (New York: Columbia University Press, 1982), p. 14.

24. Cited in ibid., p. 15.

25. For a representative example of this falsification of history, see *USA: Aspects of Social and Political Life*, Dorothea Siegmund-Schultze, ed. (Leipzig: Verlag Enzyklopdie, 1985), an East German textbook written in classic (so to speak) Leninist categories and language.

It is depressing to recall how these latter themes (particularly in terms of U.S. "militarism" and Soviet "defensiveness") were absorbed by the soft left in the West in the post-Vietnam period.

26. According to Norman Davies, professional historians were somewhat vulnerable to the Leninist siren song:

Marxism-Leninism offered several substantive attractions to Polish historians. Quite apart from its political convenience, it promised to supply that sense of organic continuity which had hitherto been signally lacking [in Polish historiography]. It promised to interpret the history of the Poles on the same basis as that of neighbouring nations, and thus to soothe their wounded pride. It promised to justify the emergence of the People's Republic as a natural stage on Poland's bumpy road to Communism, and thus to calm the chronic insecurity of the new authorities . . . . For these reasons, it stood to heal and anaesthetize and was readily adopted by a whole generation of scholars who had little ultimate faith in the validity of its precepts. (Davies, *God's Playground*: Vol. 1, pp. 14–15)

In short, the less-educated people—the greengrocers with their window signs—were not the only central and eastern Europeans to make their peace with the fissure between appearance and reality.

27. Ibid., pp. 14–15.

28. See ibid., pp. 30–31.

29. Havel, "The Power of the Powerless," p. 65.

30. Ibid., p. 45.

31. Ibid., p. 31.

32. See Václav Havel, *Disturbing the Peace* (New York: Vintage Books, 1991), p. 144.

33. Havel, "The Power of the Powerless," p. 37.

34. See Havel, "The Power of the Powerless," pp. 39ff. The pope's phrase is cited by Garton Ash in *The Uses of Adversity*, p. 48.

35. Havel, "The Power of the Powerless," pp. 42, 46, 64–65.

36. Garton Ash, *The Uses of Adversity*, p. 106. Garton Ash illustrates his principle nicely by quoting the Polish poet Ryszard Krynicki on the subject:

> *living here and now*
> *you must pretend*
> *that you live elsewhere and in other*
>   *times*
> *and, at best, fight with the dead*
> *through the iron curtain of clouds.*

37. Havel, "The Power of the Powerless," p. 82.

38. Ibid., pp. 42–43.

39. See ibid., pp. 66–67.

40. Ibid., p. 68.

41. The quote is from an interview with Václav Havel in *Newsweek*, July 22, 1991, p. 31.

42. See Garton Ash's description of this conviction in *The Uses of Adversity*, p. 212.

43. Havel, "The Power of the Powerless," p. 80.

44. Ibid., p. 81.

45. Václav Benda, "Catholicism and Politics," in Havel, *The Power of the Powerless*, p. 117.

46. Havel, "The Power of the Powerless," p. 93.

47. Cited in ibid., p. 48.

48. See Garton Ash, *The Uses of Adversity*, pp. 196ff. Michnik was particularly critical of western "peace activists" on this point: he thought they had forgotten the truth that there were things worth suffering—and dying—for.

49. G. K. Chesterton, *Orthodoxy* (New York: Doubleday Image Books, 1959), p. 41.

50. *Centesimus Annus*, 23.

51. Bronisław Geremek, "Postcommunism and Democracy," *The Washington Quarterly* 13:3 (Summer 1990), p. 127.

52. A judgment in which they were doubtless confirmed by such as Thomas Theobald, senior vice president of Citicorp's international division, who, after the declaration of martial law in Poland, had this to say about the situation: "Who knows which political system works? The only test we care about it: Can they pay their bills?"

53. Garton Ash, *We the People*, pp. 139–40.

54. Cited in Garton Ash, *The Uses of Adversity*, p. 200.

55. See Garton Ash, *The Uses of Adversity*, pp. 47–60.

56. Ibid., p. 191.

57. Cited in ibid., p. 106.

58. Bronisław Geremek described "civil society" as "the waking-up of men and women against the apathy and conformity produced by totalitarian communism. People have been awakened as citizens" (Geremek, "Postcommunism and Democracy," p. 127).

59. Adam Michnik, "Letter from the Gdańsk Prison, 1985," in *Letters from Prison and Other Essays*; for Havel, see n. 4.

60. Geremek, "Postcommunism and Democracy," p. 127.

61. Václav Havel, in fact, traces the proximate origins of Charter 77 to the 1976 prosecution by the Czechoslovak regime of a rock group, "Plastic People of the Universe." See Havel, *Disturbing the Peace*, pp. 126–32. Václav Benda agrees (interview, Prague, October 22, 1991).

62. See Garton Ash, *The Uses of Adversity*, p. 194.

63. The phrase "parallel structures" is Václav Benda's; see Havel, "The Power of the Powerless," p. 78.

Chapter 3. Catholics and Commissars: 1917–1978

1. Cardinal Casaroli's remarks on this occasion may be found in *Origins* 18:7 (June 30, 1988), pp. 101–3. On December 24, 1991, Msgr. Bačkis was appointed archbishop of Vilnius in independent Lithuania by Pope John Paul II.

2. Paul Johnson, *Modern Times: The World from the Twenties to the Eighties* (New York: Harper & Row, 1983), pp. 50–51.

3. Cited in Hansjakob Stehle, *Eastern Politics of the Vatican 1917–1979*, translated by Sandra Smith (Athens: Ohio University Press, 1981), pp. 22–23. Stehle believes that the Chicherin telegram is more reflective of Lenin's distinctive rhetorical style than Chicherin's.

4. Cited in Hansjakob Stehle, "Papal Eastern Diplomacy and the Vatican Apparatus," in Pedro Ramet, ed., *Catholicism and Politics in Communist Societies* (Durham, NC: Duke University Press, 1990), p. 347.

5. Ibid., p. 348.

6. Stehle, *Eastern Politics of the Vatican*, pp. 80–81, 128 ff.

7. Stehle, "Papal Eastern Diplomacy," p. 348.

8. Stehle, *Eastern Politics of the Vatican*, pp. 173–77.

9. See, among many other examples, Robert Conquest, *Stalin: Breaker of Nations* (New York: Viking, 1991).

10. Stehle's criticism of D'Herbigny seems driven at least in part by his interest in making the best possible case for the *Ostpolitik* of Pope Paul VI and its attempt to find a reasonable accommodation with communist regimes: a position he evidently thinks is strengthened by the deprecation of others' approaches.

11. *Divini Redemptoris*, 57–58, 80–81. *Divini Redemptoris* was issued five days after the encyclical *Mit brennender Sorge*, which condemned Nazism as fundamentally anti-Christian. According to some reports, Pius XI had prepared a third encyclical, *Humani Generis Unitas* ("The Unity of the Human Race"), which was "directed against racism, anti-Semitism, and the persecution of the Jews in Germany" (Conor Cruise O'Brien, "A Lost Chance to Save the Jews?" *New York Review of Books*, April 27, 1989, pp. 28ff). Unhappily, the pope died before this third attack on the totalitarian project could be issued.

12. Wyszyński, who is revered in Poland today as the "primate of the millennium," is occasionally chastised by western commentators for his alleged resistance to the implementation of Vatican II in Poland. It is true that the Polish primate did not approach the implementation of the Council in the same way as, say, the hierarchy of the Netherlands. But some will not regard that as a grave error. Moreover, Wyszyński and the Polish bishops practiced episcopal collegiality (meeting as a group monthly) long before the word was even bruited in American ecclesiastical circles.

Hansjakob Stehle is sympathetic to what he describes as the view in "the Roman curia" that "the Warsaw Cardinal's tactics would only be successful in the short run; that seen in the long run, the tension and 'guerilla war' between church and state would not encourage but rather exhaust the faithful" (*Eastern Politics of the Vatican*, p. 343). This view was, of course, precisely wrong, as the events of the 1980s would demonstrate. But then perhaps one should not be too surprised at this misjudgment, since it comes from an author who also argues, astonishingly, that "the 58-year-old Karol Wojtyła" had "not been an actor" in the Church's confrontation with communism, "neither as priest nor as diplomat" (ibid., p. 354).

13. Stehle charges that the critics of Paul VI's *Ostpolitik* vis-à-vis Czechoslovakia preferred "to be edified by the 'sufferings of our brothers in the East' rather than grasp a papal pastoral policy that went beyond the horizon of their always freshly painted churches" (*Eastern*

Politics of the Vatican, p. 341). This is unacceptable. It was in fact the most dynamic members of the underground Church in Slovakia and the Czech lands who were most critical of the initiatives—which they believed to be serious concessions—taken during the *Ostpolitik*. While there were surely some in the West whose anticommunism led them to excessive and unfair criticism of the *Ostpolitik*, others argued that the Montini/Casaroli strategy was mistaken precisely because they were being so informed by contacts behind the iron curtain.

14. For a thoughtful reply to these charges, see Blahoslav S. Hrubý, "Cardinal Mindszenty as a Casualty of Détente," *Worldview* 18:1 (January 1975), pp. 13–18. Mindszenty's own account may be found in his *Memoirs* (New York: Macmillan, 1974). Those inclined to dispute the honorific title "martyr cardinal" might reflect on the following passage, which is not unique, from Mindszenty's autobiography:

> The tormentor raged, roared, and in response to my silence took the implements of torture into his hands. This time he held the truncheon in one hand, a long sharp knife in the other. And then he drove me like a horse, forcing me to trot and gallop. The truncheon lashed down on my back repeatedly—for some time without a pause. Then we stood still and he brutally threatened: "I'll kill you; by morning I'll tear you to pieces and throw the remains of your corpse to the dogs or into the canal. We are the masters here now." Then he forced me to begin running again. Although I was gasping for breath and the splinters of the wooden floor stabbed painfully into my bare feet, I ran as fast as I could to escape his blows. (*Memoirs*, p. 112)

Mindszenty was, at the time of this torture, the fifty-eight-year-old cardinal-primate of Hungary.

15. See Micewski, *Cardinal Wyszyński*, p. 68.

16. Stehle, *Eastern Politics of the Vatican*, p. 311.

17. Cited in ibid., p. 296.

18. This quasi-diplomatic opening to the Kremlin was not, of course, the primary reason for the creation of the Secretariat. But it was an important by-product of Pope John's initiative that has gone largely unremarked in the West.

19. The pope's tone, in this exchange, was as different from Pius XII's as Khrushchev's was from Chicherin's (or Lenin's) in 1919.

Wrote the Soviet ambassador to Italy: "In compliance with instructions I have received from Mr. Nikita Khrushchev, may I express my congratulations to His Holiness John XXIII on the occasion of his 80th birthday, with the sincere wish for his good health and success in his noble efforts toward strengthening and consolidating peace in the world by solving international problems through frank negotiations."

The pope responded in kind: "His Holiness Pope John XXIII is grateful for your good wishes and, for his part, conveys to the entire Russian people his heartfelt wishes for the development and consolidation of general peace through positive understandings brought about by human brotherhood. For this he prays most fervently." (cited in Stehle, *Eastern Politics of the Vatican*, pp. 300–301)

20. See ibid., pp. 305–8. Stehle is, I believe, inclined to exaggerate the impact of the pope's initiative on the course of the missile crisis. It certainly did not hurt. But whether it turned the tide quite so decisively as Stehle (leaning on Norman Cousins) suggests is, as a Scots court might say, "not proven."

21. "Pope John's Opening Speech to the Council," in Walter M. Abbott, S.J., ed., *The Documents of Vatican II* (New York: America Press, 1966), pp. 712, 716.

22. *Pacem in Terris*, 159.

23. *Gaudium et Spes*, 1.

24. The exiled Polish philosopher Leszek Kołakowski (who can hardly be considered a reactionary) was not enthusiastic about the dialogue:

What . . . is called the Christian-communist dialogue is nearly always the product of deception or self-deception. Most often this "dialogue" consists of exchanging unbinding humanitarian platitudes whose principal aim is to prevent the revelation of real contradictions and to use incantations to block out the truth about historical experiences. In those cases the kinds of declarations expected from Christianity are: "Oh, yes, we, too, are in favor of social justice and man's liberation," to which the communists are to respond with assurances that "Oh, we respect your goodwill and your readiness to cooperate, even though we are guided by a scientific outlook on life," out of courtesy not stressing that the partners in this "dialogue" are the ignorant victims of medieval superstition. In today's conditions [Kołakowski was writing in 1978] this "dialogue" is a rhetorical shield which hides the murky realities of Christian life in countries ruled by communists." (Leszek Kołakowski, "The Struggle Between Caesar and God," in Robert Kostrzewa, ed., *Between East and West: Writings from "Kultura"* (New York: Hill and Wang, 1990), p. 139)

There was, clearly, more to the Christian-Marxist dialogue of the 1960s and 1970s than this. But Kołakowski's description of the basic fissure involved here, and its impact on the pattern of conversation when the dialogue partners were Marxists of a far harder sort than, say, the Frenchman Roger Garaudy, strikes me as accurate.

25. See Donald Pelotte, *John Courtney Murray: Theologian in Conflict* (New York: Paulist Press, 1975).

26. *Dignitatis Humanae*, 2.

27. Ibid., 12.

28. Reinhold Niebuhr, "Germany," *Worldview* 16:6 (June 1973), p. 17. For a more thorough discussion of the accomplishment of Vatican II

as it created conditions for the possibility of the Church's role in the Revolution of 1989, see John Courtney Murray, "The Issue of Church and State at Vatican Council II," *Theological Studies* 27:4 (December 1966), pp. 580–606.

29. See Stehle, *Eastern Politics of the Vatican*, pp. 314ff.

Chapter 4. The Woytyła Difference

1. André Frossard and Pope John Paul II, *"Be Not Afraid!"* (New York: St. Martin's Press, 1984), p. 7.

2. George Huntston Williams, *The Mind of John Paul II: Origins of His Thought and Action* (New York: Seabury Press, 1981), p. 265.

3. John Paul II, *Centesimus Annus*, 24.

4. I am indebted to Cardinal Franciszek Macharski, John Paul II's successor as archbishop of Kraków, for this image of the pope's intention—the defender of man in service to the redeemer of man—which the cardinal shared with me during an interview in the metropolitan curia of Kraków on June 12, 1991.

5. *Redemptor Hominis*, 13.

6. The Nazi occupation of Poland was particularly vicious. The Poles were regarded as Slavic *Untermenschen*, subhumans, who were to be kept alive on a subsistence diet as slave laborers for the Reich. In order to facilitate Polish subservience, the Nazis also intended to exterminate, in labor camps and death camps, the Polish intelligentsia—by which they meant everyone with a high school education. See Władysław T. Bartoszewski, *The Convent at Auschwitz* (New York: George Braziller, 1991), pp. 9–10.

7. One aspect of the future pope's activities during this terrible time has not, perhaps, been sufficiently comprehended: and that is his work in the political underground of resistance to the Nazi occupation. Here is the testimony of biographer George Blazynski:

> There was another grimmer and less well-known side to young Wojtyła's activities during the Nazi occupation. Conspiratorial university classes and clandestine theatrical performances boosting national morale were dangerous enough in themselves. But Wojtyła also lived in daily danger of losing his life. He would move about the neighboring towns taking Jewish families out of the ghettos and providing them with new identities and hiding places. He saved the lives of many Jewish families threatened with execution.
>
> Dr. Joseph L. Lichten, the representative in Rome of the Anti-Defamation League of B'nai B'rith, has confirmed that Karol Wojtyła was active in an underground group collaborating with the Christian Democratic organization UNIA, which had a record of helping Jews.

Because of this his name was placed on a Nazi blacklist. (*Pope John Paul II: A Man from Kraków* (London: Sphere Books, Ltd., 1979), pp. 49–50)

Wojtyła's efforts on behalf of the Jewish community did not end with his student days: "... Wojtyła showed his opposition to the anti-Semitism campaign of Gomułka's [communist] regime by encouraging his students to care for neglected and abandoned Jewish cemeteries" (Jan Nowak, "The Church in Poland," *Problems of Communism* 31 [January-February 1982], p. 11)

8. Quoted in Frossard and Pope John Paul II, *"Be Not Afraid!"* p. 15.
9. Quoted in ibid., p. 18.
10. Garton Ash, *The Polish Revolution: Solidarity*, pp. 28–29.
11. Cited in Garton Ash, *The Uses of Adversity*, p. 50.
12. Quoted in Frossard and Pope John Paul II, *"Be Not Afraid!"* p. 17.
13. George Huntston Williams, "Karol Wojtyła and Marxism," in Ramet, ed., *Catholicism and Politics in Communist Societies*, p. 362.
14. Quoted in Frossard and Pope John Paul II, *"Be Not Afraid!"* p. 19. The thesis involved, among other things, an effort to show the essential agreement between the mysticism of John of the Cross and classic Thomistic philosophy. Again, Wojtyła's intellectual instinct was to search out the connections between what might appear, on the surface, to be disparate realities.
15. Although his first pastor, in his days as a very junior curate in Niegowic, is said to have complained that, yes, young Wojtyła was a fine fellow, but why couldn't he have been sent someone with whom he could have had a drink, and played cards, and talked in the evening: all Wojtyła did was "read books!" Or so I was told by one of the pope's collaborators, Bishop Józef Życiński of Tarnów.
16. See Frossard and Pope John Paul II, *"Be Not Afraid!"* pp. 111, 154.
17. See ibid., p. 14.
18. Ibid., p. 56.
19. The biographical details in the preceding section, when not otherwise credited, are taken from Blazynski, *Pope John Paul II*, and Mieczysław Maliński, *Pope John Paul II: The Life of Karol Wojtyła* (New York: Seabury Press, 1979).
20. The terms *Holy See* and *Vatican* are often used interchangeably in American diplomatic, academic, and journalistic circles, somewhat to the chagrin of those to whom these terms refer.
Technically, the Vatican is simply a place, the Vatican (or Apostolic) Palace, in which the pope and his closest collaborators do their daily work. The Vatican can also be used as a shorthand term for Vatican City State, the microstate created by the Lateran Treaty of 1929, which is composed of the Vatican Palace and its immediate surroundings

(including St. Peter's Basilica), and certain other ecclesiastical properties in and around Rome that enjoy extraterritorial status.

The Holy See is the juridical embodiment, recognized as such (and sui generis in international law), of the ministry of the pope as the supreme pastor of the Roman Catholic Church. Diplomats are accredited to the Holy See, not to Vatican City State, and papal representatives abroad represent the Holy See, not the government of Vatican City State.

Thus the use of the term *the Vatican* in describing the diplomatic activities of the pope is something of a misnomer, for it tends to contribute to the impression that there are two parts to the papacy: the pope's "internal" role within the Church, and his "external" activities in the wider world. The term *the Holy See*, on the other hand, suggests (as the Church has long insisted) that it really is all of a piece. However much as that claim may have stretched a point in the days of the Papal States, when the pope was a civil ruler, it is very much the conception of his role that animates John Paul II. And thus I try to use the term *Holy See* whenever possible.

21. Agostino Casaroli was, of course, named cardinal by John Paul II, and was Archbishop Casaroli during the time when he implemented the *Ostpolitik* of Paul VI. To spare confusion, I simply refer to him as "Cardinal Casaroli" throughout.

22. These themes in the *Ostpolitik* of Paul VI have interesting parallels in the *Ostpolitik* of Willy Brandt as described by Timothy Garton Ash in "Germany and Central Europe," a lecture given at the *Institut für die Wissenschaften vom Menschen* in Vienna, excerpts of which are reprinted in the *IWM Newsletter* 28 (March/April 1991).

23. The rhetorical high point of this latter development was Paul VI's 1967 encyclical, *Populorum Progressio*. The *Wall Street Journal* was beyond the bounds of propriety (and reasonable discourse) in describing the encyclical as "warmed-over Marxism." On the other hand, there was little in the political-economic teaching of the encyclical that would have caused much distress in the Non-Aligned Movement (which was, of course, not all that nonaligned).

24. This minimalist agenda—or better, definition of "victory"—was suggested to me by Wilton Wynn, former *Time* bureau chief in Rome and a veteran observer of Vatican affairs.

25. Assuming, for the sake of argument, that this is a credible proposition, was changing the rules of this particular game part of the intention of the cardinals who broke 450 years of precedent by electing Wojtyła? Every bit of publicly available evidence suggests that it was not. Cardinal Wojtyła was elected because he was thought to be the best man for the job: and while the job description involved the public face of the Church in international relations, it most certainly did not, in October 1978, include orchestrating the Revolution of 1989. Those who

believe that the College of Cardinals is, in the final analysis, guided by the Holy Spirit in these matters will, naturally, take a more ample view of the "intentions" at work in the second conclave of 1978.

26. See Havel, "The Power of the Powerless," p. 65.

27. In the mid-thirteenth century, when Kraków was threatened by a Tartar invasion, the town watchman tried to sound the alarm from the steeple of the church, and was cut off by an arrow which pierced his throat, killing him instantly. In memory of the watchman, and as a reminder to the citizenry, the interrupted trumpet call, repeated at the top of every hour, became the aural "signature" of Kraków. It was also used as the call signal of the BBC's Polish service during World War II, and to this day is the time signal on Polish radio.

28. Jerzy Turowicz, "Karol Wojtyła," in Zbigniew Baran, ed., *Cracow: The Dialogue of Traditions* (Kraków: Znak, 1991), p. 108.

29. Wojtyła was also consecrated bishop in Wawel Cathedral amid some drama, according to biographer George Blazynski:

> It was a very dark, dull day, overcast and wet. Inside the old cathedral it was almost dark, save for the flickering candles. With great ceremony Archbishop Baziak of Kraków placed the bishop's miter on Wojtyła's head, and he, in accordance with the ceremonial rite, held it aloft for a moment, praying all the while. Suddenly—and thus are future legends born—bright rays of sunshine burst through the stained-glass windows and bathed the new bishop and his miter in clear, warm light. It was a scene worthy of great religious painters. . . . During the ceremony itself the silence in the church was shattered by a shout from one of the Solway plant workers, where Wojtyła used to work during the war: "Lolek, don't let anybody get you down!" This was received with sympathy by the congregation and by the new bishop himself. (Blazynski, *Pope John Paul II*, p. 69)

Karol Wojtyła's feelings about Wawel Cathedral are best summed up in his own words: "Within its venerable walls, Wawel Cathedral holds the entire Polish past, that most glorious and most splendid past that is truly commendable, worth[y] of following and deserving of eternal remembrance" (cited in Jan Adamczewski, *An Illustrated Guidebook to Cracow* [Interpress]).

30. "Someone once asked Wojtyła, was it becoming for a cardinal to ski? His answer was: 'It is unbecoming for a cardinal to ski badly'" (Blazynski, *Pope John Paul II*, p. 74).

31. He even used humor to good effect here: "Once, when told that no Italian cardinals skied, Wojtyła remarked innocently: 'That's funny. In Poland, forty per cent of all our cardinals are skiers.' Reminded that there were only two Polish cardinals, he smiled and quipped, 'In Poland, Wyszyński counts for sixty per cent'" (Blazynski, *Pope John Paul II*, p. 74).

32. I am indebted to a senior Vatican official and collaborator of the Holy Father for this telling vignette.

The pope spoke very directly to the Polish Church at several points during his installation homily. He cited, by name, the great Polish Nobel laureate, Henryk Sienkiewicz, whose novels had helped keep Polish historical memory alive after the partition of 1795 had ended the Polish state. He spoke of the "living, strong, *unbroken*, and deeply felt link" between Poland and the See of Rome, to which Poland had "ever remained faithful." He invoked St. Stanisław, and the Black Madonna of the Jasna Góra monastery. To western ears, these may have seemed idiosyncratic pieties. They were, in fact, wholly intentional challenges to both the Polish people and to the communist regime in Warsaw. And they were understood as such by both parties. (The homily is reprinted, in a rather bad translation, alas, in *Origins* 8:20 [November 2, 1978], pp. 305, 307–8; emphasis added.)

The officials in question were unlikely to have missed the point, since John Paul had said the following in the telegram he sent to communist party chief Edward Gierek, and the chief officials of the Polish government, in response to their messages of congratulation on his election: ". . . I want with the help of God to do all that will work for the good of my beloved nation whose thousand-year history is tied with the mission and service of the Catholic Church" (cited in ibid., p. 311).

33. The text may be found in *Origins* 8:20 (November 2, 1978), pp. 310–11.

34. Some of the relevant citations may be found in James V. Schall, S.J., *The Church, the State and Society in the Thought of John Paul II* (Chicago: Franciscan Herald Press, 1982). See especially Chapter 3, "The First Right: Religious Freedom."

35. See "Religious Freedom and the Helsinki Final Act," Pontifical Commission "Iustitia et Pax," 1981.

36. The pope's address to UNESCO is reprinted in *Origins* 10:4 (June 12, 1980), pp. 58–64.

37. See Congregation for the Clergy, "Declaration on Associations of Priests, Politics and Labor," in *Origins* 11:41 (March 25, 1982), pp. 645, 647. The Declaration was instrumental in the subsequent erosion of the numbers and influence of the "Pacem in Terris" clergy.

38. Cited in *Origins* 8:20 (November 2, 1978), p. 309.

39. John Paul II, *Centesimus Annus*, 19.

Many observers have commented, over the years, on what seems to be John Paul's hesitancy, even skepticism, about the way the West has conducted itself in the Cold War, and in the immediate post–Cold War period. The roots of that hesitancy are summed up in the symbol, "Yalta."

40. As the pope insisted yet again in the 1991 encyclical *Centesimus Annus*, in the chapter on "The Year 1989."

41. See Frossard and Pope John Paul II, *"Be Not Afraid!"* p. 23.

42. Adam Michnik, "A Lesson in Dignity," in *Letters from Prison and Other Essays*, pp. 160–68.

43. Quoted in Frossard and Pope John Paul II, *"Be Not Afraid!"* p. 251.

Chapter 5. Poland: Igniting the Revolution

1. Cited in Norman Davies, *God's Playground: A History of Poland*, Vol. 1, p. 23.

2. Cited in Norman Davies, *Heart of Europe: A Short History of Poland* (New York: Oxford University Press, 1983), p. 3.

3. Other World War II mortality rates: United States 0.2 percent; United Kingdom, 0.9 percent; Japan, 2.5 percent; Germany, 7.4 percent; USSR, 11.2 percent (figures from ibid., p. 64).

4. The figures are from Bartoszewski, *The Convent at Auschwitz*, p. 150, and Grażyna Sikorska, "Poland," in Janice Broun, *Conscience and Captivity: Religion in Eastern Europe* (Washington: Ethics and Public Policy Center, 1988), p. 166.

5. The Comintern, or Communist International (also known as the "Third International"), was one of the instruments by which Stalin controlled the communist movements of other countries.

6. Davies, *Heart of Europe*, pp. 8–9. The long-standing joke about Warsaw's Palace of Culture and Sciences went as follows: "Where do you get the best view of Warsaw? From inside the Palace of Culture and Sciences. Why? Because from there you can't see the Palace of Culture and Sciences." The Palace was modeled on the Soviet Foreign Ministry in Moscow, which a friend once described, when we were visiting the Soviet capital and ogling the floodlit ministry at night, as "the set for 'Batman.'"

7. Sikorska, "Poland," p. 178. According to Jan Nowak, a distinguished student of Polish affairs and the former head of the Polish service of Radio Free Europe, the founder of "Pax," Bolesław Piasecki, was "a former leader of the prewar fascist organization 'Falanga,' [who] had bought his life in Soviet prison by in effect offering to be a Trojan horse among Catholics" (Nowak, "The Church in Poland," p. 5). Piasecki would be a thorn in the flesh of the Polish bishops for years.

8. See Nowak, "The Church in Poland," p. 5.

9. Stanisław Barańczak, "The Cardinal and Communism," in *Breathing Under Water and Other East European Essays* (Cambridge:

Harvard University Press, 1990), p. 30. On Wyszyński as *interrex*, see also Micewski, *Cardinal Wyszyński: A Biography*, p. 48.

10. The details of Wyszyński's biography here are taken from Micewski, *Cardinal Wyszyński*, pp. 1–44.

11. Interview with Kazimierz Wóycicki, Warsaw, June 10, 1991.

12. Cited in Micewski, *Cardinal Wyszyński*, p. 52.

13. Ibid., p. 93.

14. See Sikorska, "Poland," pp. 178–79. For the text of the accord, see Broun, *Conscience and Captivity*, pp. 330–32.

15. See Sikorska, "Poland," pp. 179–80.

16. Cited in Micewski, *Cardinal Wyszyński*, p. 72.

17. Cited in Nowak, "The Church in Poland," p. 7.

18. The bishops' memorandum is excerpted in Broun, *Conscience and Captivity*, pp. 333–34.

19. See Sikorska, "Poland," p. 180, and Micewski, *Cardinal Wyszyński*, pp. 73–159.

20. See Sikorska, "Poland," p. 180.

21. Gomułka was doubtless also influenced by the demonstrations demanding Wyszyński's release that had taken place all over Poland. A million pilgrims at Częstochowa in August 1956 had put on a massive and unprecedented show of support for the interned primate. During a central committee meeting in Warsaw in October, Gomułka was confronted by thousands of demonstrators demanding the cardinal's release (see Nowak, "The Church in Poland," p. 8).

22. See Micewski, *Cardinal Wyszyński*, pp. 161, 165.

23. Sikorska, "Poland," p. 181.

24. Interview with Father Mieczysław Maliński, Kraków, June 15, 1991. Father Tischner's description of Solidarity is taken from Garton Ash, *The Uses of Adversity*, p. 106.

25. See Nowak, "The Church in Poland," p. 9.

26. Micewski, *Cardinal Wyszyński*, p. 154.

27. Cited in Davies, *God's Playground*, Vol. 1, p. 20.

28. Ibid., pp. 19–20.

29. The painting that traveled throughout Poland was a special copy blessed by Pope Pius XII at the request of Cardinal Wyszyński.

30. Interview with Father Mieczysław Maliński, Kraków, June 15, 1991.

31. Micewski, *Cardinal Wyszyński*, p. 266.

32. Bogdan Szajkowski, *Next to God . . . Poland: Politics and Religion in Contemporary Poland* (New York: St. Martin's Press, 1983), p. 22.

33. See Nowak, "The Church in Poland," p. 10.

34. See Davies, *God's Playground*, Vol. 1, pp. 20–21.

35. Interview with Father Jacek Salij, O.P., Warsaw, June 8, 1991.

36. Interview with Bishop Józef Życiński, Tarnów, June 18, 1991.
37. Davies, *God's Playground*, Vol. 1, p. 19.
38. Interview with Father Mieczysław Maliński, Warsaw, June 15, 1991.
39. Interview with Bishop Tadeusz Gocłowski, C.M., Gdańsk-Oliwa, June 13, 1991. On March 25, 1992, Bishop Gocłowski was named Metropolitan Archbishop of Gdańsk by Pope John Paul II.
40. Interview with Cardinal Franciszek Macharski, Kraków, June 12, 1991.
41. Western church "progressives" were not alone in their criticisms of the primate. It was precisely these charges of obscurantism, ultraconservatism, and authoritarianism that the Polish communist regime leveled against Cardinal Wyszyński (see Sikorska, "Poland," p. 183).
42. Szajkowski, *Next to God . . .*, p. 29.
43. Ibid., pp. 29–30.
44. Ibid., p. 30.
45. Cited in ibid., pp. 30–31.
46. Ibid.
47. Ibid., p. 43.
48. Cited in ibid., pp. 43–44.
49. The figures are from the Polish bishops' conference, and are reported in Nowak, "The Church in Poland," p. 3.
50. Cited in Grażyna Sikorska, *Light and Life: Renewal in Poland* (Grand Rapids, MI: Wm. B. Eerdmans, 1989), pp. 116–17.
51. See Sikorska, "Poland," p. 186.
52. For a splendid demolition of Rakowski (a favorite of westerners who believed in the possibilities of reform communism), see Leopold Tyrmand, "The Hairstyles of Mieczysław Rakowski," in Robert Kostrzewa, ed., *Between East and West: Writings from "Kultura,"* pp. 111–31.
53. Interview with Jerzy Turowicz, Kraków, June 15, 1991.
54. See Micewski, *Cardinal Wyszyński,* p. 205.
55. KOR later evolved into the aptly named "Committee for Social Self-Defense—KOR."
56. Garton Ash, *The Uses of Adversity,* p. 149.
57. Cited in Christopher Cviic, "The Church," in Abraham Brumberg, ed., *Poland: Genesis of a Revolution* (New York: Vintage Books, 1983), p. 100.
Michnik was even more fervent in another passage in his book when, referring to the pressures put on all the Polish people by communism, he wrote: "The children of the Church, who had grown up and departed from her, in the hour of danger returned to their mother. And although in the course of their long alienation they have changed a great deal, though they look different and speak a different language, at the decisive

moment mother and children recognized each other. Reason, law, civilization, humanism—whatever they are called—have sought and found at their source a new meaning and new strength. This source is Jesus Christ." (Cited in Szajkowski, *Next to God . . .*, p. 47).

58. Cited in Nowak, "The Church in Poland," p. 1.

59. Interview with Kazimierz Wóycicki, Warsaw, June 10, 1991.

60. Interview with Jerzy Turowicz, Kraków, June 15, 1991.

61. Interview with Barbara Paluch, Tarnów, June 17, 1991.

62. Interview with Ferdinand Chrobok, Nowa Huta, June 11, 1991.

63. Davies, *Heart of Europe*, p. 62.

64. Cited in Szajkowski, *Next to God . . .*, p. 63.

65. See ibid.

66. Ibid., pp. 61–62.

67. Cited in ibid., p. 67.

68. See ibid., p. 68.

69. Cited in ibid., p. 68.

70. Cited in Garton Ash, *The Polish Revolution: Solidarity*, p. 29.

71. Cited in ibid., p. 70.

72. Cited in ibid., p. 69.

73. Cited in ibid., p. 68.

74. Cited in ibid., p. 69.

75. Ibid., p. 72.

76. Michnik, "A Lesson in Dignity," pp. 160, 163–64.

77. Interview with Janusz Onyszkiewicz, Warsaw, June 10, 1991.

78. Interview with Cardinal Franciszek Macharski, Kraków, June 12, 1991.

79. Quoted in Slawomir Majman, "Road to Damascus," *Warsaw Voice*, June 9, 1991, p. 6.

80. Cited in Garton Ash, *The Polish Revolution: Solidarity*, p. 29.

81. Interview with Father Józef Tischner, Kraków, June 15, 1991.

82. Interview with Father Maciej Zięba, O.P., Washington, D.C., September 10, 1991.

83. Garton Ash, *The Polish Revolution: Solidarity*, p. 32.

84. Cited in ibid., p. 283.

85. Cited in ibid., p. 331.

86. Cited in *Warsaw Voice*, June 9, 1991, p. 3.

87. See Garton Ash, *The Polish Revolution: Solidarity*, and Szajkowski, *Next to God . . .*, for the basic chronology and for much telling detail. For revisionist views of the rise of Solidarity, downplaying the role of KOR and the intellectuals, see Roman Laba, *The Roots of Solidarity: A Political Sociology of Poland's Working-Class Democratization* (Princeton: Princeton University Press, 1991), and Lawrence Goodwyn, *Breaking the Barrier: The Rise of Solidarity in Poland* (New York: Oxford University Press, 1991). Lech Wałęsa's

retelling of the tale may be found in *A Way of Hope: An Autobiography* (New York: Henry Holt, 1987).

88. Cited in Szajkowski, *Next to God . . .* , p. 97.

89. Davies, *Heart of Europe*, p. 169.

90. Thanks to the efforts of the Copernicus Society of America, these novels—*With Fire and Sword, The Deluge,* and *Fire in the Steppe*—are now available for the first time in a modern English translation (from which these renderings of names are taken). Poles tell visitors that they cannot understand Poland (and especially the role of Częstochowa in Poland's national consciousness) without reading the Sienkiewicz trilogy (irrespective of its historical solecisms). Poles are right.

91. Interview with Father Józef Tischner, Kraków, June 15, 1991.

92. See Albert Camus, *Neither Victims Nor Executioners* (New York: Continuum, 1980).

93. Garton Ash, *The Polish Revolution: Solidarity,* p. 68.

94. Ibid., p. 278.

95. Timothy Garton Ash, "Poland After Solidarity," *New York Review of Books,* June 13, 1991, p. 47.

96. Ibid., p. 54.

97. Ibid., p. 57.

98. Ibid.

99. Thus on December 12, 1980, when warnings of Soviet intervention were rife, the bishops issued a communiqué that read as follows: "Action must not be taken which could drive our fatherland into danger of losing its freedom or its existence as a sovereign state. The efforts of all Poles should be directed to strengthening the already initiated process of renewal and to creating conditions for implementing the social agreement between the authorities and society. . . ." (cited in Szajkowski, *Next to God . . .* , p. 112)

100. The domino imagery was suggested to me by *Newsweek*'s central European correspondent, Andrew Nagorski, in an interview in Warsaw on June 7, 1991.

101. Garton Ash, *The Polish Revolution: Solidarity,* p. 262.

102. Szajkowski, *Next to God . . .* , p. 156. The details on the imposition of martial law are taken from Szajkowski and from Garton Ash, *The Polish Revolution: Solidarity.*

103. Davies, *Heart of Europe*, p. 3.

104. Interview with Father Stanisław Małkowski, Warsaw, June 11, 1991.

105. Interview with Janusz Onyszkiewicz, Warsaw, June 10, 1991.

As noted earlier, Jaruzelski was not far off about some western banks. Shortly after the imposition of martial law, Citicorp's Thomas Theobald seemed to confirm Lenin's prediction about the West selling the communists the rope with which it would be hung: "Who knows which political system works? The only test we care about is: Can they pay their bills?"

106. The plague imagery is from Michael Kaufman, *Mad Dreams, Saving Graces—Poland: A Nation in Conspiracy* (New York: Random House, 1989), p. 5.

107. See Garton Ash, *The Polish Revolution: Solidarity,* pp. 350–51.

108. Cited in ibid., p. 280.

109. Kaufman, *Mad Dreams,* p. 135.

110. Antonin Lewek, "New Sanctuary of Poles: The Grave of Martyr-Father Jerzy Popiełuszko" (Warsaw, 1986), pamphlet available at St. Stanisław Kostka church, Żoliborz, Warsaw.

111. Ibid.

112. Kaufman, *Mad Dreams,* p. 141.

113. Lewek, "New Sanctuary," p. 1.

114. Ibid., pp. 2–3.

115. See ibid., p. 3–4, 13.

116. Interview with Janusz Onyszkiewicz, Warsaw, June 10, 1991.

117. Cited in Kaufman, *Mad Dreams,* p. 141.

118. The quotations and data are from my interview with Father Kazimierz Jancarz at the Kolbe church on June 16, 1991.

119. Cited in Kaufman, *Mad Dreams,* p. 129.

120. Garton Ash, *The Uses of Adversity,* p. 105.

121. Interview with Father Mieczysław Maliński, Kraków, June 15, 1991.

122. Cited in Kaufman, *Mad Dreams,* p. 87.

123. Ibid., p. 93.

124. Interview with Father Mieczysław Maliński, Kraków, June 15, 1991.

125. Interview with Kazimierz Wóycicki, Warsaw, June 10, 1991.

126. For a fine evocation of the second pilgrimage, see Garton Ash, *The Uses of Adversity,* pp. 47–60.

127. Interviews with Bishop Taudeusz Gocłowski, C.M., Gdańsk-Oliwa, June 13, 1991, and with Father Mieczysław Maliński, Kraków, June 15, 1991.

128. Cited in Garton Ash, *The Uses of Adversity,* p. 279. The British historian and journalist picked up on this crucial theme in the encyclical in a way that was notably absent from most establishment Catholic commentary in the United States.

129. Ibid.

130. Cited in ibid., p. 58.

The second pilgrimage, and the to-and-fro with the regime about how many meetings the pope would have with Jaruzelski, led to a splendid joke. General Jaruzelski, the story went, requested an additional, off-the-record, "strictly private meeting" with the pope, who agreed to see him. Locked in a room at the Belvedere Palace, the general said to the pontiff, "Holy Father, you must do something for me. I am the most hated man in Poland, and I can't stand it. Please work a miracle." The pope put his head into his hands, prayed, and then said, "Wojciech, my son, you may now walk on water." The next Sunday, Jaruzelski walked down to the Vistula in a neatly pressed uniform, with ribbons and medals shined—and began to walk across the river. Two Poles were out fishing, and one said to the other: "Stasha, would you look at that dumb son-of-a-bitch Jaruzelski? He can't even swim."

131. Ibid., pp. 57–58.

132. Janice Broun, "Poland's Progress Toward Democracy," *The First Freedom* (newsletter of the Puebla Institute, Washington, D.C.), July-August 1991, p. 3.

133. Interview with Janusz Onyszkiewicz, Warsaw, June 10, 1991.

134. Interview with Bishop Józef Życiński, Tarnów, June 18, 1991.

All Poles refer to their current government as the "Third Polish Republic," the first being the old republic ended by the third partition in 1795, and the second being the interwar republic of 1918–1939. The "Polish People's Republic" is treated as if it simply didn't exist—at least as a "republic."

135. Timothy Garton Ash, "Eastern Europe: Après Le Déluge, Nous," *New York Review of Books,* August 16, 1990, p. 52.

136. Interview with Bishop Józef Życiński, Tarnów, June 18, 1991.

137. Interviews with Bishop Tadeusz Gocłowski, C.M., Gdańsk, June 13, 1991; Bishop Józef Życiński, Tarnów, June 18, 1991; and Jerzy Turowicz, Kraków, June 15, 1991.

138. Interview with Kazimierz Wóycicki, Warsaw, June 10, 1991.

139. Paweł Śpiewak, "Taking Sides," in "Clericalism: Myth or Reality?", a symposium in *Warsaw Voice,* June 2, 1991, p. 7.

Chapter 6. Czechoslovakia: A Church Reborn in Resistance

1. For a portrait of the Velvet Revolution at its most intense moments, see Garton Ash, *We the People*, pp. 78–131.

2. Interview with Father Oto Mádr, Prague, October 25, 1991 (the italicized sentence is the one stressed by Father Mádr in his recitation during our conversation). Father Mádr's assistant, Miroslav Kratochvíl, subsequently sent me the full text of the speech that Mádr had prepared for Cardinal Tomášek (letter of December 13, 1991).

3. Sadakat Kadri, *Prague* (London: Cadogan Books, 1991), p. ix.

4. Cited in ibid., p. 234.

5. Ibid., p. 103.

6. Ibid., p. 101.

7. Interview with Pavel Bratinka, Prague, October 23, 1991.

8. Stanisław Barańczak, in a review of Václav Havel's *Open Letters*, deftly summed up the Husák strategy: ". . . the rulers hold sway over the ruled by promising them a minimum of well-being and safety in exchange for a basic minimum of political obedience, and yet in reality always demand *total* obedience even though they never deliver *even that minimum* of well-being and safety they have promised" (*The New Criterion* 10:1 [September 1991], p. 156).

9. On "normalization" as creating the "Kingdom of Forgetting," see Garton Ash, *The Uses of Adversity*, pp. 62–63. Those who refused to "forget," of course, paid a steep price. In 1984 (appropriate date!), Havel described to Garton Ash "the oppressive police surveillance under which he now lives: the threat of a house search hanging over him whenever he sits down at the typewriter; the knowledge that every visitor is photographed and every conversation bugged; police narks following him wherever he goes—even into the sauna" (ibid., p. 64).

On the daily struggle for sanity in the life of a dissident, and one man's resolution of that struggle through Christian faith, see Václav Benda, "Life as a Dissident," in Broun, *Conscience and Captivity: Religion in Eastern Europe*, pp. 309–11.

10. Cited in Kadri, *Prague*, p. 223.

11. Interview with Father Oto Mádr, Prague, October 25, 1991.

12. Benda, "Catholicism and Politics," p. 113.

13. Persecution of religious orders continued without respite through the 1980s. See "The Plight of Religious Orders," a Charter 77 document, in Broun, *Conscience and Captivity*, pp. 307–8.

14. See ibid., pp. 69ff.

15. Interview with Bishop František Lobkowicz, O. Praem., Prague, October 21, 1991.

16. Cited in Broun, *Conscience and Captivity*, p. 72.

17. Interview with seminarians, Archdiocesan Seminary, Prague, October 23, 1991.

18. Broun, *Conscience and Captivity*, p. 71. Things remained very difficult in the seminaries right up until the Velvet Revolution:

In an unsigned letter from Litoměřice seminary in January 1988, students alleged that members of the secret police are being trained there. They complained that many potential students are deterred by threats to themselves and their families; that during study they are subject to police interrogation and pressure to collaborate; that many teachers are not interested in their subjects but that Marxism is taught by specialists; that their course is interrupted by two years' compulsory military service; that they are "completely cut off from the life of the Church," kept short of basic spiritual literature, and allowed only two spiritual directors; and that no religious festivals are observed at the seminary, whereas all Communist anniversaries are. (ibid., p. 77)

19. Interviews with Bishop Jaroslav Škarvada, Prague, October 19, 1991, and Václav Vaško, Prague, October 22, 1991.

20. Interview with Václav Vaško, Prague, October 22, 1991.

21. Cited in Broun, *Conscience and Captivity*, pp. 70, 72.

22. Ibid., p. 73.

23. Interview with Kamila Benda, Prague, October 27, 1991.

24. Interview with Father Oto Mádr, Prague, October 25, 1991.

25. Interview with Dr. Silvester Krčméry, Bratislava, October 30, 1991.

26. Interview with Bishop František Lobkowicz, O. Praem., Prague, October 21, 1991.

27. Interview with Father Václav Malý, Prague, October 25, 1991. Malý also had an extensive underground ministry as a priest. As he told an American visitor in 1990, "I continued my pastoral work privately in apartments. I met with laypeople, families, students, children. I lectured. I led Bible studies, theological groups, prepared people for confirmation, visited people in hospitals" (Liz McCloskey, "Václav Malý: The World of Those Below," *Commonweal*, February 8, 1991, p. 104).

28. Interview with Kamila Benda, Prague, October 27, 1991.

29. On the snubbing of the new bishops, see Broun, *Conscience and Captivity*, p. 75. On the vetting of the candidates for bishop, see Stehle, *Eastern Politics of the Vatican 1917–1979*, p. 337. Stehle states that these conversations were conducted in "uncontrolled surroundings," which strains the imagination, given standard StB practice. Stehle evidently takes seriously the claim (advanced by the clerics interviewed by Casaroli and Cheli) that, absent their episcopal ordinations, the Church would have to "forfeit its remaining pastoral possibilities." But as the Catholic reaction to the ordinations of Bishops Vrána and Feranec illustrates, the result was quite different.

30. See František Mikloško, *Nebudete ich Mócť Rozvrátiť (Secret Churches)* (Bratislava: Vydavatel'stvo ARCHA, 1991), p. 141. Dr. Mikloško reviewed these events in an interview in Bratislava on October 30, 1991. Mikloško also said that the East German and Polish hierarchies believed that the Holy See had made a serious error in stopping Korec's activities, and that Slovak priests were ordained in Poland and East Germany for service in the underground Church in Slovakia from this period on.

31. Interview with Dr. František Mikloško, Bratislava, October 30, 1991.

32. Interview with Bishop František Lobkowicz, O. Praem., Prague, October 21, 1991.

33. Cited in Broun, *Conscience and Captivity*, p. 93.

34. See Broun, *Conscience and Captivity*, p. 94.

35. Interview with Dr. František Mikloško, Bratislava, October 30, 1991.

36. Interview with Václav Vaško, Prague, October 22, 1991.

37. Interview with Father Václav Malý, Prague, October 25, 1991.

38. Interview with Bishop František Lobkowicz, O. Praem., Prague, October 21, 1991.

39. Interviews with Bishop František Lobkowicz, O. Praem., Prague, October 22, 1991, and Václav Vaško, Prague, October 22, 1991.

40. This point was emphasized by the historians Václav Vaško and František Mikloško in my interviews with them.

41. The pope's insistence on the universality of basic human rights (and not just the institutional prerogatives of the Church) was also crucial, according to Father Václav Malý, in countering the traditional anticlericalism of the Czech intelligentsia (interview, October 25, 1991).

42. Benda, "Catholicism and Politics," pp. 117, 123.

43. Interview with Father Václav Malý, Prague, October 25, 1991.

44. See Cardinal Tomášek's "Letter to the Pacem in Terris Association" demanding that the "pax terriers" submit to the Vatican's "Decree on Certain Associations and Organizations Prohibited to All Members of the Clergy," in *RCDA—Religion in Communist Dominated Areas* XXI: Nos. 10, 11, 12, 1982, p. 172.

45. Interview with Father Václav Malý, Prague, October 25, 1991.

46. Interview with Father Václav Malý, Prague, October 25, 1991.

47. Interview with Pavel Bratinka, Prague, October 23, 1991.

48. Interview with Václav Benda, Prague, October 22, 1991.

49. William H. Luers, "Czechoslovakia: Road to Revolution," *Foreign Affairs* 69:2 (Spring 1990), p. 87. Ambassador Luers's own interest in the dissidents, at a time when they were under terrible pressure from the regime in the mid-1980s, is fondly remembered today by many who had been leaders in the resistance community.

50. Cited in ibid., p. 96.

51. Benda on "framework": interview, Prague, October 22, 1991. "Frantši Tomášek": cited in Garton Ash, *We the People*, p. 99.

52. Interview with Pavel Bratinka, Prague, October 23, 1991.

53. Interview with Father Václav Malý, Prague, October 25, 1991.

54. Interview with Bishop František Lobkowicz, O. Praem., Prague, October 21, 1991.

55. See Garton Ash, *The Uses of Adversity*, pp. 214ff.

56. Interview with Pavel Bratinka, Washington, D.C., December 4, 1990.

57. Garton Ash, *The Uses of Adversity*, p. 218.

58. The demands of the third Navrátil petition illustrate the restraints

under which the Church operated in Czechoslovakia in the years immediately prior to the Velvet Revolution. That these problems remained, without any significant amelioration, also suggests the degree to which the *Ostpolitik* of the Holy See in the 1970s had been frustrated. The full text of the petition follows:

1. The fundamental demand is the separation of the Church from the state so that the state would not interfere in the church's organization and activities.
2. The state's agencies should not hinder the nomination of new bishops; this should be an internal matter for the Church.
3. The state's agencies should not interfere in the appointment of parish priests.
4. The state's agencies should not interfere in the selection of and setting of quotas for students and instructors for theological colleges.
5. The theological faculty at Olomouc should be reopened.
6. A permanent body of deacons should be allowed, in accordance with Pope Paul VI's decree of 18 June 1967.
7. All religious orders should again be allowed to function and to admit new members, as they are in the GDR and Poland.
8. Believers should be allowed to establish independent lay associations.
9. Religious instruction should be allowed to take place in churches or church premises rather than in state school buildings, as is now the case.
10. Priests should be allowed to visit prisons and hospitals when asked by patients, prisoners, or relatives. Religious ceremonies should be allowed in prisons and hospitals. Roman Catholics in prison should be allowed to take confession and spiritual counsel from priests.
11. Permission for spiritual retreats or spiritual gatherings for laymen should be granted.
12. Every parish community should be able to establish a parish council, as is the case in other countries, where laymen can assist priests in running the parish.
13. Czechoslovak Catholics should be free to get in touch with any Christian organization throughout the world.
14. Catholics should be allowed to organize and participate individually or jointly in pilgrimages abroad.
15. Catholics should have unlimited access to all religious publications; and it should be made possible to set up religious publishing houses under the guidance of Church representatives.
16. The copying and dissemination of religious texts should not be considered an illicit business activity or a legally punishable act.
17. The Church should be allowed to subscribe to religious literature from abroad.
18. It should be allowed to broadcast religious programs on the radio and television upon agreement with the Board of Ordinaries or with the chairman of the Bishops' Conference.
19. The jamming of the Vatican Czech and Slovak broadcasts and of the

RFE [Radio Free Europe] transmissions of Sunday Mass should be stopped.

20. Not only atheistic propaganda but also public promotion of Christian ideas by priests and laymen should be allowed. Since Marxists and other atheists criticize religion and the Church, Christians and people in general should be allowed to criticize Marxist-Leninist doctrine without this being considered a criminal act.

21. All confiscated church buildings that were built with the congregation's own resources and that are needed for the Church's activity should be returned to their original purpose.

22. The construction of new churches should be made possible wherever necessary.

23. The willful removal of crosses, statues, chapels, and other religious and cultural monuments should cease.

24. The power of the state Minister for Religion to interfere in the nomination, transfer, and activity of priests should be abolished.

25. Unlawfully sentenced priests, members of religious orders, and active religious laymen should be speedily and consistently rehabilitated.

26. Discrimination against Christians at work, especially in the education sector, should cease.

27. Christians should have the possibility to express their views on any subject, if it is morally justified within the right to petition.

28. All legal regulations that unjustifiably make criminal a considerable part of the activity of priests and laymen should be rescinded.

29. Articles 16, 20, 24, 28, and 32 of the constitution should be amended in accordance with the proposals made in the petition.

30. All valid laws directly or indirectly concerning religion should be adjusted to conform with the international covenants on civil and human rights.

31. A mixed commission consisting of representatives of state bodies and the Catholic Church, including laymen nominated by Cardinal František Tomášek and by representatives of the Catholic Church in Slovakia, should deal with these proposals and resolve outstanding issues. (Broun, *Conscience and Captivity*, pp. 319–20)

59. Cited in Broun, *Conscience and Captivity*, p. 97.

60. Interview with Kamila Benda, Prague, October 27, 1991.

61. Interview with Dr. Silvester Krčméry, Bratislava, October 30, 1991.

62. See Broun, *Conscience and Captivity*, p. 98.

63. Ibid.

64. Interview with Kamila Benda, Prague, October 27, 1991.

65. For further details of the *masakr*, see Garton Ash, *We the People*, pp. 79–80. At Národní 16, a bronze sculpture of outstretched hands now memorializes those beaten on the night of November 17, 1989.

66. Interview with Václav Benda, Prague, October 22, 1991.

67. Garton Ash's portrait of the revolution has been cited (n. 1). William Luers provides a useful chronology of the negotiations between regime and opposition in "Czechoslovakia," pp. 92–97.

68. Interview with Bishop František Lobkowicz, O. Praem., Prague, October 21, 1991.

69. Cited in Luers, "Czechoslovakia," p. 98.

70. Interview with Bishop František Lobkowicz, O. Praem., Prague, October 21, 1991.

71. Interview with Václav Vaško, Prague, October 22, 1991.

72. Yet another dramatic event took place three weeks after the anniversary Mass in St. Vitus's. Former president Gustáv Husák died in a Bratislava hospital on November 18, 1991—ten days after receiving the last rites of the Church from Archbishop Jan Sokol. (*Washington Post*, November 19, 1991).

73. It has also brought into view some of the complexities and difficulties of the underground Church. It now appears that there were numerous irregular ordinations to both the episcopate and the priesthood in some sectors of the underground. (These should be carefully distinguished from the ordinations to the priesthood conducted by then-Bishop Korec in Slovakia, and from the ordinations of secretly-trained Czech and Slovak priests that were carried out in East Germany and Poland.) In April 1992, the Holy See announced its new policies in respect of irregular situations in which questions of sacramental validity and/or canonical legality were involved. Single men whose priestly ordination in the underground was questionable were asked to submit to theological and liturgical examinations prior to public ordination. Married men who had been ordained in the underground were asked to function as permanent deacons in the Latin-rite Church, or to transfer to the Greek Catholic Church (strongest in eastern Slovakia), whose canons permit a married clergy. The most difficult situations involved men such as Fridolin Zahradnik and Felix Maria Davidek whose claims to episcopal ordination or canonical authority were in dispute.

There is no gainsaying the pain involved in sorting out these situations. On the one hand, the Holy See has the obligation to preserve the unity of the Church and its disciplines and the integrity of the sacramental system. On the other, the process of regularizing the Church's situation has caused resentment among some men who believe that they had served the Church faithfully, and in very difficult circumstances. (It seems that some of them may have married, for example, not to defy the Church's discipline of celibacy, but to avoid StB suspicions about the activities of single men.) On the other, other hand, it also seems clear that some clergy in the underground Church went beyond the bound-

aries of ecclesiastical discipline and propriety in their clandestine activities, even given the admittedly more elastic boundaries of "propriety" in
these exceptional circumstances; in this category, for example, would be
the attempted ordination of women to the priesthood.

Thus the effects of the communist attack on the Church will continue
to be felt for many years, as Czech and Slovak Catholics interpret and
internalize the history of the underground Church while struggling to
maintain their ecclesial unity in post-communist Czechoslovakia.

74. Interview with seminarians, Archdiocesan Seminary, Prague,
October 23, 1991.

75. Interview with Václav Vaško, Prague, October 22, 1991.

76. Interview with Václav Benda, Prague, October 22, 1991.

77. Interview with seminarians, Archdiocesan Seminary, Prague,
October 23, 1991.

78. Interview with Father Václav Malý, Prague, October 25, 1991.

79. See Andrew McHallam, "Slovakia: The First Communist Come-
back?" *European Security Analyst*, October 1991, p. 6.

80. Václav Havel, "The New Year in Prague," *New York Review of
Books*, March 7, 1991, p. 19.

Chapter 7. No Monopolies on Virtue: Christian Conviction and the Democratic Project

1. Totalitarianism's acceleration of history was directly related to its
coercive use of terror, according to Arendt:

> Terror in totalitarian government has ceased to be a mere means for the
> suppression of opposition. . . . Its chief aim is to make it possible for the
> force of nature [in the Nazi case] or of history [in the Marxist-Leninist
> case] to race freely through mankind, unhindered by any spontaneous
> human action. . . . In the iron band of terror . . . a device has been found
> not only to liberate the historical and natural forces, but to accelerate
> them to a speed they would never reach if left to themselves. Practically
> speaking, this means that terror executes on the spot the death sentences
> which Nature is supposed to have pronounced on races of individuals
> who are "unfit to live," or History on "dying classes," without waiting
> for the slower and less efficient processes of nature or history themselves.
> (Hannah Arendt, *Totalitarianism*, part 3 of *The Origins of Total-
> itarianism* [New York: Harcourt, Brace & World, 1966], pp. 162–64)

2. Pope John Paul II reflected on the modern meaning of Christian
martyrdom, and linked it to the martyrologies of the ancient Church, in
an address to an international theological congress held at the Jasna
Góra monastery in Częstochowa on August 15, 1991:

Witness [i.e., martyrdom] is a particular knowledge, an intimacy with mystery, in the global and existential sense. Let us not forget that among the written sources of Christianity there is the *"martyrologium,"* which during the course of the Church's history is constantly updated according to various geographical areas. Our century needs a new martyrology, for our continent [i.e., Europe] perhaps first of all. In it many Christians (along with others who gave their lives for the truth they professed) will be found, who are united to the recognized Tradition of the East and West. Even if the martyrology in its external form is an elementary register of persons and events, nevertheless, its deep theological content allows one to discover the very roots of every theology. The martyrology speaks of the facts of Christian experience which are especially filled and permeated by contact with the divine mystery and the presence of this same mystery.

Christ, in telling his disciples about the persecutions waiting for them because of his name, added: "Take courage, I have conquered the world" (John 16.33); and John the evangelist writes that this victory is "our faith" (see 1 John 5.4). This victory consists above all in the very experience of witnessing (*"martyrium"*). It is the experience of God's activity in man, of the power of the Holy Spirit, who "comes upon" him (see Acts 1.8). In some way the reflection of this victory is externalized and recorded in the history of the Church and in the life of societies. (*L'Osservatore Romano*, English weekly edition, September 2, 1991, pp. 8, 10)

3. See Arch Puddington, "A Turbulent Year One of the Post-Communist Era," *Freedom Review* 22:1 (1991), pp. 51–54.

4. I am indebted to Archbishop Miloslav Vlk of Prague for this image of "inner migration."

5. "Address to the Diplomatic Corps" in Budapest, August 17, 1991, reprinted in *L'Osservatore Romano* (English weekly edition), September 2, 1991, p. 5.

6. See *Lumen Gentium*, the Dogmatic Constitution on the Church of the Second Vatican Council, 1.

7. Ibid.

8. Wolfhart Pannenberg, "The Present and Future Church," *First Things* 17 (November 1991), p. 47.

9. Pope John Paul II spoke to a cultural symposium held prior to the 1991 Special Assembly for Europe of the Synod of Bishops (which met to consider the theme, "We Are Witnesses of Christ Who Liberated Us") in these terms:

European culture is marked by the sense of the transcendence of the human person, for it is rooted in the fertile soil of the Christian faith, according to which the human person is a being created in the image and likeness of God, a child of the heavenly Father through grace who has been called to share in his supernatural happiness. Through the mystery of the incarnation, through his passion and resurrection, *Christ opens up time to the dimension of eternity*; he also gives meaning to suffering and his strength to the struggle against sin.

Atheistic ideologies, imposed by the force of totalitarian powers, systematically sought to destroy this culture which believers had forged. But Europeans resisted with the strength of their moral conscience and their spiritual freedom, as persons formed by the two hands of the heavenly Father, the Son, and the Holy Spirit, as St. Iranaeus called them. (*L'Osservatore Romano*, English weekly edition, November 12, 1991; emphasis added)

10. Pannenberg, "The Present and Future Church," p. 49.

11. James H. Billington, "The Crisis of Communism and the Future of Freedom," in *Ethics and International Affairs* 5 (1991), p. 88.

12. Ibid., p. 95.

13. Ibid., p. 97.

14. *Redemptoris Missio*, 39.

Six months later, in the encyclical *Centesimus Annus*, the pope developed the point further:

Nor does the Church close her eyes to the danger of fanaticism . . . among those who, in the name of an ideology which purports to be scientific or religious, claim the right to impose on others their own concept of what is true and good. Christian truth is not of this kind. Since it is not an ideology, the Christian faith does not presume to imprison changing sociopolitical realities in a rigid schema, and it recognizes that human life is realized in history in conditions that are diverse and imperfect. Furthermore, in constantly reaffirming the transcendent dignity of the person, the Church's method is always that of respect for freedom. (*Centesimus Annus*, 46)

15. *Centesimus Annus*, 46.

16. John Paul II, "Religion's Role in a Free Society," an address to the cultural and scientific leaders of Hungary, August 17, 1991; reprinted in *Origins* 21:13 (September 5, 1991), p. 209.

17. Ibid.

18. Ibid.

19. Ibid.

20. The pope expressed these concerns in 1991 to a meeting of European Christian Democrats:

. . . [The] relationship between democracy and Christianity must be rethought and studied by each generation, particularly at this time.

In fact, there exists a temptation today to establish democracy on a moral relativism which goes so far as to reject all certitude about the meaning of human life and dignity, about human rights and fundamental human duties. When this sort of mentality takes hold, sooner or later democracies undergo a moral crisis. Relativism impedes the exercise of the necessary discernment between various demands which are expressed at the root of society: between good and evil. A society's life depends on decisions which must presuppose a firm moral conviction. When there is no more trust in the very value of the human person, one loses sight of what constitutes the nobility of democracy; it is then ready to give way to various forms of corruption and manipulation of its institutions. Christians who are involved in politics have the precise duty of fighting to protect the respect due to the human person who has been created and loved by God. Contrary to what one sometimes hears stated, a sincere faith does not necessarily lead to fanaticism or contempt for different convictions. We think that the human person reaches the true and the good through the use of his intellect and will, helped by divine grace. The sure foundation of democracy lies in this approach. (*L'Osservatore Romano*, English weekly edition, December 2, 1991, p. 3)

21. The use of Holocaust imagery in relation to the abortion debate is understandably controversial. For a brilliant discussion of the Holocaust and abortion, sensitive to the grave moral issues engaged by the comparison, see James Tunstead Burtchaell, C.S.C., *Rachel Weeping: The Case Against Abortion* (San Francisco: Harper & Row, 1984), pp. 141–238. On abortion as a civil rights issue in the American context, see my chapter, "The Abortion Debate and the Hospitable Society," in *Catholicism and the Renewal of American Democracy* (New York: Paulist Press, 1989), pp. 121–38.

22. This charge is frequently leveled by so-called post-communists whose disentanglement from their former ideological convictions is not altogether certain. Maciej Ilowiecki, president of the Polish journalists' association, identified this, and the Church's difficulties in presenting itself as a moral mentor to a new democracy, as two related problems of democratic consolidation in Poland, in "History's Bad Joke," *The [Warsaw] Insider*, No. 20 (June 20, 1991), p. 4.

23. Interviews with Father Jacek Salij, O.P., Warsaw, June 8, 1991; Cardinal Franciszek Macharski, Kraków, June 12, 1991; Jerzy Turowicz, Kraków, June 15, 1991; Barbara Paluch, Tarnów, June 17, 1991; Václav Vaško, Prague, October 22, 1991; Václav Benda, Prague, October 22, 1991; Kamila Benda, Prague, October 27, 1991; František Mikloško, Bratislava, October 30, 1991.

24. See my essay, "The *Tranquillitas Ordinis* Debate: A Memoir with Prescriptions," in *Freedom and Its Discontents: Catholicism Confronts Modernity* (Washington, DC: Ethics and Public Policy Center, 1991), pp. 53–75.

25. Waldemar Chrostowski, "The Desert and After," *Warsaw Voice*, June 9, 1991, p. 10.

26. Reprinted in *RCDA—Religion in Communist Dominated Areas* XXIV:1 (Winter 1985), pp. 6–7.

27. Barańczak, "The Cardinal and Communism," p. 32.

28. *Centesimus Annus*, 45.

29. Cited in Stehle, "Papal Eastern Diplomacy," p. 341.

30. Cited in ibid.

31. "Declaration of the Special Synod Assembly for Europe," *Origins* 21:29 (December 26, 1991), p. 457.

32. John Paul II, "On the Threshold of a New Era," an address to the bishops of Hungary, August 20, 1991, reprinted in *Origins* 21:13 (September 5, 1991), p. 207.

Index

Acton, Lord, 84
Agca, Mehmet Ali, 144
Agnes of Bohemia, Saint, 185
Alexeeva, Ludmilla, 27
"Anatomy of a Reticence, The"
    (Václav Havel), 23–25
Andropov, Yuri, 18, 35, 143
Arendt, Hannah, 38, 191
Aristotle, 54
Ark Church (Church of the Ark
    of Our Lady, Queen of
    Poland), 92–93, 132, 151
Arnold, Stanisław, 46
Association of the Friends of
    Children, 110
Augustine, Saint, 7, 10, 12
Auschwitz-Birkenau, 32

Bačkis, Audrys, 59, 220n.1
Ball, John, 6
Bar Kokhba, Simon, 7
Benda, Kamila, 160, 170–71,
    181–82, 186, 192
Benda, Václav, 51, 160, 167,
    170, 175–78, 182, 184,
    186–87, 189, 220n.61
Benedict, Saint, 98
Beran, Cardinal Josef, 65, 74–75,
    167, 172
Besançon, Alain, 148
Bierut, Bolesław, 105, 111
Billington, James H., 5, 10–11,
    13, 17, 197–98

Bismarck, Prince Otto von, 35
Blachnicki, Franciszek, 125–26
Black Madonna, 16, 44, 93, 99,
    104, 108, 114, 116–17, 137,
    148, 228n.32
Blumenthal, Sidney, 18
Bockelson, Jan, 6, 8, 10
Bohemian Taborites, 6, 8
Bolesław the Bold, King, 91
Bolesław the Shameful, Prince,
    103
Bonaparte, Napoleon, 60
Bonner, Yelena, 27
Bonneville, Nicholas, 10
Bratinka, Pavel, 160, 164, 177,
    179–80, 186, 188–89
Brezhnev, Leonid Ilyich, 16, 20,
    27, 124, 143–44, 212n.29
Brezhnev Doctrine, 19, 23, 27,
    30, 86–87, 161
British Broadcasting Corporation
    (BBC), 216n.24
Brzezinski, Zbigniew, 17
Bujak, Zbigniew, 139, 143, 153,
    217n.5
Bukovsky, John, 172–73
Buonarotti, Filippo, 10
Bush, George, 18

Camus, Albert, 140
"Caritas," 106
Čarnogursky, Ján, 189
Carter, Jimmy, 33

Casaroli, Cardinal Agostino,
    59–60, 86–87, 95, 101, 172
Catholic University of Lublin,
    105, 109
Ceaușescu, Nicolae, 75
Centesimus Annus (Pope John
    Paul II, "On the Hundredth
    Anniversary of *Rerum
    Novarum*"), 96–97, 199–200,
    216–17n.3, 244n.14
"Challenge of Peace, The" (Na-
    tional Conference of
    Catholic Bishops), 215n.19
"Charter 77," 27, 49, 51, 165,
    173, 175, 177, 205
Cheka, 12
Cheli, Giovanni, 172
Chesterton, Gilbert Keith, 53
Chicherin, Georgiy Vassiliyevich,
    61–62
*Church, the Left, and Dialogue,
    The* (Adam Michnik),
    127–28
Christian-Marxist Dialogue,
    70–71, 223n.24
Chrobok, Ferdinand, 129
City of God, The (Saint Augus-
    tine), 7
Civic Forum (*Občanske Forum*),
    161, 184
Civil society, 50–56, 101, 194,
    220n.58
Clubs of the Catholic Intelli-
    gentsia (*KIK*), 92, 112, 128,
    138
Cohn, Norman, 9, 211n.6
Commentary, 164
Commission on Security and
    Cooperation in Europe (Con-
    gressional Helsinki Commis-
    sion), 28
Committee for the Defense of
    Workers (*KOR*), 55

Communism, 11–12, 161
    acquiescence to, 47–50
    and history, 45–47, 151
    and human relationships,
        43–44, 52, 55, 194
    and language, 47, 194
    and law, 44–45
    as threat to peace, 23–25,
        96–98, 203–5
    atheism and, 206–7
    culture of the lie in, 37–38,
        41–48, 79, 194
    economic backwardness of, 30,
        37
    effects of, 37–38, 47–48, 161
    pseudo-religious nature of,
        11–12, 35, 42–43, 55,
        193–94, 206–7
Comte, Auguste, 9
Conference on Security and
    Cooperation in Europe
    (CSCE), 26–30, 33, 75
    "Basket Three" of CSCE Final
        Act, 27–29, 33, 75
    CSCE review conferences,
        28–29, 94
Copernicus, Nicholas, 80, 98
Covenant on Civil and Political
    Rights, U.N., 30
Cuban Missile Crisis (1962),
    68–69
Cyril, Saint, 98, 179
Czechoslovakia
    Catholic Church in, 160–61,
        166–74, 179–90
    communism in, 161–66,
        168–70, 236–37n.18,
        238–40n.58
    democratic prospect in, 185–90
    Soviet invasion of (1968), 143,
        161, 163
    "Velvet Revolution" in,
        183–85

Częstochowa. *See* Jasna Góra monastery

Dahrendorf, Sir Ralf, 17–18, 20
Davies, Norman, 105, 119, 129
"Day After, The," 23
"Declaration on Religious Freedom." *See Dignitatis Humanae*
Democracy
   consolidation of, 195–99
   truth and, 199–203, 244n.14, 244–45n.20
D'Herbigny, Michel, S.J., 62–64
Dignitatis Humanae (Vatican II "Declaration on Religious Freedom"), 71–74, 120
   impact on Revolution of 1989, 73–74, 120–21
   themes, 72–74, 120
Diocletian, persecution of, 65
Divini Redemptoris (Pope Pius XI, "On Atheistic Communism"), 64
Dostoevsky, Fyodor, 5, 98
Drummer of Niklaushausen, The, 6
Dubček, Alexander, 34, 180, 184
Dzerzhinsky, Feliks, 12

Einstein, Albert, 101
Erasmus, 98
Essenes, 7

Feranec, Josef, 172
Fichte, Johann Gottlieb, 9
"Final revolution," 3, 5–6, 13–14, 16, 34, 50–55, 102, 104, 119, 133–34, 136, 158, 191–93, 199, 209
"Flying University," 55
Foreign Affairs, 15, 17
Frank, Hans, 81

Frossard, André, 77, 89
Fukuyama, Francis, 31–33

Gandhi, Mohandas K., 153
Garton Ash, Timothy, 17, 34, 48, 54, 81, 127, 136, 140–42, 152, 156, 180, 213n.4
Gasparri, Cardinal Pietro, 61
Gaudium et Spes (Vatican II "Pastoral Constitution on the Church in the Modern World"), 70, 120
Gdańsk, 54, 112, 122–153
Gdynia, 122, 153
Geremek, Bronisław, 39, 53, 55–56, 127, 138, 155, 220n.58
Gielgud, Sir John, 82
Gierek, Edward, 75, 123, 131
Ginzburg, Alexander, 27
Glemp, Cardinal Józef, 143, 147, 150
Gniezno, 107, 133
Gocłowski, Tadeusz, C.M., 120, 157
Gojdic, Pavol, 168
Gomułka, Władysław, 35, 44, 112, 118, 122
"Good Friday of Bratislava," 182–83
Gorbachev, Mikhail, 18–21, 33, 59–60, 98, 182
Gottwald, Klement, 161, 163, 166–67
"Great Novena," 100, 113–20, 129, 192
Grechko, Andrei, 164
Grigorenko, Petyor, 27
Gromyko, Andrei, 74
Gulag, 32, 74

Halík, Tomáš, 177
Haraszti, Miklós, 39

Hašek, Jaroslav, 163
Havel, Václav, 23–25, 27–28, 34,
    37–42, 45, 47–48, 51–52,
    55, 89, 159, 165–66, 178,
    190, 220n.61
  analysis of communism of,
    38–50, 217n.5
  in Velvet Revolution, 159, 178,
    184–85
  on western peace movements,
    23–25
Hegel, G.F.W., 9, 31–33
Helsinki Final Act. *See* Confer-
    ence on Security and Cooper-
    ation in Europe
Helsinki monitoring groups,
    27–30, 33
Helsinki Watch, 28
Hlond, Cardinal August, 108
Holy See. *See Ostpolitik* of the
    Holy See
Honecker, Erich, 20, 35
Howard, Michael, 18–19
Hus, Jan, 161
Husák, Gustáv, 20, 161, 163–66

Intermediate-range Nuclear
    Forces (INF), 22–23
International Physicians for the
    Prevention of Nuclear War,
    23

Jagiellonian University, 80, 151
Jakeš, Miloš, 184
Jancarz, Kazimierz, 151–52, 192
Jankowski, Henryk, 138, 151
Jaruzelski, Wojciech, 20, 145,
    154–55, 234–35n.130
Jasna Góra monastery, 16, 44,
    104, 108, 117, 138
Joachim of Fiore, 6, 9, 10–12
John of the Cross, Saint, 84

John XXIII, Pope (Angelo Giusep-
    pe Roncalli), 67–69, 87
John Paul II, Pope (Karol Józef
    Wojtyła), 16, 48, 52–53, 57,
    59, 77–86, 88–102, 121–22,
    126–28, 130–37, 147, 174,
    195, 225n.15, 227n.30,
    227n.31
  1979 Polish pilgrimage of, 57,
    129–37, 141, 143, 176,
    205
  1983 Polish pilgrimage of, 54,
    148, 153
  1987 Polish pilgrimage of, 153
  assassination attempt on, 144
  Christian humanism of, 78–79,
    93–95, 100, 131–32
  election of, 79, 88, 97, 101,
    128–29, 174–77,
    226–27n.25, 228n.32
  evangelical message of, 77–79,
    95–97, 101–2, 131–33,
    135, 149, 175, 199–203,
    242n.2, 243–44n.9,
    244n.20
  impact of, 88–90, 93–96,
    101–2, 129–37, 140, 143,
    153–55, 174-77, 199,
    238n.41
  millennialism of, 100–101
  Ostpolitik of, 85, 88–90,
    93–102, 175–77, 208
  popular piety, views on,
    98–100
  preparation of, 80–85, 90–93,
    224–25n.7
  Yalta, views on, 96–98, 131,
    133, 137, 228n.39
Johnson, Paul, 60
Joseph, Saint, 64

Kaczmarek, Czesław, 108, 112
Kaczmarek, Lech, 138

Kaczorowska, Emilia, 80, 91
Kádár, János, 75
Kafka, Franz, 164–65
Kaiser, Robert G., 19
Kania, Stanisław, 145
Kaufman, Michael, 149
Kazimierz the Great, King, 103
Kennedy, John F., 22, 128
KGB, 12
Khrushchev, Nikita, 68–69, 111, 162
Khomeini, Ayatollah Ruhollah, 100, 196
Kinga Chapel, Wieliczka, 103
Kirkpatrick, Jeane J., 17, 213n.8
Kis, János, 39
Koestler, Arthur, 38
Kołakowski, Leszek, 38, 128, 206–7, 223n.24
Kolbe Church, Nowa Huta, 148, 151–52
König, Cardinal Franz, 70
Konrad, György, 39
Korec, Ján Chryzostom, S.J., 160, 172–73, 182–83, 186, 237n.30
Kostka Church, Warsaw (*see* Popiełuszko, Jerzy)
Kotas, Jan, 187
Kraków, 90–93, 227n.27
Krčméry, Silvester, 160, 171, 182, 186
Kréková, Marie Ruth, 178
Krupskaya, Nadezhda, 60
Kuroń, Jacek, 39, 56, 127, 141, 155

Laborem Exercens (Pope John Paul II, "On Human Work"), 144–45
Lenin, Vladimir Ilyich (Ulyanov), 5, 6, 11–12, 16, 46–47, 60–61, 207

Lenin Shipyards, Gdańsk, 3, 54, 56, 122–23, 128, 137–41, 154
Lenin Steelworks, Nowa Huta, 92, 151
Leo the Great, Pope, 135
Lessing, Gotthold Ephraim, 9
"Letter from the Gdańsk Prison, 1985" (Adam Michnik), 55
Lewek, Antonin, 149–50
"Light and Life" movement, 125–26
Lincoln, Abraham, 200
Lithuanian Catholic Religious Aid, 28
Lobkowicz, Bishop František, O. Praem., 168, 171, 174–75, 185–86
Luers, William H., 178
Luke, Saint, 116

Macharski, Cardinal Franciszek, 120, 134–35, 157
Mádr, Oto, 159–60, 166, 170–71, 177, 184, 192
Malia, Martin, 20
Maliński, Mieczysław, 116–17, 120, 152–53
Małkowski, Stanisław, 145–46
Malraux, André, 38
Malý, Václav, 34, 159–60, 171, 175–77, 179, 184, 187–89, 192, 204–5
Marchenko, Anatoly, 27
Maritain, Jacques, 66
Marx, Karl, 5, 6, 207
Mazowiecki, Tadeusz, 39, 56, 128, 138, 141, 155
McNeill, William H., 19
Methodius, Saint, 98, 174, 179
Micewski, Andrzej, 114
Michnik, Adam, 28, 39, 52, 54–56, 100, 127, 134, 152, 231–32n.57

Mickiewicz, Adam, 46, 139
Mikloško, František, 160, 175, 182, 186, 189, 237n.30
Millennium and millenarianism, 4–14, 32–33
  in Middle Ages, 6–9
  in modern times, 5, 10–12, 100–101
Miłosz, Czesław, 38
Mindszenty, Cardinal József, 65, 74–75, 222n.14
Molotov-Ribbentrop Pact (1939), 96
Montini, Giovanni Battista. *See* Paul VI, Pope
Murray, John Courtney, S.J., 71, 202
Mussolini, Benito, 207

National Endowment for Democracy, 25
Navrátil, Augustin, 180–81
Navrátil petition for religious freedom, 180–82, 238–40n.58
Nicholas II, Czar, 35
Niebuhr, Reinhold, 33, 73
NKVD, 12
Nonviolence, 53–55, 101–2, 135, 139–40
North Atlantic Treaty Organization (NATO), 22, 110
Novak, Michael, 153
Nowa Huta, 52, 92–93, 105, 154

"Oasis" summer camps, 125
Onyszkiewicz, Janusz, 134, 146, 150, 154–55
Opletal, Jan, 183
Orbán, Viktor, 39
Orlov, Yuri, 27
Orwell, George, 38, 47

Ostpolitik of the Holy See
  under Pope Benedict XV, 61–62
  under Pope Pius XI, 62–64, 97
  under Pope Pius XII, 64–67, 97
  under Pope John XXIII, 67–70, 87
  under Pope Paul VI, 59–60, 65, 74–76, 85–88, 101, 121, 172–73, 176
  under Pope John Paul II, 88–90, 93–102, 175–77, 208

Pacelli, Eugenio. *See* Pius XII, Pope
Pacem in Terris (Pope John XXIII, "Peace on Earth"), 69, 75
"*Pacem in Terris*" movement ("Pax terriers"), 44, 87, 95, 168–69, 173, 177, 186
Palach, Jan, 164
Paluch, Barbara, 129
Pannenberg, Wolfhart, 195, 197
"Pastoral Constitution on the Church in the Modern World." *See Gaudium et Spes*
Patočka, Jan, 51, 165
Paul VI, Pope (Giovanni Battista Montini), 65–66, 69–70, 74–76, 86–88, 101, 117–18, 172
Pax Christi, 204
Pax movement, 44, 106, 110
Physicians for Social Responsibility, 23
Piasecki, Bolesław, 108, 229n.7
Piłsudski, Józef, 35, 46, 107
Pimen, Patriarch, 59
Pius XI, Pope (Achille Ratti), 62–66, 70, 75, 97, 208

Pius XII, Pope (Eugenio Pacelli), 62–70, 75, 87, 97, 108
Pizzardo, Giuseppe, 62
Podgorny, Nikolai Viktorovich, 75
Poland
  as trigger of Revolution of 1989, 56–57
  Catholicism in, 103–4, 118–22, 125–28, 131–33, 140, 147–52, 156–58, 198, 201–2, 207
  communism and, 104–6, 110–12, 114, 118–19, 122–24, 128–33, 145, 155, 235n.134
  democratic prospect in, 155–58
  Marian piety of, 99, 108, 113–117
  Romantic tradition in, 99, 139–40
Polish United Workers' Party, 110
Polityka, 126, 131
Popiełuszko, Jerzy, 148–50, 152
"Power of the Powerless, The" (Václav Havel), 39–51, 55, 125, 217n.5
Public Against Violence (*Verejnosť Proti Násiliu*), 161, 184

Radio Free Europe (RFE), 216n.24
Rakowski, Mieczysław F., 126, 131
Rapallo Conference, 62
Reagan Doctrine, 25
Reagan, Ronald W., 18, 21–26, 33
Religion in Communist Dominated Areas — RCDA, 204
Rhapsodic Theater, 82
Rokossovsky, Konstantin, 112
Roncalli, Angelo Giuseppe. *See* John XXIII, Pope

Rousseau, Jean-Jacques, 10–11
Russicum (Russian College in Rome), 62

Sakharov, Andrei, 18, 23
Salij, Jacek, O.P., 119
Salisbury Review, 164
Sapieha, Cardinal Adam, 81–82, 84, 92
Scheler, Max, 83
Schelling, Friedrich Wilhelm Joseph von, 204–5
Schillebeeckx, Edward, O.P., 204–5
Scientists for Sakharov, Orlov, and Sharansky, 28
Second Vatican Council (Vatican II), 68–75, 119–22, 129, 138–39
  and Catholic human rights revolution, 72–75
  impact on Poland, 119–22, 221n.12
  on communism, 72
  on religious freedom, 71–74
Secretariat for Christian Unity, 68
Secretariat for Non-Believers, 70
Sharansky, Anatoly (Natan), 27
Sicarii, 7
Sienkiewicz, Henryk, 46, 139–40, 228n.32, 233n.90
Silone, Ignazio, 38
Slavorum Apostoli (Pope John Paul II, "The Apostles of the Slavs"), 98, 179
Slipyj, Cardinal Jósyf, 65, 74
Sobieski, King Jan, 99
Social Self-Defense Committee— KOR, 55–56
Solidarity (*Solidarnosc*), 27, 49, 56–57, 141–43, 152–55, 165
  Gdańsk strike of 1980, 137–41

John Paul II and, 140–41
Lech Wałęsa and, 56, 138, 141
moral character of, 54–55, 113,
    139–40
workers and intellectuals in, 138
Cardinal Wyszyński and,
    138–39, 142–43
Sollicitudo Rei Socialis (Pope John
    Paul II, "On the Social Con-
    cerns of the Church"),
    153–54
Solovieff, Vladimir, 62–63
Solzhenitsyn, Aleksandr, 22, 38, 54
Spellman, Cardinal Francis, 66,
    71, 87
Stalin, Josef, 13, 16, 19, 27, 46,
    60, 64–66, 69, 96, 104, 108,
    144, 161
Stanisław, Saint, 91–92, 96,
    99–100, 129–30, 228n.32
Stehle, Hansjakob, 63–64, 66,
    221n.10, 221n.12, 223n.20,
    237n.29
Stepinac, Cardinal Alojzije, 65, 74
Strategic Defense Initiative (SDI),
    25–26, 214–15n.19
Synod of Kraków, 100
Szajkowski, Bogdan, 133

Tardini, Domenico, 66–67
Tehran Conference (1943), 118
Tischner, Józef, 39, 45, 54, 113,
    126, 136, 140, 154
Tiso, Jozef, 189
Tito, Marshall, 65, 74–75
Tomášek, Cardinal František, 34,
    159–60, 173–74, 176–78,
    181–82, 184–85, 190
Turowicz, Jerzy, 90, 98, 126, 129,
    130, 157
Tygodnik Powszechny ("Universal
    Weekly"), 126–28, 130, 153

Tyranowski, Jan, 81, 84

UNESCO, John Paul II at, 94
Universal Declaration of Human
    Rights (1948), 30, 131
Ursus tractor factory, 124, 127

Václav I, King, 185
Vaško, Václav, 169, 175, 186
Vatican. *See Ostpolitik* of the
    Holy See
Vatican Radio, 216n.24
Velehrad, pilgrimage to, 174–75,
    179–80
Villot, Cardinal Jean, 27
Vlk, Miloslav, 168, 186
Vrána, Josef, 172

Walentynowicz, Anna, 137
Wałęsa, Lech, 18, 56, 138, 141,
    145, 149–50, 151, 154–55
Wawel Castle, 81, 91
Wawel Cathedral, 47, 91, 93, 99
Wieliczka, 103–04
Więź ("Link"), 128
Wildavsky, Aaron, 17
Williams, George Huntston, 83
Wojtyła, Edmond, 80, 91
Wojtyła, Karol (father of John
    Paul II), 80, 84, 91
Wojtyła, Karol Józef. *See* John
    Paul II, Pope
Wóycicki, Kazimierz, 128–29,
    157–58
Wyszyński, Cardinal Stefan, 44,
    65–66, 74, 87, 93, 107–24,
    127, 144, 147–48, 192, 207
as Polish *interrex*, 107, 148
early life of, 107–8
Great Novena of, 100, 113–20
"Non possumus" of, 110–11, 207
Solidarity and, 138–39, 142–43

Yalta agreements (1945), 46, 53,
    86, 96–98, 142, 228n.39

Zhivkov, Todor, 75
Zięba, Maciej, O.P., 136–37

Znak ("Sign"), 112
Zvěřina, Josef, 177
Życiński, Józef, 119, 157,
    218n.19